THE NURSERY WORLD OF DR BLATZ

JOCELYN MOTYER RAYMOND

# The Nursery World of Dr Blatz

UNIVERSITY OF TORONTO PRESS

Toronto Buffalo London

© University of Toronto Press 1991
Toronto Buffalo London
Printed in Canada
Reprinted in 2018
ISBN 0-8020-2793-8
ISBN 978-1-4875-8543-3 (paper)

(∞)

Printed on acid-free paper

**Canadian Cataloguing in Publication Data**

Raymond, Jocelyn Motyer
  The nursery world of Dr Blatz

  Includes bibliographical references and index.
  ISBN 0-8020-2793-8
  1. Blatz, William E., 1895–1964. 2. Child
  development – Canada – History. 3. Child
  psychology – History. 4. Psychologists – Canada –
  Biography. I. Title.
  BF721.R38 1991      155.4'092      C91-093053-8

PICTURE CREDITS: The nursery program was a balance of structured and unstructured activities (photo by George Rutherford Studio, Church Street, Toronto); the adult's role in routines AND nursery children relaxed on their mats (photos by Gordon H. Jarrett, Toronto). All of the photographs appear courtesy of the Thomas Fisher Rare Book Library.

This book has been published with the help of a grant from the Social Science Federation of Canada, using funds provided by the Social Sciences and Humanities Research Council of Canada. Publication was also assisted by the Canada Council and the Ontario Arts Council under their block grant programs.

To my husband, Richard

# Contents

# Preface

William E. Blatz guided the hands that rocked the cradles of a whole generation of Canadian children. From the mid-1920s to the mid-1950s Dr Blatz was Canada's own world-renowned expert on raising children. When Blatz spoke parents listened, invariably with fascination, though not always with approbation.

In the early days Blatz and his ideas were frequently equated with the devil and his works. He chipped away at the tradition of iron-fisted parental authority and seemed to threaten the whole order of civilization with his emphasis on teaching children to think for themselves. Throughout most of his career, however, Blatz was in full control as the celebrated child psychologist whose opinions, while often momentarily surprising, were generally considered sound enough to be sought by press and public. Today many of the dangerous viewpoints that once startled another generation have become so familiar and tame that few people under the age of fifty have ever heard of Blatz. But his influence echoes still in schools, pre-schools, day-care centres, guidance clinics, juvenile courts, and social agencies. Indeed, whether our parents and grandparents approved of him or opposed him, Blatz at least indirectly had a great deal to do with the way we were raised.

Blatz grew up in the secure nest of a large German immigrant family, with four older sisters to lavish attention on their little brother. He enjoyed a playful childhood but caught early glimpses of the raw world outside through the ministrations of his parents to the sick and troubled. Out on his own, his eyes were further opened when he worked with injured veterans and perceived the relationship between healing the wounds of war and the early development of healthy children. As a medical doctor turned psychologist, he had the endorsement of several organizations that were working to improve the world by enhancing the lives of children.

Blatz was always able to keep alert to a wide variety of activities at once, and his world extended far beyond his home ground at the University of Toronto. He was a popular writer and a charismatic speaker, in demand all over North America and in Great Britain. He became the particular pet of the Toronto establishment, which admired him and, in any matters of particular interest to Blatz, treated him with absolute deference. He was a sharp adversary in debate but never lost his dignity by fighting tooth and nail; he preferred instead to tease and test his opponents until they admitted defeat. He had the knack of turning his own disappointments into fortunate diversions. If thwarted by circumstances he could focus his full attention on something else, as happened when he was turned out of the Dionne nursery and soon after tackled an even greater challenge in wartime Britain.

When he died, the Senate of the University of Toronto made a resolution of tribute to him. It contained these words: 'Dr Blatz started on a forty-year career which was to bring him international recognition as lecturer, author, child-expert, parent-educator – and general all-round disturber of the intellectual peace.'

Blatz's profound influence on changing attitudes towards children has helped to make us who we are today.

# Acknowledgments

In their retirement, two of Blatz's most faithful disciples, Mary Northway and Dorothy Millichamp, gathered his books, letters, papers, photographs, and files for safekeeping in the Thomas Fisher Rare Book Library at the University of Toronto. They also interviewed his family, friends, and colleagues, recording these recollections on tape. Either of them could have written a biography of Blatz, but they deferred to a future biographer who might judge the Blatz era from a greater distance. To them, my friends and former teachers, I acknowledge a very great debt.

Douglas Myers arranged for me to interview his father, Roger Myers, as well as the Honourable Walter Gordon, both of whom added intelligent comment and detail. Blatz's sister, his widow, and his daughter (Lee Nihill, Anne Blatz, and Gery deRoux) recalled Blatz at home, while several of his protégés – J.D. Griffin, Don Atcheson, Nick Laidlaw, and Michael Grapko – described his work. Some of his long-term colleagues – Margaret Fletcher, Mary Wright, Betty Flint, Nan Foster, Carroll Davis, and Eleanor Hamilton – talked vividly about Blatz, and someone who had never met Blatz but has developed a major scholarly interest in him, Richard Volpe of the Faculty of Education at Toronto, was a thoughtful and stimulating person to interview.

Katharine Martyn and the staff of the Thomas Fisher Rare Book Library have gone out of their way to make my research visits pleasant and productive. I thank them particularly.

In Halifax, Doug Myers, Judith Newman, Tony Burton, Malcolm

Ross, Anne Wood, Doris Hirsch, and Joyce Stevenson encouraged me to get to work. My husband and son insisted I keep going, and my daughter obligingly attacked an earlier draft with her sharp red pencil. Marie (Milton) Davis (who once studied and worked with Blatz) put the manuscript into her word processor and provided invaluable critical comment, while Winnifred Lecky and Andrew Robertson helped to keep household chaos at bay during its writing. Dalhousie University and the Social Sciences and Humanities Research Council of Canada provided support for the project in its initial stages.

I thank them all, though I am sad to know that it is no longer possible for Mary Northway, Margaret Fletcher, Roger Myers, Walter Gordon, Lee Nihill, or Nick Laidlaw to know my gratitude.

# Chronology

1895 Born in Hamilton to Leo and Victoria (Mesmer) Blatz.
1916 BA, University of Toronto.
1917 MA in physiology, University of Toronto.
1917–18 Worked with injured war veterans at Hart House, University of Toronto.
1919–21 MB, University of Toronto Medical School.
1921–4 PH D in psychology, University of Chicago.
1922 Married Margery Rowland, 24 January.
1924 Head of new child study project at University of Toronto (founded by Laura Spelman Rockefeller Memorial and sponsored by Canadian National Committee for Mental Hygiene).
1924 Assistant professor in Department of Psychology, University of Toronto.
1925 St George's School for Child Study started in November.
1925 Research director for CNCMH (until 1935).
1925 Psychological consultant to the Juvenile Court of Toronto.
1925 Began Regal Road Public School research project for Mental Hygiene (continued to 1933).
1926 Official opening of St George's School in January.
1928 Published *Parents and the Pre-School Child*, with co-author H.M. Bott (Toronto: Dent).
1930 Visited nursery schools in Europe and Russia.
1930 Published *The Management of Young Children*, with co-author H.M. Bott (New York: Morrow).
1931 Director of Windy Ridge Day School.

1935 Educational consultant on Dionne quintuplets (research terminated in 1938).

1937 Organized Conference on Research Studies on Dionne Quintuplets, Toronto, October 1937.

1937 Published *Collected Studies on the Dionne Quintuplets*, as senior co-author, among others (Toronto: University of Toronto Press).

1938 Published *The Five Sisters* (Toronto: McClelland and Stewart).

1938 Karl Bernhardt replaced Helen Bott as head of parent education division.

1939 Bought farm at Caledon East.

1939 Kindergarten-Primary Specialist Course started.

1940 Published *Hostages to Peace* (New York: Morrow).

1941–2 Surveyed need for child services in wartime Britain, with C.M. Hincks and S.K. Jaffary, under the auspices of CNCMH (November 1941 to March 1942).

1942 Canadian Children's Services Overseas founded.

1942 Returned to England with staff of five to set up Garrison Lane Nursery Training Centre in Birmingham (May).

1944 Published *Understanding the Young Child* (Toronto: Clarke, Irwin).

1944 Graduate Diploma in Child Study program started.

1946 Advised on Ontario legislation to set standards and regulations for day nurseries.

1946 Married second wife, Anne Harris.

1951 *Twenty-Five Years of Child Study, 1926–1951* published (Toronto: University of Toronto Press).

1953 New institute building opened on Walmer Road, amalgamating Windy Ridge and St George's Nursery School. Institute operated under federal mental health grants, 1953–8.

1956 *Well Children ... a progress report* published (Toronto: University of Toronto Press).

1960 Retired as director of the Institute for Child Study. Became director emeritus.

1963 Retired as professor of psychology.

1964 Completed draft for *Human Security: Some Reflections*.

1964 Died 1 November.

1966 *Human Security: Some Reflections* posthumously published (Toronto: University of Toronto Press).

In the Second World War, W.E. Blatz, a physician and psychologist, advised on the adjustment of children in wartime Britain. Shown are some of the overseas corps from the Canadian Children's Services who helped him start the Garrison Lane Nursery Training School in Birmingham: Mary Wright, Dorothy Millichamp, Anne Harris (Blatz), Margaret Fletcher, and Mary McFarland (Smith).

Staff Sergeant W.E. Blatz worked on the rehabilitation of nerve-damaged veterans during the First World War.

The nursery program was a balance of structured and unstructured activities. On their playground at the University of Toronto, children settle to play in the sandbox.

BELOW (LEFT):
At St George's Nursery School the day started with a quick health check before the children played outdoors.

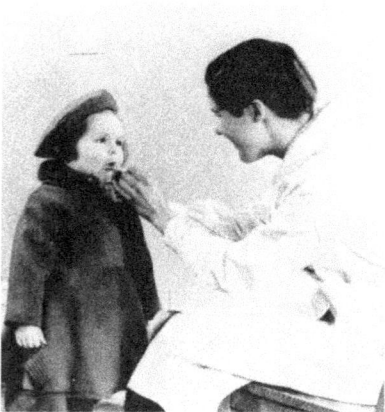

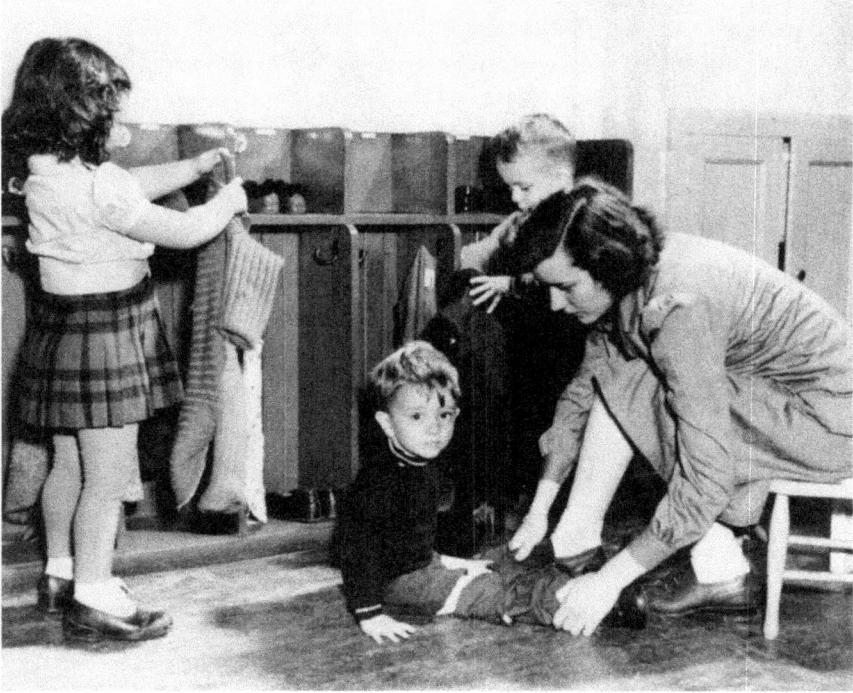

Undressing after outdoor play followed a specific sequence of steps with an adult on hand to give help and instruction.

OPPOSITE (RIGHT):
Art activities were left to the children's own initiative and kept entirely free of adult interference.

Sometimes a few children were gathered to discover the possibilities of new materials.

The morning of active play was arranged to become progressively quieter as the children settled with picture books before lunch.

The adult's role in routines was friendly but businesslike. Here, Margaret Fletcher helps three-year-olds with the techniques of getting washed.

The nursery children relaxed on their mats for a short rest at the end of the morning.

Daring jungle gymnasts of the early nursery world learn both to test the limits of adventure and to extricate themselves safely.

Lunch was served cafeteria style with as many small servings as the children wanted, but with a little of everything, every time.

The university's offer of the Leighton McCarthy house allowed Blatz to raise money in a personal campaign and to add both a new wing and an elementary school to his nursery.

At the celebrations marking twenty-five years of child study at the University of Toronto, Blatz told the guests that it was the first time in his life he had ever addressed an audience that was entirely friendly.

# THE NURSERY WORLD OF DR BLATZ

# 1 The Educator Educated

William Blatz first helped to deliver a baby when he was eleven years old, and he was so calm and competent that his mother decided he was destined to become a doctor. He did indeed fulfil her ambition, but not as the family practitioner or obstetrician she might have imagined, for as soon as he completed his medical training in 1921 he went on to take a psychology degree and became known far and wide as Dr Blatz, Canada's innovative child psychologist.

After the First World War the public mood, even for the victorious, was more bruised and disillusioned than happy and glorious. It was evident that new ways would have to be found to discover what had upset an apparently stable world and to circumvent further similar troubles. It was necessary to improve people in general and would be most efficient to start by working on children in particular. But where to begin?

For those who were searching for a way forward, the new science of psychology beckoned invitingly. From it some caught a glimmer of knowledge so small that it shed no useful light on their problems. Some groped about, misinterpreting what they found. Others were so dazzled by psychology's terminology and formulae that they forgot to temper their adherence to it with their own good sense. Clearly, psychology needed an interpreter to meet the public's demand for accessibility and to prevent it from being turned into little more than a party game.

Young Dr Blatz was ready with his message just as the world was searching for new answers. People were ready to listen to him, though not necessarily to agree. Before long, in Canada, in much of North America, and in Europe, he had become one of the general public's main interpreters of child psychology.

Blatz was prepared to throw over traditional patterns of child raising that seemed unproductive and to refurbish those that seemed worth keeping. For every person ready to embrace Blatz's ideas, however, there were as many others who were highly offended by them. His main aim as a speaker and writer was to sweep away complacency and replace it with rational thought. Never at a loss for words or practical suggestions, and a charismatic speaker who could be counted upon to be scintillating and amusing, he was much in demand. He was tenacious in an argument (until triumphant) and always perfectly self-confident, sometimes to the point of bumptiousness. His saving grace was that in the midst of jousting, if his opponent grew disturbed, Blatz could become instantly warm and humane. He aroused strong feelings of adulation in his admirers and outrage in his antagonists, and, simply by provoking people to examine their ideas, had a profound effect on the upbringing of a whole generation of children in North America and Great Britain.

Blatz's career was a many-faceted one. He was involved in nursery education, progressive education, and teacher education. He was a clinical counsellor for the Toronto Juvenile Court, social work agencies, and a hospital school, as well as for a number of people who sought his help. He worked closely with both the mental hygiene movement and the Child Study Association, he travelled and lectured, and he wrote eight books and numerous articles, many of them for popular journals. He spoke on both CBC and BBC radio and appeared on early television. He helped with the rehabilitation of war veterans and set up a pre-school program for the Dionne quintuplets. During the Second World War he led a group of Canadians overseas to develop training programs for day-care workers in Britain. He taught at the University of Toronto and was founding director of its Institute of Child Study. Throughout his working life he was engaged in longitudinal studies, and he developed an overall theory of the development of security that linked together his experience and his research.

Blatz grew up in a family where people took responsibility for themselves, for each other, and for members of the outside community. Hard work and efficient management kept the family in comfortable though never wealthy circumstances, and they were highly respected leaders in the neighbourhood.

All Leo and Victoria Blatz's nine children were well mannered and sensible, but it was the youngest, Wilhelm, whom Victoria judged to be the most level-headed. She gave him an early – if informal – start on his medical training. His parents were the neighbourhood trouble-shooters; when people needed advice it was the Blatzes' counsel they sought. When a medical emergency arose, Victoria Blatz was the one called to help until the doctor could get there, and usually she took one of her children with her as an assistant. Each child had a turn at helping, but she found her youngest son best suited to the work of soothing the troubled, arbitrating family battles, coping with medical emergencies, and helping to act as midwife. He started accompanying her on her rounds before he was eleven and thus learned at an early age to stay calm, self-controlled, and helpful in any situation, including childbirth and medical or emotional crises.

If family tradition had held sway, 'Helm' as family members called him would have become a tailor, not a doctor. His mother's grandfather, great-grandfather, and great-great-grandfather had all been tailors, while their wives were all dressmakers who sewed for the most fashionable women in France and Germany. His father, Leo Blatz, had originally trained as a brick glazer, but long before he met his wife he had changed to tailoring.

Blatz's mother, Victoria Mesmer, was born in Alsace-Lorraine in the town of Mainz-on-the-Rhine. Her mother's family name was changed back and forth from the French name 'Becaume' to the German 'Bilz' to reflect the political fortunes of the area, and she grew up fluent in both French and German. Victoria's father, Johannes, was a descendant of the Franz Anton Mesmer who had enjoyed a flurry of fame and won himself a dubious reputation as a magnetic therapist in eighteenth-century Vienna.[1]

Victoria was named after the queen of England, with Her Majesty's specific permission. It happened that Victoria's mother, Christina Mesmer, was in charge of the ladies' official costumes at the court of Saxe-Coburg-Gotha when Queen Victoria of England married Prince Albert of Saxe-Coburg. The young queen apparently took note of Christina Mesmer's work, for she usually arranged to have a stylish costume or two designed by Christina. In 1855, when working on a dress for the visiting Queen, Christina mentioned that she had just given birth to a daughter and asked Victoria's permission to name the baby after her. The Queen gave her consent.[2]

Like many Germans of the time, however, the young Mesmer family developed a strong desire to seek the apparent prosperity and stability of North America. Rising prices and social and political unrest in Germany, along with reduced fares for the ocean crossing and active recruitment of immigrants for the New World, made emigration attractive. Certainly the United States, with its highly organized immigration policies, attracted the majority of Germans, but by the middle of the century, Canada began to attract more, most of them from the Mainz area.[3] When Victoria was less than a year old she moved to Canada with her parents and maternal grandparents. She used to say afterwards that they went to avoid the unrest at home and because friends of her parents who had emigrated had quickly made good. They left Germany in 1855 with a group of Bilz relatives, most of whom went on to Toronto and then north to Barrie and Huntsville. The Mesmers, however, chose to settle in Hamilton.

In the mid-nineteenth century Hamilton's fast growing population and prospering businesses earned it the label of 'an ambitious little city.' But suddenly in 1857 a depression struck, the city's population declined and land values also fell. The city was unable to collect enough taxes to cover its debts and went bankrupt.[4] There was no work for young Mesmer and his wife, and though they struggled on for another two years, just four years after they had first come to Canada with bright hopes, the three-generation family found little choice but to cross the Atlantic again to return to Germany and to Mainz.

Back in Germany and back at work, Johannes and Christina Mesmer prospered enough to be able to educate young Victoria at a convent, the School of the English Ladies (known in Canada as the Sisters of Loretto). Already fluent in French and German, Victoria added English to her languages at school. (In later years her youngest son would, quite perversely, describe his family as a humble one. Among the myths he perpetrated was that his mother could speak little or no English. When his book, *Understanding the Young Child*, was translated into German, he made much of his delight that at last his mother would be able to read one of his books, when actually she was perfectly capable of reading it in the original English.)

The family spent eleven years in Germany. Then, when Victoria was fifteen, Johannes, Christina, and Victoria crossed the Atlantic once more and settled again in Hamilton. This time they were able to make a comfortable living and become part of the German community living there. They joined the newly formed Germania Klub, a cultural and athletic organization, and it was there, a year later, that sixteen-year-old Victoria met young Thomas Blatz. His real name was Leo Platz, but through various confusions in the course of immigrating, his name had undergone several changes.

Leo had never intended either to emigrate to Canada, or to become a tailor, or to change his name. His parents, George Thomas Platz and Anna Wander, had died before he was ten, leaving him with two older brothers and a sister. They were taken to live with relatives who had a farm near the small town of Helmstadt in Bavaria. As well as helping with farm chores and learning such basic skills as carpentry and gardening, the children were taught marketable trades. When Leo was twelve and being trained as a brick glazer, an invitation came for an older brother, Thomas, to join a relative in the United States. (The relative was a Platz cousin who had migrated earlier to Buffalo and prospered there as a tailor.) Thomas accepted the invitation to go to Buffalo to learn the tailoring trade, and his papers were prepared. But when it came time to depart Thomas had second thoughts: he was afraid of the sea and decided that he would prefer to stay in Germany and remain a farmer. However, so that his ticket and papers would not go to waste, he proposed that his brother, Leo, should use them. Leo, aged twelve, duly sailed for the United States under the name of Thomas Platz. After he had spent a year in Buffalo learning the rudiments of tailoring, his American relatives arranged for him to finish his apprenticeship with an acquaintance of theirs in Hamilton, Ontario. The Hamilton postmaster happened to register Leo's name with a 'B' instead of a 'P,' and thus, officially, he became Thomas Blatz. He continued to use his own name, Leo, with family and friends, but avoided the red tape involved in changing his name back from Blatz to Platz. (Blatz was pronounced 'Blots.')

Although Leo was only twelve when he travelled to the new world, his fate was very different from that of most other little immigrants of his day. Many of the children who were 'rescued' from urban poverty in one country were transferred to rural deprivation in another. They were casually supervised by their sponsoring organizations, and many were set to hard labour without the opportunity to learn a skill.[5] Leo, however, made his own decision to leave Germany and to leave the farm for city life. Furthermore, he was sponsored by a relative who was well established in North America, and he was apprenticed to a specific trade that made him employable in an urban environment.

In Hamilton he quickly established himself as a competent tailor and an energetic member of the German community. At age seventeen he was one of the founding members of the Germania Klub and, by the time he met young Victoria Mesmer in 1871, at the age of twenty, he was an established tailor with his own small shop, ready to marry and raise a family.

Their wedding portrait shows a moustached and curly-haired Leo seated squarely in an armchair, wearing a well-cut three-piece suit. Victoria is beside him, dressed in many layers of pleats and ruffles, her hair in corkscrew ringlets crowned with a wreath of flowers holding profuse fluffs of veil. Although she is standing and he is seated, she must reach quite high to put her hand on his shoulder, for she is five feet tall and he over six.

Hamilton was still largely a city of immigrants and remained that way until well into the second half of the nineteenth century. Ethnic groups did not usually gather into ghettos, with the possible exception of the Irish, who dominated an area known as Cork Town. Of the various immigrant groups, the Irish and the Catholics seemed to fare the worst. At mid-century, a quarter of Hamilton's labourers lived in Cork Town, and they were generally among the most economically disadvantaged. Nevertheless, despite the poverty, there was a high incidence of home ownership in Cork Town, reflecting the propensity of the Irish to buy their own homes, however humble they might be. Though the poorer Irish settlers tended to cluster at the foot of the mountain, the area was not entirely homogeneous, for a significant number of the élite traded the convenience of a mid-town residence for a scenic location at the base of the mountain. It was highly characteristic of Hamilton to have a mixture of poor and affluent houses on the same street.[6]

At the foot of this mountain, in Cork Town, Leo Blatz bought his first house. He was not wealthy, but business was good, and his circumstances grew increasingly comfortable. Although tailors at the time were generally not as well off as those in the construction trades, Leo Blatz was one of the more successful tailors in town and was able to provide well for his family. Victoria helped in the business from the start, keeping the books and managing the office.

The Blatzes were not Irish, of course, but they were strong Catholics and their integration into Cork Town life was smooth. Their first home was a cottage near the 'steps' at the foot of the mountain. It was called 'Kehr Ein' (Turn In), and indeed quickly became the place where neighbours went for advice and assistance.

They had been married for five years before their first child, Eva, was born. She was followed, at two-year intervals, by Adam, Christine, Charlie, Rosalie, and Louis, and then, at three-year intervals by Elizabeth (known as Lee), Leo, and finally the youngest, Wilhelm, in 1894.[7]

Wilhelm was born at home on a Sunday morning. That day Leo took the youngest children to Mass, then for a long walk on the mountain, and after that, most unexpectedly, to a restaurant for a round of cream sodas and poppyseed rolls. When the children arrived home, they were astounded to find that they had a new baby brother.

Little 'Helm' was a source of worry at first, for he was a small and sickly baby, breathing only with difficulty. His eldest sisters, Eva and Christine, aged nineteen and fifteen, were perfectly happy to undertake the care of the new infant, putting his bed near the oven to keep him warm and lavishing attention on him. Victoria, who was then forty and the mother of nine children, took a long time to regain her strength, and, by the time she did, Helm's care had been taken over almost entirely by the eldest girls.

As the business prospered and the family grew, it became both possible and desirable to move to a larger house. Leo found one nearby on a larger lot, razed it to the foundation, and then himself planned, supervised, and did much of the building of the new version of 'Kehr Ein.' It was in this new house that Wilhelm Blatz was born.

The house was built into the slope of the ground on two and a half levels. It combined ornateness with comfort and efficiency. The parlour boasted such Victorian splendours as a huge, gilt-framed mirror, a marble mantle, gilded chairs, long sofas, a grand piano, collections of sea shells and curios, and an abundance of bric-à-brac covering every available surface. In the main hall was a heavy sideboard bearing a silver punch-bowl and the family Bible. On this floor were Leo's office, bedroom, and bathroom, and a sunroom for his plants. On the upper level Victoria had her own room, which she shared with the current baby. Nearby were separate dormitories, one for the boys and one for the girls of the family, each with its own toilet and wash-basin. In summer the whole family moved to a sleeping porch that was open to the air. There were also a guest-room, a large hall with room for the children's books and games, and an alcove for Victoria's sewing-machine.

Half a level down from the main floor were the children's playroom, the kitchen, breakfast-room, and dining-room, and a conservatory for plants, vegetables – and a family treasure: the icebox. Outdoors there was a cement patio with benches and a rotating stone table, invented by Leo, for family activities. There were garden sheds, the root cellar, and a child's wonderland of rock gardens for flowers and herbs, grape arbours, an orchard, a vegetable garden, and – special favourites with the children – a grotto with step-seats and a play yard complete with sandbox, swing, see-saw, and a square of cement for skipping or bouncing balls. William Blatz's sister and niece recall a childhood of playing 'school' on the grotto steps, making sand gardens with twigs and pebbles in cigar boxes, and hours of play with the dollhouses and barns built for each child by their father and decorated by their mother. An elaborate game of train travel invented for the children by Victoria would have done credit to the imaginative powers of the most devoted grade school teacher of today. Under their mother's eye, the children made tickets with the names of all the stations on their proposed route. Then they worked out schedules and train connections, purchasing their tickets with play money from the conductor of the day. Part of the game was to pack themselves an appetizing and nutritious lunch from the icebox and root cellar, and to think how they would react to any travel contingencies.

A favourite game when father was out, and thus unable to forbid it, was 'speeching.' Each child in turn would climb on to the dining-table to give a speech on a given topic. Only German could be spoken from the table; if a word of English was uttered, pandemonium broke out, for the penalty was to receive bashes on the legs from rulers and wads of paper. (Despite William Blatz's later picture of the family as German speaking, both Lee and niece Victoria – who was only ten years younger than her uncle – describe this game of playful but clandestine German speaking as a family tradition – in a family that tried to speak English at home.)

The Blatz family put a big emphasis on parties and picnics in the hearty Bavarian style with lots of music, laughter, and food. Young Helm would perform magic tricks or present his monologue about Johnny Smoker, which invariably convulsed his audience and made the family and friends think that perhaps he should be headed for the vaudeville theatre rather than the operating theatre.

The family picnics started well before the First World War. The Canadian relatives would gather in Berlin (now Kitchener) one year and in Buffalo the next. After 1915 the annual picnics moved to Victoria Park in Niagara Falls on the last Saturday of May. Everybody contributed sausages, German potato salad, large pots of baked beans, pies, and cakes.[8]

Apart from parties and picnics, it was very much a home-based family, as Blatz's sister Lee recalls. When Eva, the eldest daughter, married, she and her husband bought the adjoining property and made the two gardens into one. The youngest Blatz children grew up with nieces and nephews of the same age, inviting friends to play, but rarely playing on the streets.

The family had a tradition of order and 'good form.' The children were expected to present guests to their mother, to shake hands with or kiss relatives as required, to eat what was put before them, to speak only when spoken to, and to accept the ritual of settling around the dining-table for homework each night, with their mother on hand to supervise. Victoria herself was quick and clever and read a great deal. In later years her son remarked that she always gave him full acclaim for everything he did, and he had a strong desire to please her.[9] There was organization but no feeling of constraint. It was quite obvious that there was love enough for all, and there never were serious family quarrels with Victoria 'at hand as the solvent, the humourous [sic] peacemaker, the judge.'[10] Family members recall the day Leo brought home two dozen prize hens he had bought from a friend, declaring they would be an easy way to provide fresh eggs for the family. Victoria had no interest in raising hens but listened and said nothing. The next Sunday two roast chickens appeared at dinner, and more the next week, until there were no more hens and no further discussion. Victoria (or 'Nomie' as her family called her) was usually dressed in soft colours, her skirts widened with multiple petticoats, and the long-sleeved blouses she always wore decorated with a jabot of lace or embroidery for the regular afternoons she was at home to callers. She was very fond of cats, and the family always had at least one, as well as a dog, which was Leo's special pet.

Although both Leo and Victoria became naturalized Canadian citizens, European customs were observed for festive events. Christmas and New Year's meant not only traditional German stollen and Lebkuchen, but also French croissants, a suckling pig or a goose decorated with oranges and onions, and the silver punch-bowl filled with fruits soaked in wine. Victoria usually had at least some of her children with her while she prepared these treats or daily meals; and, perhaps because cooking was a part of the German male tradition, she departed from then-current North American customs and included her sons as well as her daughters in the cooking instruction.

Leo's business developed into a custom-tailoring shop for a larger company. It occupied four houses, converted into a single building. From the outside it looked like a row of cottages with flower boxes on the window ledges and a garden in back with benches and tables for the workers to use at lunch-time. Eventually it employed forty men and women.

Helm attended St Patrick's Separate School until the age of twelve and then Central Collegiate until he was sixteen. Along the way he helped out in the tailoring shop. As a pre-schooler he learned to pull the basting threads; later, as an errand boy, he carried parcels of goods back and forth. He also learned to sew quite well. (In later years, when he was at the pinnacle of his career, he still found time to make many of his own daughter's party dresses and other special clothes.)

The house was usually filled with people: relatives and Irish and German friends visited often, and parties were frequent. So many children visited that daughter Lee has commented that Leo Blatz sometimes confused his own nine children with others. Often the visitors were people in distress. Both Victoria and Leo were good listeners with a fund of common sense and inventive knowledge, and the community often turned to them for help with their personal problems. Both remained active in the Germania Klub. Leo, then several of his sons in turn, acted as its president, while Victoria, and then two of her daughters, were presidents of the ladies' group. All the children joined in its choirs and theatrical events.

As Wilhelm (Helm) accompanied his mother on her visits to help out in neighbourhood emergencies, he learned a good deal about the symptoms and management of various diseases and injuries from accidents; this undoubtedly helped to lay the foundation for his later medical training. His real forte, however, seemed to be as an entertainer. He was in demand as an actor for school performances, and at parties he could act as a magician or stand-up comedian. Had he decided to go on the stage no one would have been surprised, his sister says.

His mother, however, had her heart set on his becoming a doctor. He seemed to have the necessary academic ability, for he was invariably at the top of his class in school. His sister recalls another bright child's complaint that 'the Blatz boy wins all the prizes.' She does not recall that he was in any way unusual, however, except for being exceptionally witty and always a tease. Victoria put a strong emphasis on academic endeavour and simply assumed that all her children would do well in school; and all of them did.

Wilhelm finished Central Collegiate at age sixteen and reported to the University of Toronto, but was advised to wait until he was a year older. He spent the intervening time at school as a teacher's helper, assisting other students and marking papers. At that time he began to take a special interest in his niece, Victoria Mueller, who had been crippled since birth. During his university years they kept in close touch, and he set up special study programs for her.

Wilhelm (by now more frequently called Bill) entered university the next year. He was a religious boy who attended Mass almost daily for several years and had even seriously considered the priesthood. At the University of Toronto, however, he did not attend the Catholic St Michael's College. He claimed later that when standing in line to register he simply chose the same college as the person in front of him. It was Victoria College, the college of the Methodists, and gradually he drifted away from the Catholic church.

At that time few first-generation immigrants went to university unless their families had been well-to-do or educated in the Old World. Wilhelm Blatz was the only child in his family to go on to university, although all had gone to high school. The eldest boy, Adam, became an organist and choirmaster, Charlie and Louis joined forces as building contractors, while Leo became an electrician. The eldest sisters married young, but Lee, the youngest girl, trained as a nurse before she married.

At university, Bill Blatz embarked on his studies in physiology in preparation for becoming a doctor, just as he had promised his mother. One of his first extracurricular activities was to try out for the Varsity football team. He managed to get a football letter as centre scrimmage, but as he stood only five foot seven and weighed 108 pounds, it was generally agreed that he could be of most use in team management.

In the eyes of his nieces and nephews of the same age in Hamilton, he cut a dashing figure. Sometimes when he went to Hamilton he would stay at his sister Christine's rather than going home, where he would have had to give an account of himself to his mother. His sister, accustomed to mothering him since he was little, would tidy him up and launder his clothes before sending him back to university. One week she received a postcard of his football team, showing the players leaning on each others' shoulders. One or two wear helmets, though most are bareheaded; Blatz alone wears a dark knitted cap, which almost entirely covers his eyes. Among the players stand six young women, all smiles, wearing broad-brimmed hats, fox furs, and feathers. The inscribed message sounds a frantic note: 'Dear Tina, Will be at your place Thursday about 7.00 p.m. as there is a dance at the club. Do not say anything to anybody at home. Helm. P.S. If there is a dance at the club, I want to go for I got to learn to dance by Friday night.'[11]

As well as enjoying the social whirl, Blatz managed to find time to do very well in his studies, to teach a night school class in chemistry at the technical school, and to write a weekly column on motoring for a Toronto newspaper. In the summers he joined his brothers as one of the Blatz Brothers Builders. One summer they were building a five-room cottage on the Hamilton mountain and Blatz was installing the windows. He put the glass in the sashes and planned to paint the next day, but that night there was a heavy rain and the sashes warped, breaking all the glass. He walked home in tears. His mother made him coffee and an egg and told him to go back to get more window glass, but advised him to paint the sashes first this time. It was a lesson in practical sympathy and a step towards learning to cope with disappointment.[12] It was this kind of practical help that Blatz would later give to people in distress when they came to him for assistance.

Blatz Brothers Builders lasted only a few years, but during its operation the brothers built another cottage on Hamilton Beach, several more-substantial houses on the mountain, and a small manufacturing plant in Brampton. Blatz developed enough dexterity at carpentry, along with the sewing and cooking he had already learned, to maintain all three skills as lifelong interests.

Blatz received a BA in 1916 and an MA in 1917. His thesis involved an effort to produce Addison's Disease artificially in laboratory rats by tying off the adrenal glands. He was headed for medicine, as his mother had planned, but the First World War was by then in progress and would intervene. Earlier he had been exempted from military service because of his employment as a medical research student, but now he sought to enlist and to go overseas with the Royal Naval Air Service.

In December 1916 he had requested a copy of the regulations for special entry in Canada into the RNAS. The regulations declared that candidates must be of a pure European descent and the sons either of natural-born or naturalized British subjects. In doubtful cases, the burden of clear proof would rest upon the candidate.[13]

That seemed to present no problem, however, for even though both his parents were German-born they were both loyal to king and country and had been naturalized in Canada as British subjects. Furthermore Blatz's grandmother had made dresses for the king of England's grandmother and had even been allowed to name her daughter (Blatz's mother) after Her Majesty, Queen Victoria.

A month after his application for overseas duty he received notice from the naval recruiting secretary in Ottawa that his name had been placed on the list of accepted candidates for the Royal Naval Air Service. On the date of his departure from Canada he would be entered as a probationary flight officer.

On 15 March 1917, Vice-Admiral C. Kingsmill, director of the Naval Service of Canada, wrote to Whitehall confirming that W.E. Blatz was booked for passage to England on a transport leaving Canada about 20 March.

Almost immediately, though, the decision was reversed. It was discovered that Blatz was of German descent, and the burden to prove otherwise would rest with him. It was an unanswerable fact, and so he was refused entry both to the RNAS and to the Royal Naval Volunteer Reserve as a surgeon probationer.

Kingsmill wrote a letter for Blatz to clear his name and explain the situation:

> This is to certify that Mr. Wilhelm Blatz made application to this Department for entry as a Probationary Flight Officer in the Royal Naval Air Service. He fulfilled all the requirements as to physique, education, etc., and produced excellent references from people of the best standing.
>
> He was accepted for entry and was about to leave for England when it was ascertained that this gentleman was of German extraction on his father's side. Mr. Blatz was perfectly frank on this point and made no attempt to conceal it.
>
> Though this Department has no reason whatsoever to doubt his loyalty to the Crown, and very much regrets the action which it is compelled to take, it was forced to carry out the instructions from the Admiralty not to enter any persons of enemy extraction.

Mr. Blatz also applied for entry as a Surgeon Probationer, RNVR, but the same reason prevented this also.[14]

It was a great blow to Blatz to be rejected for overseas service, but it marked a turning point in his life. Left at loose ends, he met by chance on the university campus the man who was to have a large and continuing part in his future career.

This was E.A. (Ned) Bott, a psychologist on the staff of the University of Toronto. Bott himself had been rejected as a recruit because of his poor eyesight and had turned to civilian war work, organizing a group of volunteers to work with soldiers who had returned from France. He was chiefly interested in trying to treat chronic cases with some physiological involvement: nerve injuries, so-called shell-shock, and amputations. Bott was renowned for his mechanical inventiveness and had devised gadgets to help reactivate damaged muscles. The university campus's newest architectural jewel, Hart House, was turned over for teaching the volunteer staff to work with Bott's patients; the actual rehabilitation work took place at Christie Street Hospital.[15]

Shortly after Blatz accepted Bott's invitation to join the Hart House re-education team, the project was taken over by the Royal Canadian Army Medical Corps. As this type of service need not involve going overseas, Blatz was allowed to move sideways, continuing the same job but enlisting in the forces. He was appointed a staff sergeant in functional re-education and placed in charge of the physiological laboratory. His duties involved teaching the volunteers a detailed anatomy of limbs, working directly with the veterans to demonstrate techniques of physiotherapy to the volunteers, and working at research in the laboratory. Margaret Fletcher, who studied with him in preparation for volunteer service, recalls his classes as the favourite with her group of fellow students. It was a short course but very rigorous. Blatz and Bott together gave intensive instruction in the anatomy of arms and legs, and Bott illustrated the lectures with his albums of glossy photographs of the layers of muscles. Physiotherapy could make the muscles work, but the problem was to persuade the soldiers to follow through independently. Fletcher spoke of Blatz's ability to challenge those men whom no one else could help. Blatz would be called upon to demonstrate how to work with difficult cases. He would be quite confident that the patient could perform the exercise and would look him right in the eye and almost will him to go through the motions that had seemed too difficult before. Blatz was always very definite that the patient had to concentrate on what was happening, and the man would find himself doing well when he had been ready to give up.[16]

To Blatz it was quite obvious that the key to success in physiotherapy was motivation; the patients would have to concentrate on what was happening, want very much to succeed, and become participant learners in order to master their limitations and develop the ability to meet future situations with confidence. He found himself dealing with what he described as a phenomenon more elusive than any other – consciousness. He also developed an overriding interest in motivation – in explaining why some would work hard in rehabilitative therapy while others would soon give up.[17] It seemed to him that Bott's field of psychology was the most promising place to look for the answers to such questions. Interest in early learning was a natural stage in this long quest, because, as Bott wrote later, motivation, with the emphasis on self-direction and progressive achievement, would be much the same in children as in veteran patients. With younger subjects, however, the task would be simpler and, presumably, easier to study.[18]

Blatz's first two scholarly publications were prepared during these army years. They were jointly written by F.A. Hartman, Staff-sergeant W.E. Blatz, and L.G. Kilborn and focused on the influences of treatment on denervated muscle. The first paper concerned circulatory changes that take place when the nerve to a muscle is severed, and the second paper discussed the effect of massage (finding it to be slightly helpful but otherwise of inconclusive benefit).[19]

Blatz was discharged soon after the war. By then he had decided that psychology interested him more than physiology. Bott urged him to finish his medical studies first, however, in order to lay a strong foundation for work in the new kind of psychology, which was moving away from philosophy. Blatz also had an obligation to his mother, whose heart was still set on his becoming a doctor.

He returned to the University of Toronto's medical school for his clinical work and received the MB degree in 1921.

Despite the rigours of his medical studies, he still found time for three major interests. He was courting Margery Rowland, whom he had met on a blind date when they were both students at Victoria College; he was editor of the medical students' magazine, *Epistaxis*; and he was manager of the Varsity football team, which won the Grey Cup in 1920. (His contacts with the football team led to one important phase of his later career. He became a friend of Bill Dafoe, the bright younger brother of a country doctor, Allan Roy Dafoe, of Callander, Ontario, who some fourteen years later brought Blatz to work with the Dionne quintuplets.)

The two examples of medical collegiate humour attributed to W.E.B. in the 1921 edition of *Epistaxis* are parodies of a litany and a medical student's credo. They are full of such heavy ironies as: 'Every neophyte at the shrine of Hippocrates solemnly believes that surgeons receive fabulous sums for the most trivial operations, *ergo* and *propter hoc* surgery is the only field to master ... that medicine is certainly no profession for women, and hence look [*sic*] askance at all freshettes ... that the first two years are on the calendar so that they would not be too young when graduating.'[20] (Much of Blatz's later career was spent with highly competent female colleagues, so it is not entirely surprising to find the little jokes about women doctors. Besides, his fiancée was a lawyer by profession, having studied law at Osgoode Hall.)

Both while he was at Hart House, and in medical school, Blatz continued his work with his niece Victoria Mueller. She was the child of his sister Christine, who had virtually raised Blatz as a baby. Victoria, who was just ten years younger than her uncle, had been born with a dislocated hip, and her right leg had nerve damage and a rigid ankle. She remembers when she was about five overhearing her fifteen-year-old Uncle Helm discuss her future with a distant relative. She spoke only German and French at the time, but could understand Blatz when he said in English, 'She will make it because she has a brain. I'm watching her.' And indeed he did watch her and guide the course of her education.[21]

While at Hart House Blatz tried some of the newest physiotherapy techniques on his niece. Her foot was motionless but she recalls his trying to get even a tiny motion in a toe, then recording its extent on a gauge. The slightest movement would thus encourage her to try harder. He made a game of it, and she was happy to carry on. In a letter to her, dated 25 April 1919, he discusses her dismay at the need to wear heavy orthopaedic boots and writes:

> I can readily appreciate Victoria dear how you feel about these boots, but remember there are lots of things worse than unsightly boots. You deserve a great deal of credit for your sunny disposition in the face of many trials and you should treasure that more than anything else on earth. Also Victoria remember that you are blessed with parents who have done and will do all they can to alleviate what seems to you

naturally to be a very hard lot. You will have learned by now that it is some such trial that inspires genius. The poet Byron was lame just as you are, Milton was blind, Carlyle was a confirmed dyspeptic, George Eliot an invalid, Poe practically insane and look at their success ...
Learn all you can of everything, and about everything, don't just learn what the teacher says. When you are knitting think of where the wool comes from, when did they first begin to knit, why use wool instead of cotton and so on ... this system will lead you into many fascinating byways ... when you get on farther in your studies you will find that the true enjoyment of life is the appreciation of literature, art and music ... it is only by eternally seeking that we are eternally busy learning more.[22]

In another letter, a year later, he writes: 'the more one busies oneself in interests other than actual school study the broader and more cultured does one become. An educated man does not necessarily mean one who knows what is inside of books. School is only to show the students how to study and to teach the essentials. Do not let any opportunity pass to learn of other things.'[23]

After medical school Blatz was able to turn to his newer and now major interest: psychology. His medical training had done little to foster this interest in the workings of the mind: it included only four lectures on psychiatry, none on psychology, and one demonstration of a delusional patient. 'Thus my decision was strengthened to find out exactly what psychology had to offer in the understanding of human beings.'[24] Most specifically, he wanted to learn more about the way mental processes operate and the way people are motivated to direct their attention to solving problems. Bott arranged for him to study at the most appropriate place and with the most suitable person to develop his interest in motivation. This was at the University of Chicago, where Harvey Carr was head of the psychology department.

The University of Chicago was virtually an instant university, fashioned in 1892 from the remnants of a defunct theological seminary and nourished with liberal applications of money from the founder of Standard Oil, John D. Rockefeller. The young university had soon earned a reputation for academic innovation, especially in the social sciences.[25]

Philosopher-psychologist John Dewey spent ten of the early years at Chicago and started a laboratory school where he developed some of the progressive ideas that still influence today's education. In psychology itself, the name of the university became attached to a particularly American approach to the subject, a distinct departure from the traditions established when Wilhelm Wundt set up his psychology laboratory at Leipzig in 1879 and ushered in 'scientific psychology.' Wundt and his students concentrated their efforts on trying to analyse the building blocks of consciousness. They developed rigorous techniques of introspection, systematically examining their own sensations and feelings, convinced that virtually all experiences could be reduced to simple elements, which would then reveal the basic structure of consciousness.

Although the orthodox definition of psychology as the science of consciousness continued without challenge for several decades, in practice many psychologists soon looked beyond the mere facts of mental phenomena to the way these functioned. They became interested in finding explanations for what people do, how they do it, and why.[26] This was true of psychologists on both sides of the Atlantic, but particularly of those in the United States, and especially at the young University of Chicago. Both Dewey and James Rowland Angell, head of the psychology department, had been pupils of the pragmatist William James at Harvard and shared his viewpoint that the value of ideas should be judged by their usefulness.

It was left to the Oxford-educated Edward B. Titchener, a stern adherent of Wundt's psychology, to point out the error of their ways, and thus to split psychology asunder. Titchener, thwarted in his effort to interest a British university in starting a psychological laboratory, had settled for the United States and Cornell. (His arrival in the United States coincided with the founding of the University of Chicago.) Although a person of broad cultural interests (for a while at Cornell he had also acted as professor of music), his view of psychology was as narrow as the edge of a knife.

Titchener watched with growing disapproval as American psychologists galloped too far ahead of what he considered to be the proper pursuits of basic psychological investigation. At Chicago, for example, psychology was being put to practical use, especially in the field of education,[27] and the whole emphasis of psychological investigation was on adaptation, action, utility, and practicality. Titchener did not approve of an approach that looked at how things work and how things might be used while seeming to ignore the vast territories still uncharted in the structure of consciousness.

Titchener operated decisively to divide psychology in two. In 1898 he published the first of his papers, calling the true followers of the way of Wundt 'structuralists' and dismissing the other brash adventurers as 'functionalists.'

Although Angell rarely became ruffled, he felt compelled to fight back in defence of American psychology, making a declaration of the positive importance of functionalism. Functional psychology, he said, was not as interested in the mere contents of experience as it was in singling out and describing mental operations in their whole setting and in light of their goals.[28]

Angell became the most prominent spokesperson for functionalism, and American psychology in general and University of Chicago psychologists in particular were associated with the functional school. The focus was on adjustment to the physical and social environment as a person's major task. Initially, for instance, conscious processes would be used in making adjustments, but eventually new sensory-motor co-ordinates would become established in familiar situations. Later, as these were perfected, the mental aspects of the process would diminish and the co-ordination would become completely automatic.[29] Thus habits are formed. (This interest in habit formation was a legacy from William James, passed through Dewey and Angell to Carr and thence to Blatz, who applied it as the basis of his earliest ideas in child raising.)

When Angell was elevated to the presidency of Yale University, Harvey Carr, one of his former students, took his place as head of psychology at Chicago. Titchener at Cornell continued to attack Carr at Chicago, encouraging Chicago further to define its position.

Functional psychology went on studying consciousness, but looked more at how consciousness developed and operated than at its make-up. Introspection was supplemented by objective observations of behaviour, until eventually the process was reversed, and it became more usual for direct observations to be supplemented by introspection. Introspection was used to give on-the-spot accounts of experiences while they were still fresh in a person's mind. In his 1925 book (written while Blatz was studying with him) Carr defined psychology as the study of mental activity. In his studies he explored the relationship between physiological reactions and such mental processes as acquiring, retaining, organizing, and evaluating experiences. These processes would be used in order to adapt or adjust. The studies of mental activities (such as memory, attention, sensation, and perception) were interpreted in the light of their contribution to total behaviour rather than as separate and isolated faculties. Throughout Carr's work, the role of motivation was emphasized.[30]

It was obvious to Blatz that Chicago and Carr could offer useful insights into the driving force in human behaviour. The young Canadian doctor was one of the first doctoral students in psychology at Chicago after Carr became head of the department, but already under Angell Chicago had trained a productive group of psychologists who were prepared to apply their knowledge to useful pursuits. Some, like L.L. Thurstone and Walter V. Bingham, had gone on to develop intelligence tests (although this interest in testing was not typical of the group, because generally Chicago was more interested in conduct than in capacity).[31] Helen Thompson Woolley, who set dazzling academic records at Chicago, was a distinguished child psychologist before her untimely illness. Beardsley Ruml turned from his doctoral studies in the measurement of intelligence to administering money for the Rockefeller family foundations. John B. Watson built up the animal laboratories while he was a student at Chicago and stayed on to develop them further. In 1913, at Johns Hopkins University, he made his own declaration of independence from functionalism by redefining psychology as an objective natural science. The same methods could be used for studying both people and animals, so there was room neither for introspection nor for the study of consciousness in Watson's behaviourism.[32] Watson did, however, retain the functionalist's interest in habit formation.

Chicago had a profound influence on Blatz, an influence that showed in his work throughout his life. Apart from the obvious interest in progressive education based on an understanding of a child's needs and the emphasis on individual problem solving, Blatz was perfectly in tune with Dewey's pragmatic approach to testing ideas by their consequences. While he was at Chicago he worked in the animal laboratory that Watson had organized, and he produced a publication concerning the learning performance of white rats.[33] Like Watson, he made habit training an important part of his early plan for raising children; but he remained a functionalist, and thus always assumed that learning was a more active matter than behaviourists held it to be. For Blatz, as for other functionalists, people were viewed as being active in their adaptations, rather than as victims of circumstance or as manipulated into learning by others. Habits were acquired as an efficient way to expedite routine situations; but functionalists always allowed the learner the element of conscious choice. Consciousness occupied a prominent place in Blatz's last book, when he laid the foundation for the statement of his developmental theory of security. Blatz used introspection to amplify his objective observations of later events in his life (such as going through an air raid) in much the same way that he used introspective recall in his doctoral research.

His thesis was a classical functionalist experiment, with objective observations of a physiological reaction under varying conditions. It was followed with subjective reports of what went through his subject's mind immediately afterwards.

The thesis was 'concerned with the investigation of the cardiac, respiratory, and electrical changes which could be observed during, and subsequent to, the arousal of the emotion of fear. This emotion was induced by the removal of the subject's body support in an unexpected manner.'[34] The subjects were seated in a collapsible armchair, invented by Blatz. The chair pivoted on an axle and would fall forward when released by the experimenter. It would free fall through about sixty degrees, then would be brought to rest gradually, and safely, with the help of a pneumatic door check. Blatz observed reactions and also recorded them on photographic film, on an electrocardiograph, and on an electric pneumograph. Introspective reports by the subjects indicated that they experienced, in all cases, a genuine emotion of fear. Variations of the experiment with loud bells and with or without the falling chair showed some evidence that prior experience and the removal of the element of surprise made the subjects report less fear than before, although their physiological responses remained remarkably similar. (Even when the subjects thought they no longer felt any fear, their breathing and heart rates continued to be more rapid.)

Blatz's thesis brought instant attention. *Popular Science* wrote asking for photographs of the device with a person seated in position, together with a view showing the chair after it had collapsed. Blatz replied that no photographs were available, but that the *Journal of Experimental Psychology* would have a full report on the thesis at some future date.[35] It was published in the *Journal* in the spring issue of 1925.

The Chicago years had been exhilarating ones intellectually, but lean ones financially. Blatz had married Margery Rowland and the two were living more cheaply than anyone would choose to live. He had been granted a fellowship of $250, with the assurance that it was possible to manage quite comfortably in Chicago on $30 a month. When he discovered that the fellowship covered only his fees, he wired a friend for assistance and was loaned $200. It took the young couple nine years to pay this back. They shared a small flat with two other friends in a five-storey walkup, and in later years Blatz told apocryphal tales of making a thirty-nine-cent package of apricots last for two years and buying two cans of navy beans at a bargain, opening one and finding it not very good, but saving the second as a symbol of having something in reserve for a real emergency. When he finished his degree in 1924 they were expecting a baby. Clearly it was time to get to work, and preferably to find that work back at home in Canada.

The challenge awaiting Blatz in Canada was that of organizing a child study centre at the University of Toronto. This undertaking was to become the cornerstone of his career.

# 2 Childhood Ready for Change

When Blatz graduated from Chicago there were already several organizations whose aim was to change the direction of family and child life in North America. These both supported each other and prompted Blatz to play his own part in helping to turn child care and parenting into professionally directed productions. The efforts of the Canadian National Committee for Mental Hygiene (CNCMH), the emergence at the University of Toronto of psychology as a subject apart from philosophy, the influence of the Rockefeller Foundation, and the evolution of the child study movement in North America all combined in 1925 to introduce the young Dr Blatz and his St George's School for Child Study to the city of Toronto.

Pre-scientific psychology had been taught at Toronto since the mid-nineteenth century, and in 1889 James Mark Baldwin, a disciple of Wundt, set up a laboratory there that Baldwin described in his autobiography as 'the first anywhere on British soil.'[1] When Baldwin left Toronto a few years later for Princeton, Edward B. Titchener applied (unsuccessfully) for his post in an attempt to obtain a position somewhere in the Empire.[2] The person who did succeed Baldwin conducted research at Toronto in his first years but soon began to spend increasing amounts of time in Germany. It was E.A. (Ned) Bott, first as a student, then as a member of the philosophy staff, who managed to keep the laboratory afloat. At the beginning of the First World War, Bott turned the laboratory into a rehabilitation clinic and, when it needed more space, had the veterans' project transferred to Hart House. Blatz, of course, worked with him there.

After the war Bott returned to the university as lecturer in philosophy and 'assistant' in the psychology lab, although he was, in fact, in charge of it. Psychology quickly became one of the most popular post-war undergraduate courses, and it was soon necessary for Bott to negotiate its expanding budgetary needs directly with the university president. By 1920 psychology had grown numerically larger than philosophy and became a 'subject' on its own, with its own staff. When the two disciplines separated, Bott chose psychology. The psychology faculty remained in the faculty of arts, but, in a bid for clear independence from all things philosophical in the first few years, aligned themselves with the medical faculty. Although Bott did much of the administrative work for the subject (and was named its head when psychology became a department in 1926), in 1920 the name at the top of the psychology staff list was that of C.K. Clarke. Clarke was then dean of medicine, professor of psychology, superintendent of the Toronto General Hospital, and medical director of the Canadian National Committee for Mental Hygiene.[3]

Earlier, when Clarke had been superintendent of the Toronto Hospital for the Insane, he had grown particularly interested in the study of 'feeble-mindedness.' He was one of the founders of the mental hygiene and eugenics movement, which has been described as 'an amalgam of humanitarianism, patriotism, science and pseudoscience ... [with] one of its major concerns [being] the mental health of children.'[4] Clarke's emphasis was on hereditary factors, and the whole thrust of the early mental hygiene movement was towards containing any problems that might arise from feeble-mindedness. He was joined in his crusade by Dr Helen MacMurchy, chief of the Division of Child Welfare in the Dominion Department of Health, who used statistics and even story-books to warn of the dangers of allowing 'mental defectives' to mingle with the general community. In her book *The Almosts: A Study of the Feebleminded*, she told the stories of a series of characters from novels, adding the brisk comment that 'so far at least we do not seem to have taken mentally defective persons in the world as seriously as the great writers.'[5]

The committee worked to exclude mentally defective children and adults from entering Canada; advocated separate classes for the feeble-minded, well away from other children; was intent on establishing relationships between feeble-mindedness and juvenile delinquency;

and warned that the feeble-minded should be sterilized lest they produce offspring with similar deficiencies.[6]

The co-founder of the CNCMH, along with Clarke, was Clarence M. Hincks. Hincks was a general practitioner who was also a medical officer in the Toronto school system. His interest in the relationship between physical and mental disorders widened to include mental hygiene when he became a consultant to the newly organized Toronto Juvenile Court in 1913. His interests converged with Clarke's at the court, although he met Bott quite independently of Clarke when he assisted in some research in the psychology laboratory at the end of the war. (Both Clarke and Hincks knew indirectly of young Blatz's wartime work at Hart House. It is also likely that Bott's advice to Blatz to become a physician before studying psychology reflected the way psychology at Toronto was distancing itself from philosophy and marching with medicine.)

In the United States a National Committee for Mental Hygiene had been formed earlier through the efforts of a former mental patient, Clifford Beers, and with the support of such groups as the Rockefeller Foundation. Hincks sought the help of Beers in organizing a Canadian equivalent, and in 1918 the Canadian National Committee for Mental Hygiene was formed, with Clarke as its medical director and Hincks as secretary.

Hincks's life was governed by his moods, which ran in cycles from euphoria to the depths of depression. When he was feeling elated he could sweep others along with his grand designs, but when he felt low he was certain he had overstepped the mark. At those points he would drop out for a while, taking refuge at his Muskoka cottage while his fellow workers toiled to tidy up his enterprises and get them properly launched. This would make Hincks feel so much better that he would go on to his next great vision. Thus the CNCMH grew, not in a smooth sequence, but, literally, by leaps and bounds.

Hincks was a charismatic fund raiser and was able to get support from some of the wealthiest families in Toronto and Montreal: the Eatons, the Masseys, the Beattys – of the department store, farm-machinery, and railway industries, respectively – while his first patron was the governor-general of Canada, the Duke of Devonshire, who was one of England's wealthiest peers. All gave generously to the cause of mental hygiene.[7]

The other two groups that influenced the direction of Blatz's career were the child study pioneers and the Laura Spelman Rockefeller

Memorial fund. Both shared an enthusiasm for studying child development with a view to improving the next generation, and both were committed to teaching parents wise ways of raising children.

In the United States and Canada there had been an interest in learning formal parenting skills since before the turn of the century when groups of mothers first met to discuss the work of G. Stanley Hall. Hall, considered the founder of child psychology in North America, believed that the stages of a child's growth recapitulated the history of mankind. He engaged parents and teachers in filling out lengthy questionnaires, assuring them that he had 'overwhelming evidence that to know a child better is to love it more.'[8]

In 1901, William Scott, the Scottish-born principal of the Toronto Normal School, wrote with enthusiasm that child study has 'freshened and heightened our interest in children. The child is now understood as never before ... What is the meaning of Mothers' Clubs, Mothers' Congresses, Mothers' Reading Circles, Art Leagues, but increased interest in children? Dr. Stanley Hall says that the movement has increased matrimony and the desire to rear children.'[9]

Hall's genetic psychology represented yet another approach to psychology, one that used laboratories and conducted research but showed more interest in theory than in practice. Baldwin was enthusiastic about it for a while and arranged for the Toronto philosopher Frederick Tracy to study for a PH D with Hall at Clark University and suggested he write his dissertation on child psychology. Hall, at Clark University, had a different point of view from Angell and Carr at Chicago, looking at development as a predetermined process, with very little room for adaptation. It was a logical step for Hall's later followers to become concerned with tests and measurements and to stress the overriding influence of heredity upon capacity.[10]

Among the groups of American mothers discussing Halls' work was the Society for the Study of Child Nature, formed in 1888 as part of the Ethical Culture Society of New York. Over the next two decades the group shifted its interest to more 'scientific' writers, such as Dr L.E. Holt, who gave authoritative instructions for the physical management of children in his *Care and Feeding of Infants*. With their new sophistication went a new name, the Federation of Child Study of New York. The group was intelligent and eager to learn and a few years later took on yet another name and another role.

In the universities child study was also getting under way. In 1911 Arnold Gesell started the Yale Psycho-Clinic to study mental development, and in 1917 the University of Iowa received a grant from the Women's Christian Temperance Union to form its Child Welfare Research Station. At much the same time, in New York, the Bureau of Educational Experiments opened the Harriet Johnson Nursery (which later became the Bank Street School and today is the Bank Street College of Education).

After the war there was a surge of interest in child guidance, university nursery schools, parent education, and child development research. These new areas of interest all reflected a general ambition to improve mankind. In 1922 Abigail Eliot opened a nursery in Boston that became the Eliot-Pearson School at Tufts, and in the same year the Merrill-Palmer School of Motherhood and Home Training opened its nursery. Merrill-Palmer conducted research on physical development and nutrition, and its first director, Helen Thompson Woolley, a Chicago graduate, undertook studies of personality development.

In the area of child guidance to prevent delinquency the National Committee for Mental Hygiene in the United States and later its Canadian counterpart were soon firmly launched and receiving funds from major philanthropies to sustain research and clinics.

For instance, John D. Rockefeller, Sr, had been told by his adviser (former clergyman Frederick E. Gates) that his fortune was rolling up, in fact rolling up like an avalanche: 'You must distribute it faster than it grows! If you do not it will crush you, and your children, and your children's children.'[11]

Part of the Rockefeller effort to sidestep such a fate was the establishment of a fund in memory of J.D. Rockefeller's wife, Laura Spelman Rockefeller, to promote the welfare of women and children.[12] In the first years, its funds had made lump-sum payments to already-established child welfare organizations. When Beardsley Ruml became its director in 1922, he at once reoriented the aims of the memorial to focus on a reform of the social sciences to make them apply more directly to improving childhood. He enlisted the help of the economist Lawrence Frank, who was becoming known for his writing on school reform and progressive education as doors to a better world, and who was a close friend of the founders of the Bureau of Educational Experiments in New York.

Frank presented a comprehensive plan to Ruml for what was to become the parent education movement in North America. The Laura Spelman Rockefeller Memorial would establish child development research centres in a group of major universities, centres that would, in turn, provide information on the science of child study to mothers who would meet in small groups to learn more about children. Frank has been called 'the apostle of the "progressive" home, the visionary who started a whole social movement virtually at rock bottom and eventually transformed all social institutions.'[13]

One of the first steps of the Ruml-Frank team administering the memorial fund was to develop a core group of people interested in parent education. They selected the Federation of Child Study, gave it professional management, and broadened its range beyond New York City to turn it into the Child Study Association of America. Teachers' College at Columbia University was given the first money for a research centre in child development, and the memorial was ready to look further for other similar projects. In Toronto, the Rockefeller Foundation itself was already helping mental hygiene to subsidize both psychology at the university, and, from there, a program of research in the schools. Explaining mental hygiene's concentration on psychology, Clarence Hincks wrote in his (unpublished) autobiography that this was due to a hunch of his at the beginning of the century. 'I felt the twentieth century would be a century for psychology – revealing to us the nature and possibilities of man in regard to his intellectual, emotional and behavioural potentialities.'[14] It was time, Hincks thought, for child study to be established in Canada.

Hincks knew the Rockefeller Foundation directors very well, and when he met Ruml of the Memorial, Hincks was asked to address a group of Bronxville mothers. Ruml would not be there, but his wife, as president of the group of women, would report to him afterwards. Hincks talked about child development, telling the women about Canada's Osler family, Sir Edmund, Sir William, and the Honourable Featherstone Osler, and their two 'unusually able' sisters. He attributed their success in life as stockbroker, physician, and judge, to a highly intelligent father, who had lived as an itinerant preacher, and a mother of strong character and constant influence, and he was eloquent in expounding to his audience that the early years in life determine what children will be when they grow up.

That afternoon, after his wife had talked to him, Ruml travelled down Fifth Avenue in a taxicab with Hincks. He said: 'Hincks, how much money do you want from the Laura Spelman Rockefeller Memorial as our initial payment?' They settled on $150,000, though Hincks said he always insisted on matching all American grants dollar for dollar with Canadian in order to assure continuity and Canadian in-

volvement. (The funds in this case were supplemented by the Metro-
politan Insurance Company.) Hincks was taken to meet Lawrence
Frank, who urged him to help raise the level of effective living of all
people, well and sick alike, preaching (to Hincks, the converted) that
Hincks must help create the science of human development and learn
the factors that influence development from birth to death.

To begin work in the child study field in Canada, Hincks decided
on two projects, one at McGill and the other at the University of Toronto.
He planned to appoint the paediatrician Dr A.B. Chandler to initiate
studies at McGill, but was at a loss about Toronto. He consulted Bott,
who reminded him about William Blatz, the young man who had
worked with the veterans and who was doing post-graduate work in
Chicago. Hincks asked Blatz to meet him in New York, and the two sat
on a park bench in the Battery in lower New York and discussed the
possibilities of the project at length before meeting with Ruml. Ruml
was apparently not impressed with the brash young Blatz.

After he had met Blatz, Ruml told Hincks: 'I am making no size
up of Blatz. My job is to give money away. Your job is to assemble
suitable staff. If you are fortunate in your selection, that is fine. If you
are not fortunate that is your funeral and I don't want to share it.'[15]
Hincks's judgment prevailed, and Blatz was appointed for the research
work in Toronto. He returned to Canada to develop projects largely
funded by the Laura Spelman Rockefeller Memorial and affiliated with
mental hygiene and psychology. The St George's School, with its emphasis on research and parent education, was to absorb his main effort,
but along with the child study went child guidance work in the Juvenile
Court and consultation with social work agencies.

Back in Toronto, Blatz and his wife found an apartment on
Homewood Court in time for the birth of their daughter. Hamilton
was an easy day's return journey by train, so Blatz was able to keep in
touch with his childhood home, and his parents were full of pride in
their youngest son, now a fully qualified physician and psychologist.
Even so, Blatz would tell of the day when his brother Adam's four-
year-old fell off a table and Blatz was checking her over. 'Mother came
in from an adjoining room, having heard the uproar, and, seeing her
grandchild lying inert on the floor, immediately said, "Get a doctor!
Get a doctor!" ... it is a little difficult for parents to think of their
children as quite grown up.'[16]

In 1925 Blatz had no cohesive theory of child raising to help him
start on his work, but his own childhood had laid some ground rules

for what he considered to be a fair and reasonable approach to children. His parents always combined affection with efficient management, respecting each child's interest and encouraging independence. 'I don't think I can remember any time when either Mother or my Dad visited us with unfair or unjust discipline. I know that on no occasion has she ever interfered with the direction of my own thinking.'[17] Chicago had provided him with some additional basic beliefs, in such things as the practical value of forming habits, the importance of making decisions, and the role of consequences. Independence, efficiency, habits, choices, consequences, and individual interests were all to be incorporated in the basic formulation and later elaborations of Blatz's theory over the years.

In his first months back in Toronto, while Bott carried out negotiations with the university to convert a house on the campus into the school for child study, Blatz made several trips to the United States to learn what he could about other established nurseries and progressive schools. He also started his lifelong association with the Toronto Juvenile Court Clinic, organized a series of case discussions with social workers, and joined a mental hygiene research project that was looking at the behaviour of children in a large public school. These activities, which started early in his career, gave him an opportunity to begin to tie together some of his evolving ideas on child raising with the work of mental hygiene.

One of mental hygiene's primary interests was the prevention of delinquency. Through the efforts of such earlier reformers as Ontario's J.J. Kelso, children in trouble with the law were beginning to be heard in their own courts. In theory, at least, the juvenile courts had turned from punishment to treatment in hopes of avoiding further trouble.

By the time Blatz arrived in Toronto, the CNCMH, supported in large part by Rockefeller funds, was already involved in a variety of projects aimed at averting delinquency. Blatz took part in most of them, in the court, in social work, at Regal Road Public School, and in parent education.

Certainly the most basic step towards prevention was to begin early, and right in the home, to guide parents in raising their children. Dr Helen MacMurchy had started already with her *Little Blue Books* series, which specified 'the Canadian Way' of managing every aspect of a child's life, from imposing a standard schedule within hours of the baby's birth ('Keep right to the time table');[18] to sex education ('Perhaps you should have a happy but serious little talk with them before they go to school, so that they will be prepared. Encourage them by assuring them that Mother and Father know all about it, and will tell them all about it whenever they want to know, but that they better run away and play if other children begin to tell them things that are not nice');[19] to the virtues of fresh air ('Last night you left the window open a wee little bit. It was zero last night. Sometimes it is zero in winter and that is one of the things that make us Canadians what we are').[20]

Blatz's approach was absolutely down-to-earth; he encouraged parents in the full disclosure of information when the children asked. He believed in schedules, but felt that daily routines should be set only after observation of each baby's needs, then followed carefully. It was the approach of a researcher – to examine a situation before drawing conclusions or making plans. At the new St George's School he was preparing to study children from their earliest days at home and to follow them later in the laboratory nursery school. Meanwhile, he would educate parents by encouraging them to think through situations rather than to follow instructions blindly. What was learned at St George's School about building positive mental health in childhood could then be applied in different cultural or economic circumstances.

The study of Regal Road Public School for mental hygiene purposes was already well under way before Blatz returned to Toronto. This sweeping study of the population of a large elementary school focused on misdemeanours as early warnings of problems that could be treated before they turned into full-blown maladjustments or delinquencies. Blatz spent eight years at Regal Road gathering material and counselling parents. He published an interim report of his own findings, but the group as a whole never managed to put the study together or to draw overall conclusions.

Another mental hygiene project that interested Blatz right from the start was the training of social caseworkers as part of a team trying to prevent early difficulties from turning into serious problems.

The crucial development in social work between 1880 and 1930 had been the emerging belief that social work was headed towards a scientific understanding and control of behaviour.[21] There was a growing conviction that insight into emotions and psychic life would prove to be the key to skilled casework.[22] Clinics broadened their scope to deal not just with economic dependency and relief but also with problems of mental health and emotional adjustment. During the First World War, mental hygiene proposed that training in psychiatric social work and in related casework should be extended to offer courses in mental hygiene to all other social workers.[23]

No longer was the compassion and personal charity of volunteers enough; social work was becoming professional, and for this training was required. In 1914, J.J. Kelso of the Children's Aid Society persuaded the University of Toronto to commence a new social service course.[24] Another push towards professional social work was the formation in 1920 of the Canadian Council on Child Welfare (CCCW) to act as a co-ordinating body for child welfare services. Charlotte Whitton was its driving force, and the CCCW received annual federal grants to examine all aspects of child life and to disseminate information on maternal and child care. Whitton was committed to the idea that social work should be in the hands of professionals and, as the power of the council spread, she used the opportunity to place trained social workers in key positions.[25]

Although by the 1920s social work was evolving as a profession and was no longer exclusively in the hands of the volunteer altruist, volunteers were still needed, but only if they worked under professional leadership. Social work agencies used volunteers selectively by carefully screening and supervising their efforts.[26] At the same time, professional social workers were trying to establish a body of knowledge and methods for themselves, based upon the latest 'scientific knowledge.'[27] They looked for support and guidance from experts in related fields.

Blatz was one of those experts. As a part of the CNCMH, he helped in the training of social work students and consulted in the professional development of those already working with children in social agencies or the juvenile courts.

A good deal of the work at the Toronto Juvenile Court as well as at social agencies was able to focus on education for the prevention of trouble, but sometimes problems were found so late or were so extreme that more drastic measures were taken.

There were two forceful ways that earlier social reformers had used to break family patterns in their efforts to keep young people from being swept into delinquency. The first, and most obvious, was to remove children from their home and its influences. Initial efforts of child-savers had been to rescue children from what seemed to be inappropriate situations and to place them in institutions. This gave way to boarding children out with foster families, which was the general Children's Aid approach to child welfare.[28] (At the time Blatz started his work in Toronto, however, the realization was dawning that it might be possible to strengthen the family itself with casework and counselling.)[29]

The second, and more insidious, method of changing family patterns was to try to prevent people from reproducing who might provide an undesirable heredity for their offspring. This was the early orientation of mental hygiene and of both C.K. Clarke and Helen MacMurchy. The retarded, the insane, the epileptic, and the criminal were judged to be cast from the same mould. MacMurchy's book *The Almosts* warned of 'what feeble-mindedness costs in hard cash, in self-respect, in social degradation – and degeneracy.' Early court and social work efforts concentrated on removing every feeble-minded person from society 'to keep away from him evils and temptations that he never will be grown-up enough to resist.' Furthermore, 'marriage with a mental defective brings the curse of mental defect upon the children ... We do wrong when we permit a mental defective to be a parent.'[30]

Eugenics held that the basis of all traits, mental and physical, was laid down at birth and that there was a direct relationship between conduct and intelligence. Tales of generation after generation of the Kallikak and Jukes families seemed to lend substance to the argument that behaviour is inherited and that controlled breeding should make it possible to raise superior human beings. Eugenics enjoyed a wild surge of popularity in the first two decades of this century, and even George Bernard Shaw entered the debate with *Man and Superman*, although it has been said that Shaw was probably more interested in promoting sexual freedom than in taking part in a scientific revolution.[31]

In the United States, the first intelligence tests were used to classify mentally handicapped school children. They were developed further during the First World War, and after the war further tests showed delinquents, immigrants, and minority groups falling short of the standard of the middle-class Americans who set the tests. This seemed to prove a relationship between intelligence and morality, and at the same time to warrant dismissing minority groups as undesirable.[32] In Canada, eugenics groups worked to restrict immigration and to ensure that the feeble-minded were locked away, sterilized, or segregated by sex in their reproductive years so that there would be no danger to society from them. Taken to its logical conclusion, hereditarian-eugenics thinking led to oppression; only another short step or two led to the

Nazi attempts to breed the race they wanted and eliminate anyone who differed from their requirements.

When Blatz finished his graduate work, however, the breezes of change were taking a fresh direction. In the mid-1920s genetic theory had outstripped eugenic thought, and research was showing genetics to be a far more complex subject than eugenics could accommodate. It was quite evident that nature and nurture were not in opposition to each other; each played its role, depending and acting upon the other. The eugenics movement was becoming an embarrassment to most working geneticists.[33]

Sociologists at the University of Chicago were studying deviance from a cultural and environmental perspective and undertook studies in delinquency under the sponsorship of the Laura Spelman Rockefeller Memorial (LSRM).[34] It is not surprising that the University of Chicago should emphasize environment so strongly, for it had itself outstripped its own rather unpromising origins when it received lavish nurturing from Rockefeller and imaginative guidance from its first president, and had grown to be liberal and innovative. It was the essence of functional psychology to stress processes and adjustment to the cultural environment. Although it is true that some of the early graduates in psychology from Chicago had become interested in tests, there was general skepticism about inferences from the results. Dewey was critical of racial testing, Woolley was one of the first to comment that intelligence is only one factor in success,[35] and Angell wrote in his autobiography that functional psychology seeks longitudinal rather than transverse views of life.[36] The whole effort of the LSRM, too, was based on being able to make changes, and thus it needed to shift public attention away from the early type of child study and genetic psychology where mothers simply watched spellbound while a child's personality unfolded. It was ready to study more vigorous interactions between the child and the world. Lawrence Frank and the LSRM promoted longitudinal research rather than short observations or tests. At the same time that they were starting child study centres in North America they also helped the European functionalist Edouard Claparède to found the J.J. Rousseau Institute in Geneva to promote progressive education and study the science of the child. Claparède later invited the Swiss psychologist Jean Piaget to become the institute's director of studies.[37]

By the time Blatz returned to Toronto, Clarke had died, the eugenics ideas of Helen MacMurchy were being questioned, and Clarence

Hincks was shifting his thinking into a new alignment. Blatz brought further change and another new voice to the CNCMH as its research director. In those early days he was very much a product of Chicago thought, clever at combining ideas, applying them, and bringing them to public attention. At a time when heredity was still generally considered to be the stern warden that guards a lifetime's ambitions and attitudes, Blatz set about at once trying to open doors in the name of the environment.

He was adamant, for example, that patterns of behaviour can be shaped only by the environment. In one of his earliest social work meetings he argued with the district medical officer, who was still clinging to the arguments of many middle-class reformers. The medical officer was sure that feeble-minded women were very likely candidates for prostitution.[38] Here is the interchange between them:

Dr. A.: I think she has inherited low morals.

Blatz: Do you think you can inherit a low moral proclivity?

Dr. A.: Yes.

Blatz: I wonder if we can substantiate that? Do you mean to say that if that girl had been taken away from that home and sent to school that she would have been a prostitute?

Dr. A.: I would be very much afraid of it if the father was low grade mentally. According to statistics the majority of prostitutes are of low mentality.

Blatz: I think the statistics show it is the low grade ones who are caught.[39]

In his own answer to the Kallikak and Jukes family studies, Blatz plotted a family tree from five generations of his own family, showing the random branches and twigs of the good, the bad, and the indifferent. But apart from these strong convictions that there is no relationship between intellectual ability and morality, Blatz paid relatively little attention to other aspects of the intelligence question. He was more interested in studying children's healthy social and emotional adjustments than in noting their intellectual accomplishments, although he recognized that these usually developed together and looked for progress in all areas. He used standard intelligence tests in all his work, early and late, to establish a baseline for understanding personal adjustment and in order to supplement the data from his longitudinal research. He thought tests were useful to help children in school find their educational niche and to reduce unfair competition, but he never treated the tests with the same reverence that the schools and some educational psychologists, such as Peter Sandiford at the University of Toronto showed to them.

Although from time to time he expressed doubt about the validity of an actual IQ score, he continued to use tests because he thought a certain basic ability was inherent and should be known if at all possible. It would round out the picture. However he did not share the then-prevalent (and still persistent) view that a particular measurement must limit a child's potential. There was usually room for extensive manoeuvreability in his assessments of intelligence because he considered that interests and motivation would play more important roles than innate capacity.

Although, later, he proposed an elaborate school system with placement based on extensive testing, he also took account of interests and accomplishments to make sure that the schooling suited each child. He also expected tests to change with different circumstances in the child's life and was delighted to see that children living in otherwise deprived conditions who were given a rich pre-school experience could show a steady rise in their IQ scores.

Blatz's social concerns ran strongly parallel to his more flamboyant efforts, but he did little to draw attention to them. Certainly he is most often associated with the model school at the university, which became the mecca of Toronto's middle-class mothers. In his research at St George's he studied children whose family lives were generally stable enough to give a reasonable likelihood of mental health. These children provided a relatively unclouded picture for his basic research and allowed him to identify some of the principles of healthy child development. At the same time, as research director for CNCMH, he was able also to apply his knowledge gained at St George's School to help other children who found the world a tough and complicated place. The Toronto Juvenile Court, a downtown school, crèches and day-care centres, the slums of Birmingham, a hospital school for emotionally disturbed children, the training of social workers, and clinical counselling were all important but little-publicized parts of Blatz's professional life.

Upon his return to Toronto, Blatz was immediately in demand as a public speaker and adviser to groups concerned with child welfare. The relatively small and tight-knit circle of professionals involved in social work and the prevention of juvenile delinquency readily stretched to encompass the new addition to the staff of the CNCMH (also known simply as 'Mental Hygiene') and of Psychology. The mental hygiene movement held a bright promise, and social workers welcomed its help with enthusiasm. Blatz, as one of the young lions of the CNCMH, was readily embraced by the representatives of Toronto agencies. As a physician and psychologist he seemed the perfect expert to help them improve both their techniques and their understanding of human behaviour.

He was appointed to the Toronto Juvenile Court as psychological consultant for particularly perplexing cases and was chairman of the court committee, which consisted of a judge, a physician, a clergyman, teachers, and social workers. (In the United States, the National Committee for Mental Hygiene had already set up a series of such guidance clinics for courts in several American cities with the mandate to delve into the background of individual problems and to make recommendations for children who were either neglected or in trouble with the law.) Blatz served on the Toronto Juvenile Court Clinic committee for most of his active career and is credited with being the driving force that kept it going during the Second World War, when most of the younger staff members were in the services.

At the same time he organized a series of social studies conferences with the bold purpose of 'clarifying some of the factors in modern social work practice.'[40] In these social studies conferences Blatz met every two weeks with a keen little group of social workers, nurses, field workers, and district medical officers representing the Department of Public Health, the Gerrard Street Girls' Home, the Infants' Home, the Hospital for Sick Children, Catholic Welfare, and the Jewish Federation. They hoped to discuss with him their more puzzling cases and through this method to further the development of professional social work in three specific directions. First of all they would focus on an examination of problem behaviour and study both its causes and its cures. Secondly they would try to polish the techniques of social work, particularly those that involved interviewing and recording. And, at the same time, the conferences would attempt to co-ordinate the activities of workers in a wide variety of fields, such as those concerned with juvenile delinquency, child placement, relief for dependents, and infants' care. This third goal was coupled with a rather vague statement that the workers would try to 'disentangle agencies,' presumably to clarify functions of the various agencies while they were co-ordinating activities.[41]

Reports of the discussions give direct insight into attitudes towards children at the beginning of Blatz's career and show how Blatz was starting to put together his views on child life. With such matters as lying, sibling rivalry, inconsistency, and consequences he focused on practical and efficient ways of coping. Beyond this, he demonstrated an awareness of the deeper questions that could underlie obvious problems, and he was ready to enlist the aid of parents as effective observers in the search to understand their children.

The conferences were also an opportunity for Blatz to sharpen his skills as a teacher, making strong and surprising statements in order to shift perceptions, and using a series of staccato questions to force his students to rethink their positions. Those attending the conferences were professionals in the field, but they were clearly eager to defer to Blatz, and the last word was usually his. (In a more formal teaching setting one of the first courses to be given at the St George's School for Child Study was offered to social workers.)

Most of the cases of juvenile delinquency brought to the court or social work conferences involved truancy, vagrancy, and incorrigibility. They are sad sagas of broken homes, low-paid jobs, absent fathers, mental illness, unwanted pregnancies, deaths in childbirth, venereal diseases, alcoholism, mental retardation, unemployment, and subsistence on the dole that passed for welfare.

Some of the misbehaviour was considered to be a problem simply because children and not adults were involved. Even today the world of the child and the world of the adult are governed by different sets of rules. If an adult stays out late at night, does a little gambling and drinking, or chooses companions unwisely, it usually evokes little comment. If an adult misses work he may lose his job, but it is most unlikely that he will be picked up by the police and required to explain his absence. Similar roustabout behaviour or simple truancy in a youngster, however, will very likely lead to great concern and perhaps intervention by a social agency or the courts. The child is indeed young, his way of life is still relatively unformed, the rules are more precise, and intervention may improve his approach to the world. Today, as in Blatz's time, similar misdemeanours are the focus of concern.

To get the conferences under way, Blatz used the discussion of a young truant to help the social workers develop a method of history taking. The picture should be as complete as possible, he said, and obtained from a variety of sources. Although parents might not be able to answer precise questions about physical growth, they were the best source of information about such things as labour and childbirth, method of feeding, the sequence of diseases in infancy, when the child got the first tooth, when the child walked and talked, whether the mother perceived any differences compared with siblings, whether there were temper tantrums, the method of discipline, if the baby had been picked up whenever it wanted, and if there was any inconsistency in parental treatment.

Even with this recording, outside observations of the little truant would be needed. 'Suppose the mother says the boy is mischievous. The father says he gives no trouble. We need other opinions. We want the opinion of the nurses who came in contact with him. We also want to know how the parents discipline the boy.'

The explanation from the workers told of a chaos of wavering expectations. They explained that the mother dragged the boy back to school by the hand and vowed to strap him. But her resolve weakened on the way, and instead she gave him a taffy apple. Another day, while being forced back to school, the boy broke away. The mother chased him for a while, but decided it was beneath her dignity to continue. Eventually, another boy caught him in the neighbouring woods, and this time he was strapped.

Blatz took the opportunity to point out the confusion such inconsistency could bring to a child's life. 'Imagine a boy being dragged to school and being told in front of the teacher that he was to be strapped and instead being given a taffy apple. Next time he was brought back and received a strapping when he may have been expecting another apple.' Before it could attempt to give an opinion about the boy's problems, Blatz said, the conference would need to know how often the child was *permitted* to stay home, and for what reasons, the boy's attitude towards school (in detail), his recreation, companionship, and home adjustment, and his own story of the truancy and lying. It appeared that the mother was shielding the children from their father. Was this because he punished too severely? Did the father purposely avoid an interview with the school nurse, or was the mother perhaps trying to keep him out of the way?

In the 1920s it was considered perfectly acceptable for a parent to hit a child. Blatz's ideas to the contrary were radical and subversive, and his public crusade for an alternative to harsh punishment was supported only by bold thinkers. It was unusual in the 1920s for adults to regard children as human beings or to allow them their dignity; unusual to encourage them to make decisions and to think for themselves, as Blatz advocated. He was ahead of his time in his sensitivity to children and his insistence that fear is no way to help a child to learn.

Even so, in very recent years there has been increased awareness of the harmful effects of parental severity. Adults in contact with children are now learning to be alert to the sort of clues that may indicate family violence or abused children. The 1925 reports of the court clinic or social studies conferences reveal the halting phrases that often point to maltreatment. There is the tearful child who begs not to be sent back to her alcoholic stepfather, the care-worn woman who is in fact a battered wife, or the frightened boy whose father is abusive in the name of parental authority.

Although social work was beginning to make efforts to strengthen family life and keep a child at home rather than use foster care, Blatz was not always convinced. If strong action was needed he often chose to change the circumstances of the child's life. Sometimes it involved nothing short of taking the child away from an unhealthy situation. For instance, when members of the Toronto social studies conference decided to remove a girl from her home, Blatz heartily approved of the idea. 'If we could do what we want,' he went as far as to say, 'we would take them all away.'[42] Judge Ben Lindsay in Chicago had already advocated making parenthood a profession with companionate marriage preceding it. Those couples who seemed suited to be responsible and effective parents would be licensed to have children. The others would simply go on living together.[43] In 1934 Blatz spoke in much the same vein when he called the marriage certificate a meaningless and inadequate preparation for parenthood. This drew fire from a canon of the church who declared Blatz to be a blot on the landscape.[44] Again, much later, in *Maclean's* magazine (September 1945), Blatz described the court's purpose as working unceasingly to repair some of the social damages that arise out of lack of preparation for family life.

'The state, if it has a responsibility for legislating divorce, has also a responsibility for legislating courses in preparation for marriage. The technique for this educational programme cannot be thought out in a moment. The need for research in human problems has never been more pressing.'

A look at the 1925 records of court and agency gives a view of how children who were without benefit of a family to anchor them could be buffeted about just beyond reach of the social workers' outstretched hands.

In the Juvenile Court Blatz rarely dealt directly with the troubled youngsters. Instead, he mobilized his clinic team of judge, priest, doctor, social worker, and probation officer to try to resolve problems.

In the case of a fifteen-year-old boy who had been brought before the court for petty thievery and incorrigibility Blatz was anxious to bring a standard system to bear upon his misdemeanours. The first priority would be to get an objective summary of the case in both chronological and topical order. It would also be important to be quite specific in classifying the charges. Blatz had high hopes: 'We are continually trying to get at the motive. If we could standardize these delinquencies into categories then we could see at the end of the year whether we can find that there is a general trend in the delinquency in specific cases.'

The home should be investigated, too, to find out what advice was given to the child there. 'Have you anyone whose judgment you can trust to tell you whether that home is impossible or not?' he asked the meeting. What was needed, said Blatz, was someone who could go into the home and manufacture the proper environment for dealing with the conditions that might exist there.

The boy's life had been a traumatic series of events: his mother had died when he was a baby, he had grown up in an orphanage, and he had been badly burned as a child. He had come to Canada recently to join his father, but had met with only a harsh reception.

Someone mentioned that deportation had been suggested in the boy's case. Blatz was firm in his conviction that this would not be a good idea: 'Deportation would be a solution to us, not the boy.' The problem was really one of finding a way to deal with difficult cases when there weren't enough staff to give them proper attention. The focus would have to be on discovering how to develop specific procedures and methods for dealing with groups of similar cases. More efficient methods were needed.

The next week, Blatz's style of chairing the clinic discussion was quite different. This time he made few comments and no lengthy summaries. Instead he put a barrage of questions to the committee and, by the end of the meeting, led its members to settle on a temporary resolution with regard to the fifteen-year-old Dennis.

Dennis always seemed to be afraid of something. When a neighbour had sheltered him 'he broke down when he was treated kindly.'

> Blatz: He is unhappy in his home. There is no affection from father or [step]mother. More than that he sees others are getting affection and he is not. What can we do? Can the boy go back into that home?

Some members of the clinic committee thought at first that he could. Perhaps the father could be brought to a realization that his past attitudes had been responsible for the boy's attitudes now. Perhaps they could become pals and co-operate, someone suggested. Even though admittedly the father had an ungovernable temper, he was, after all, 'a good temperance man.' Perhaps the social worker could talk to him about 'what a boy should do.'

Blatz's questions were relentless. 'How?' and 'Is it practicable?' he asked. Five times he put the same question: 'Should the boy go back home?' Each time the answer was more qualified. Eventually the group agreed that, although Dennis's return to his family might be the ultimate goal, it was inadvisable until there was evidence of major changes in the way his father would treat him. Meanwhile the court priest would arrange a boarding home for him.

It was easier said than done. Dennis had sought refuge with a family that the social worker judged to be living in deplorable circumstances. The Gintys kept an untidy home, they had 'horsey companions,' the woman was unintelligent and not even a Catholic, as Dennis was. Perhaps it was the kind of shiftless life he enjoyed, riding about with Mr Ginty and working in his livery.

The court priest reported that he had found what he described as a splendid boarding home for Dennis, but had little hope that he would stay there. For Blatz some values could override the more obvious ones. Of the Ginty's home he said, 'This home is not Catholic. The mother is feeble-minded and very untidy. He would have no room to himself. *But these are the people to whom he likes to go.* If Dennis wants to go [to] the Gintys, let him.'

Nevertheless, Blatz thought a question still remained about the boy's own home and his father and mother, and suggested that the court 'should start attacking the home right now.'

The social worker visited Dennis's home at the request of the clinic and interviewed his father, his stepmother, and an aunt. His father declared that the boy had given trouble ever since he arrived in Canada and had been particularly difficult in the last few months. He would agree to have him at home, except that he could not control him. He would be willing to have him work outside the home, but would never consent to Dennis's paying a specific sum towards his board and keeping the remainder of his money. He declared that this system was the ruination of Canadian boys and that for his part he would expect Dennis to give him all his wages out of which he would supply the boy with what he required. He would make no allowance for the fact that Dennis had been brought up in an institution, for he knew perfectly good men who had survived the same circumstances.

The aunt who lived nearby told the social worker that she had met Dennis on the street a few weeks before. 'He looked very ill, had a bad cough, was very untidy, and looked as if he had been sleeping in a stable with animals.' He was cold and hungry and started to cry as soon as she spoke to him. She took him home and gave him some food.

The arrangement with the Gintys did not work for long. Dennis was beyond the age for child welfare assistance and was not holding a steady job, which meant that the Gintys could not afford to keep him. Mr Ginty was out of work, and the family had even had to sell their horses to keep going. Mrs Ginty's mother started telephoning the court and insisting that Dennis must leave her daughter's house, as the family was in need and she refused to assist them while Dennis was there. She declared that she herself was quite offended by his presence.

The court social worker took Dennis to see Dr Blatz. Blatz's report was succinct and practical. Here it is:

> Dennis seemed cheerful, well provided for and at ease.
> Asked Dennis if he wished to go back home. He said 'No.'
> Pointed out:
> (a) That now his stepmother had made arrangements for her own sons he had better make up his mind to *start for himself.*
> (b) That he was over 16 and out of Juvenile Court jurisdiction.
> (c) That we were now his friends and he should come to us when he felt need for advice.
> Arranged after consulting Dennis for the social worker to help him:
> (a) Get a position – one at hand – $12.00 per week. Suggested Aunt to take $5.00 (and that he would board there).
> Bank          $5.00
> Keep out      $2.00

(b) The court worker was to send Dennis a few books of adventure.
(c) To take Dennis to the Boys' Club and if he likes it to have him join.
(d) Companions – arrange for Dennis to have a few boys in to play checkers, etc.
(e) That the Court worker was to see him weekly – not to spy, but to hear his troubles, if any.
(f) That he is to phone me every week.

Dr W.E. Blatz.

Another record gives a glimpse of attitudes of the time towards intelligence testing, illegitimacy, institutional care, and infant adjustment. It is a sad sequel to a decision made some twenty years beforehand to bring a ten-year-old girl from England and to place her in a series of foster homes and domestic positions. Norman MacDonald, writing as recently as 1966, hailed the bringing of children to Canada to labour on farms and in private homes as an act of mercy. Dr Barnardo's work he considered 'synonymous with humanitarianism of the best kind.'[45] In the last few years, however, serious doubts have been raised about MacDonald's assumption that the children were transferred 'from misery in England to comfort in Canada.' Kenneth Bagnell, in his book *The Little Immigrants*, credits men such as Blatz with helping to bring about a change in attitudes towards children:

> The society [in 1905] in which these youngsters were about to begin their lives as Canadians did not dislike children, but in its treatment of them – especially those who were the offspring of unknown and distant parents – it seemed bent on thwarting any self they may have had, any tendency to feel special worth ... The notion that the raising of children was a serious and involving task, a notion that thirty years later would evolve into the field of child psychology, with its scrutiny of parental influence by men such as William E. Blatz of Toronto and its examination of the impact on children of rejection, dominance, and hostility, was a world away from all but a few children, and especially distant from the world of immigrant children.[46]

The problem facing the conference was how to plan for the two-year-old child of a woman who had died unmarried the year before. The child's mother had been born in England in 1896. She was said to know nothing about her own father, and her mother had died when she was a child. She and her sister had been brought up in the Barnardo Home, coming to Canada when she was ten. The two children had been separated and placed in different farm homes and later took domestic positions. When she was twenty-five, the woman became pregnant and was admitted to a shelter, where she remained for a year. Her baby was adopted, and she took up a new position in domestic service. Three years later she became pregnant again, was admitted to the shelter, gave birth to a little girl, and died a few months later of pneumonia.

There were strong discrepancies in the records of the mother's life, with the Barnardo Home presenting a far rosier picture than did the agency. It was, after all, the Barnardo policy to open its doors to any young person in need. To avoid the crush, the open entrance had to be coupled with an open exit, and an open exit often meant a quick exit and final drop into space. The agencies overseeing child immigration were often sketchy in their follow-up care and record keeping. Indeed, agency records often painted a picture more rosy than realistic. The immigration agencies had a stake in helping their young dependents move into the work-force. In this particular case, too, there were sharp contradictions between the Barnardo evaluations and those of the social work agency that followed later.

The Barnardo Home records had deemed the mother's work satisfactory, adding that she worked willingly and well. At age twenty-three she had been earning eighteen dollars a month. After her baby was born out of wedlock and placed for adoption, her work record deteriorated. The home for unmarried mothers reported that she had changed jobs frequently and that her work had become unsatisfactory.

The agency reported that, although her health appeared to be normal, she was of diminutive physique. Barnardo Home records had declared her to be a good, healthy girl. The Barnardo records showed 'good attendance' at school, church, and Sunday school. Later records at the agency shelter considered her 'practically illiterate.'

Records by Clarke at the Toronto General Hospital had measured the mother's mental age at nine years and recommended institutional care for her. It is very probable that she was one of the 125 wards of the Barnardo organization examined by Clarke at the Toronto General Hospital between 1917 and 1924. Of these, 77 worked as domestics and 11 in factories. Clarke considered only 5 of them to be normal, with 5 judged to be mentally ill, 37 undiagnosed, and the others mentally defective.[47]

There were words too about the girl's 'disposition.' When she was still under the wing of the Barnardo organization at age twenty-one she was described as 'well-behaved' and 'a very nice little girl.' The worker at the shelter described her as neatly dressed, rather attractive, reserved, and gentle, but quite determined. She was considered to have been neither vicious nor immoral, although very anxious to be married. The worker at the shelter described her as being 'of the clinging sort who aroused a sympathy in the men she met. This she mistook for love and would not be advised to the contrary.'

It is hardly surprising that the girl sought affection so eagerly after such an unstable childhood. In her discussion of the plight of labouring immigrant children, Joy Parr has remarked that 'to be young, a servant and a stranger was to be unusually vulnerable, powerless and alone.'[48] Added to this was the fact that when it became publicly known (usually through pregnancy) that a young woman could no longer be considered virtuous, she was ostracized and usually had difficulty finding either steady employment or a husband.[49]

This is just what happened to the girl after her first pregnancy. She drifted from job to job and dropped a few notches on the scale, from being considered a good and willing worker to an unsatisfactory one. Eventually she met a widower with three sons. The man was interviewed after her death, and the social worker pronounced him to be a well-dressed, well-spoken, and intelligent man with a good job. 'He admitted that he had improper relations with her and would have married her if she had been normal mentally,' the social worker reported. As it happened, of the man's older three sons, two were already in the Institute for the Feeble-Minded in Orillia. A request went off to find out more about these children and their family history.

By the 1920s adoption was becoming increasingly popular,[50] but social agencies still considered adoption of 'feeble-minded' children to be out of the question. The social workers had been liberated enough from fears of heredity to place the woman's first child for adoption, but they were not so sure about the second. The baby was two years old, but had still not tried solid food and seemed to lag in development. She had such a happy disposition, though, that the workers called her Sunshine and conceded that 'she might be rather attractive if fixed up.'

Blatz wondered if the child could reasonably be placed in a boarding home. 'Is feeble-mindedness a factor in returning children to the shelter?' he asked.

The worker from the Infants' Home replied: 'Last year out of seven or eight hundred wards only two were returned on account of being feeble-minded.'

That confirmed it for Blatz: a proper environment could accommodate children of all ranges of intelligence. 'When you have a feeble-minded child in a normal, good home it does not usually give trouble.'

But one worker ventured further, and prophetically, into possible causes of retardation. 'We feel those children may be the result of an institution,' she said.

Blatz was adamant. He was and always continued to be convinced that, even though the environment was all-important and would influence almost every area of a child's life, there was nevertheless an inborn capacity that set the ground rules and that could not be changed. 'The institution should have nothing to do with fundamental capacity.'

But the worker persisted. 'It certainly retards physical development and we thought perhaps it might affect intelligence. Would lack of stimulation affect a child?'

Blatz had no answer for that. He recommended home care for the baby, but this was for humane and practical reasons, not because he thought it could increase the baby's potential for intellectual growth.

The worker's question, however, showed insight that has since been validated by today's knowledge of how infants learn. Intelligence, as such, was of relatively little interest to Blatz; he was more concerned with children's social adjustment, emotional health, and physical well-being. Today's knowledge, which shows an interdependence of all four factors in a balanced life, has come through investigations of the effects of institutional placements; and John Bowlby's work on maternal deprivation has done a great deal to alter the care of infants both at home and in social service settings.[51] Eventually, Blatz's own security theory, presented in its final form, called for sound adult-child relationships as a signature of mental health in all areas of a child's life.

That came much later, however. In 1925 he was poised at the beginning of his career.

Throughout this career, Blatz worked very much on his own, surrounded usually by a band of eager co-workers. Blatz was always in charge, however. He was not a political person or a joiner of organizations. His interest in education never extended to involvement with school boards. While both Blatz and Whitton were in the public eye at about the same time, they played very different roles. Both were aware of the needs of children, but Blatz's work was at a more personal level. Blatz was always more interested in research and education than in public policy and legislation.

# 3 The Blatz Babies

In 1925 it seemed almost beyond belief that two-year-old children, virtually babies, could be expected to leave their comfortable middle-class homes to go to school. This seemed to threaten all established practices of keeping both mothers and young children tethered to home and apron strings.

One of Margaret Hincks's earliest memories was of hearing her father talking at the dinner table about the latest development at the Canadian National Committee for Mental Hygiene. Their project involved a Laura Spelman Rockefeller Memorial grant to establish a school for child study at the University of Toronto with young Dr Blatz as its director. The youngest Hincks baby was on the list to be enrolled there, and Margaret Hincks remembers that her mother attended classes for parents at the school and kept detailed records of the infant's life for a full three days of every month, while from time to time toys and baby equipment arrived on loan for the family to evaluate. When little Barbara Hincks reached two and was ready for nursery school, Margaret remembers her mother's tears of anguish at the parting. Three years later there were more maternal tears, for it was time for Barbara to leave the St George's School.[1]

Although Blatz's nursery school drew the most public attention and comment, the nursery was only one of two divisions in the new St George's School for Child Study. The other formal division was parent education, and the entire staff participated in the research program. This was, of course, the main emphasis in the Lawrence Frank—

Beardsley Ruml plan for the Rockefeller Memorial: to educate parents in the newest, scientifically based ways of raising children. The university child study institutes, which the memorial sponsored, were designed to support the cause of parent education by creating laboratory schools and research programs to develop a theoretical and practical framework for parent discussion and enlightenment.

Teachers' College at Columbia University had already established such an all-encompassing program the year before, and the Laura Spelman Rockefeller Memorial was in the process of starting child study at Minnesota and the University of California (Berkeley), as well as financing a widened program at Iowa. At the same time it was introducing two Canadian centres at the University of Toronto and McGill, and arranging with Yale for its new programs, which followed nearly two years later. The focus of research and parent education in all the centres was on physical health, child development, and mental hygiene.

The idea of initiating child study at some of the other universities had met with resistance at first, with various schools and departments declaring it a waste of money to study children when other established research programs needed support. At Minnesota, the School of Education wanted child study under its sole jurisdiction, but Frank insisted that child study should be autonomous, or at least semi-independent, in order to encourage interdisciplinary studies.[2] At Toronto, negotiations went smoothly and swiftly because both Bott and Hincks had paved the way, and psychology had already demonstrated its own ability to exist as a subject without a department, able to call upon expertise from both the arts and the medical faculties.

Child psychology, of course, was no stranger to the University of Toronto. The protégé of James Mark Baldwin, Frederick Tracy, had written *The Psychology of Childhood* in 1893, a work that was popular enough to reappear in seven editions and to be translated into German. Although Tracy had been a fellow in psychology at Clark University under G. Stanley Hall, and although he was interested in psychology, he taught ethics at Toronto and had never worked in any practical way either in the laboratory or with children.[3] Tracy's book, a romantic but detailed account of the 'unfolding of the mental life' of children, drew upon the meticulous observations of such authors as Charles Darwin to outline the development of the senses, the intellect, the feelings, the will, and language, as well as aesthetic, moral, and religious ideas, and concluded with a lengthy treatise on psychopathic

conditions in child life.[4] Accessible information about child development had been in short supply, and Tracy's book at the turn of the
century had a following among well-educated people who were interested in childhood as a relatively abstract subject of study. Later Tracy
turned his attention to teacher training and, in 1909, along with Samuel
Bower Sinclair of MacDonald College, wrote an introduction to educational psychology. Peter Sandiford was prominent in educational
psychology as well, but by the time Blatz returned to Toronto the field
of child psychology itself was virtually deserted.

Upon his return to Toronto, Blatz was appointed to the staff of
Psychology, and the nursery school became one of the central laboratories for Psychology (which was on the verge of acquiring its own
status as a department). The St George's School was administered by
the Advisory University Committee on Child Study with representatives from Psychology, Medicine, the Ontario College of Education,
and the Department of Psychiatry, under the immediate guidance of
the Department of Paediatrics and the Department of Public Health.

'Such was the setting of the St. George's Nursery School. Its objectives lay in mental hygiene; its foundation was the human sciences;
its professional status was university level; its educational associates
were teacher-training organizations; and its students were parents.'[5]

Although Psychology, as such, did not participate in day-to-day
decisions about running the school, Bott had a major role, informally
but directly, in the school's early days. His wife, Helen McMurchie
Bott, MA (no relation to Dr Helen MacMurchy), was sent to New York
to spend a week with the Child Study Association as her preparation
for taking charge of the parent education department; his daughter,
Elizabeth, was one of the first children enrolled in the nursery, and
Blatz was still somewhat Bott's protégé. And, of course, there were
strong links among Mental Hygiene, Psychology, and Child Study, with
Mental Hygiene controlling the budgets of both.

In preparation for the opening of the nursery, Blatz made several
visits to the United States, particularly to Columbia University's Institute for Child Welfare Research, the Lincoln School in New York
(famed for progressive education), the Bureau of Educational Experiments (later Bank Street School, and then College of Education), and
the Merrill-Palmer School in Detroit. Merrill-Palmer (today the Merrill-
Palmer Institute) had been under way for three years, and its program
and facilities were sufficiently well developed for Elizabeth Cleveland,
supervisor of girls' and women's activities in the Detroit Public Schools,

to set forth its general principles in her 1925 book, *Training the Toddler*.[6] The book, a highly practical guide to the young child's day at school or at home, gave notes on nutrition, with sample meals, descriptions of a nursery classroom and playground, and advice on manageable clothing and on the day's routine, which she insisted should be one of 'unrelenting regularity.' Her suggestion that working in the kitchen at measuring ingredients and mixing batters could provide important educational experiences for the very young was not adopted by nursery schools in general for another forty years or so, but other parts of the book are dated by a heavy layer of sentiment and an emphasis on cheerfulness at all costs, with children expected to wrap their negative feelings in polite disguise.

At Columbia University Blatz consulted the laboratory's copious research forms involving physical and medical histories, motor tests, nursery menus, and parent interviews, and at all the schools he visited he looked at the logistics for research organization and record keeping.

In Toronto there was already a history of pre-school care as part of the system of welfare, and there were also kindergartens for five-year-olds. The Victoria Crèche had been opened in 1892 and the West End Crèche in 1907. Both were day-care centres, although their care was more custodial than educational. Kindergartens had been introduced into Ontario by Toronto school inspector J.L. Hughes in 1883 and recognized as part of the public school system in Ontario by the Department of Education two years later.[7] But there were no child-centred programs for the very young, so Blatz and his staff were left to their own devices to develop the St George's School.

Mental Hygiene rented a house from the university to house Child Study at 47 St George Street, directly opposite the window of the university's president, Sir Robert Falconer. (Mental Hygiene itself was located at 111 St George Street in an Edwardian house.) Bott designed the playground and constructed its swings, slides, jungle gym, sandbox, see-saw, building blocks, playhouse, large wooden platform, and storage shed with the help of the university maintenance staff. The inside of the house was remodelled to make one large playroom, a washroom, a dining-room, and a kitchen. The second floor was given over to parent education rooms, a library, rooms for research, and staff offices.

Throughout the nursery school, each child had a picture symbol to help in identifying any furnishings set aside specifically for his or her individual use. A drawing of a flag, a bluebird, a pine tree, a toy train, etc. would be fastened to each coat cupboard, washbasin, towel rack or camp cot to help the children, who were too young to read, to find their personal equipment. Everything in the nursery was child-size and designed for safe use.

The nursery rooms were painted in light colours with filmy curtains to allow maximum light and air, and roller blinds darkened the rooms at naptime. Kindergarten chairs, wide-stanced and made of wood, were set at cut-down wooden tables, the table-tops covered in pastel oilcloths. Toys were stored on low shelves in individual boxes, again kept well-ordered, painted, and washed. Curtains could be pulled across the front of the toy shelves to remove distractions when it was not playtime. The floors were covered with pastel linoleum to provide splinter-free space for sitting or kneeling to play with large blocks or the Noah's ark.

The first toys at the school were such traditional playthings as blocks, wooden trains, puzzles, dolls, and zoo and farm animals; some were borrowed from other educational systems (such as Montessori's pink tower or the boxes of Froebel's gifts), but were used in a less structured manner. There were very few books available beyond *Peter Rabbit, Mother Goose*, and books of fairy-tales, although in the United States Lucy Sprague Mitchell of the Bureau of Educational Experiments had, just a year or two before, written a realistic series of pre-school-level picture story-books about everyday life, and the genre soon became popular. Artwork involved plasticine or large paper and thick paint with large brushes, and the children were free to paint or model what they liked. To balance the spontaneous choice in artwork, the children, boys and girls alike, learned the basics of carpentry in a course that was highly structured to help them to develop enough skill to use small-scale but genuine saws, hammers, nails, and screwdrivers with safety.

Such blocks, dolls, and art materials are still the basics of nursery school equipment sixty or more years later, but today there is usually much more of everything and more variety. Today we know how difficult it is for the very young to share and take turns, so, wherever possible, schools try to have more than enough to go around. In the early exploratory days of the St George's School there was very little equipment, but the staff at first thought this almost a virtue, for they hoped the children would learn to take turns. (In a year or two the adults learned that co-operation is not taught by competition for a limited supply of playthings. In a staff meeting of 19 January 1927, the staff was specifically searching for wagons or steam-shovel toys, in the hope of encouraging children to play together with materials that would be more enjoyable to use with someone else than alone.)

The St George's Nursery School opened very late in 1925 with a timetable that arranged for four adults to be always on duty and a capacity originally planned for eighteen children. The first few weeks were very tentative, with few children in attendance, and the school did not really begin to function fully until early in 1926. By Easter, fourteen children were enrolled, although there was an average daily attendance of only eleven. Most of the parents were connected with the university, Mental Hygiene, or the medical community. They tended to be well-educated, in fairly comfortable circumstances, and a trifle adventurous in choosing 'modern ways' over accepted practices. The first staff consisted of Della Dingle, who had worked in the nursery connected with the College of Home Economics of Cornell University, as the head, assisted by M. Goodeve. They were supplemented at all times by at least two other people, some drawn from parent education, some part-time workers. In the early days Blatz worked directly with the children and trained the staff on the job. He was barely thirty, still of wiry build, and dressed always in perfectly tailored suits and high, starched collars. (He retained a lifelong fondness for well-made clothes, as befits the son of a tailor, although later he exchanged the high collar and wide tie of his youth for a bow-tie (worn always), along with three-piece suits set off with a gold watch chain, which was stretched tighter and tighter across the waistcoat as he added a few more pounds over the years.)

When the nursery opened, Blatz was a long way from developing any cohesive approaches for understanding young children. The general attitude was one of, 'Let's watch the children and find out.' But from the children's point of view the nursery program was carefully planned and, although the adults may have felt confused at times, the children's days were calm and orderly. In June 1926 Blatz wrote in the *University of Toronto Monthly*: 'A special technique for dealing with children of this age has to be evolved. In the meantime the children, mostly *only* children and hence *lonely* children, are enjoying an atmosphere of freedom, self-dependence, regulated habits, adequate social contacts – and of serenity. The latter is a *sine qua non* of any well-conducted nursery school.' (When Blatz did begin to develop his security theory some ten years later, serenity was one of its cornerstones.)

In starting the school, a smooth-running routine had been the first consideration, and 'everything was done with the greatest punctuality in order to train the children in the habit of regularity.'[8]

The children arrived at school between 9:00 and 9:30 and were given a quick check by a public health nurse. Any who seemed to be suffering from a cold or the beginning of an illness were sent right home with their mothers. If all was well, the children would take off their outer clothing and store it in their individual wooden lockers, which had a series of shelves and hooks at child height so everything could be put away neatly. Winter clothing could involve coats (often of fur or chinchilla cloth with elaborate buttons), hats, gloves, leggings, and overshoes with metal buckles. In the early days of the school the children were left to struggle with their clothes so they could learn by trial and error and become independent.

Looking back on it years later, one staff member observed that the cloakroom routine was one instance where, without a theory, reasonable hunches were tested and sometimes found wanting. After several years of having the children work on their own in this way the staff noticed that 'the children were apparently unintentionally being "taught how to dawdle"; at which point a change was made to helping as necessary, but with insistence on the child attending to the process, and encouraging self-effort.'[9]

Indoors, the children amused themselves with toys and games while the others were arriving. The adults kept well out of the way, interfering only if absolutely necessary. When all the children were assembled, there was a short period of group games and songs with musical accompaniment, followed by fruit or vegetable juice at ten o'clock. Then it was back into their outdoor clothing to play in the garden with the large equipment designed by Bott. The wooden platform allowed outdoor play even in wet weather. (There was scrupulous attention to climate, however; temperatures inside and outside the building were recorded regularly at 8:30 a.m., 11:00 a.m., and 1:00 p.m. so that the doors and windows could be adjusted and the children's clothing modified accordingly.)

At twelve o'clock the children returned inside to get ready for dinner. It was not easy to use the toilet when underwear usually involved a union suit with drop seat or, worse still, a combination vest and underpants with buttons to be undone at the shoulders. Short trousers, bloomers, rompers, or skirts were often held up by a series of buttons around the waist of the underwear. Straps of overalls were difficult to buckle and failed to stay in place unless crossed tightly and uncomfortably, and those little girls who were not wearing overalls had to struggle with lisle stockings and dangling garters.

The washing routine was broken into a series of steps to encourage the children to manage on their own. There was a long bench in the washroom with an area for each child's metal washbowl and marked with each one's special symbol. Above it hung a towel, face-cloth, comb, tooth-brush, and mug. The children carried their basins back and forth to the sink (which was equipped with a long-handled tap), helping themselves to the cold water (the adult adding only the hot), and emptying the basin both after washing their hands and again after washing their faces. They learned to comb their hair at a low mirror and to keep their own washing areas tidy; if they spilled water they simply used the short-handled mop to dry it up, with no comments from the adults. After washing came a few minutes of relaxation before lunch, with the children lying on their own mats and listening to a story or music.

The meal was served at small tables, five children and one adult to a table. The diets were prescribed by the Department of Paediatrics, with typed copies sent to the parents so that home and school meals could be co-ordinated. The children were expected to finish at least one serving of the first course, no matter how small, before dessert, but could have a second helping of either dinner or dessert if they liked. The nursery technique soon became one of removing practically all traces of a resisted food from the plate, leaving just a morsel, perhaps a single pea, to taste. One child (who eventually grew to accept most foods) started by peeling and discarding the skin from the pea and scraping off a tiny bite of the pulp, thus calling the meal finished. It was considered to be a step in the direction of acceptance.

For the afternoon nap the children all had their own cots, which consisted of folding wooden frames with canvas covers. A sheet was tied over the stretcher, and the children were given soft blankets but no pillows. The beds were low enough for them to get in and out quite easily, but there was always a teacher in the room keeping records of the length and quality of each child's sleep. The recording was detailed enough to require its own shorthand, and eventually a list of eighteen symbols was evolved to describe the children's tossings, turnings, murmurs, sneezes, and snores. Those who did not sleep were expected to rest quietly without disturbing anyone else.

After an hour and a half the children put on their shoes (invariably high, laced boots for the youngest, oxfords for the four-year-olds) and went to the dining-room for their afternoon glass of milk. Then came dressing in outdoor garments again and playing outdoors, or inside with all the windows open, until they were collected to go home at three o'clock.

One mother wrote ecstatically about the school for *The New Outlook*: 'It is a busy, orderly happy day of play with other children. A day free from querulous "Don'ts" and irritated scoldings. A day in which there is plenty of time to finish one's block castle or learn the joy of putting on one's very own shoes. The serene atmosphere prevents the over-stimulation of the child which so many people dread, and nothing could be further removed from the regulation "children's party." '[10]

In the first few years there was a constant need to justify the idea of the nursery. 'It was viewed as another institution making inroads on the home; or as a species of day nursery, where the woman of leisure could leave her child, thus ridding herself further of family responsibility.'[11] Another Blatz stalwart commenced her defence of the nursery by countering the litany of the critics ('What will happen if the babies follow the flappers and the grandmothers out of the home? Our mothers will degenerate into mere social parasites.') with the terse comment that the same hue and cry went up long ago when it was first suggested that a trained teacher in a school would be better equipped than parents at home to teach children.[12] Blatz went on record as saying that there was no need to spank a child; instead, 'the big secret is to last longer than he does. If corporal punishment is administered at home we tell the parents we would rather not have the children in the nursery school.'[13] An 'old-fashioned mother' was quoted the next day as saying that while the ideal method certainly is to escape spanking the child, she thought that if fewer mothers would tire themselves out going to clubs, fewer children would be spanked. 'I know I am very old-fashioned and backward in saying this, and all my friends disagree with me, but you see women going out day after day, giving their energy to a group of women, and leaving their babies at home with a maid. Then they come home at night, tired out, and "fly off the handle" as they say, too readily.'[14]

In talking to the press and the public, Blatz and his followers took great care to stress that mothers were not frittering away their time while their pre-school children were at the nursery. They had records to write and nursery meetings and parent education classes to attend to keep them fully occupied and absorbed in the serious business of raising children. 'The nursery school has a distinct value as a demonstration where parents of the children attending may be taught the fine points of their job, so that instead of being an excuse for neglecting their offspring, it becomes a stimulus to greater interest and understanding. Through study groups which they attend, home records which they agree to make periodically, and various contacts with the school, possibilities for self-education are unlimited.'[15]

One of the best defences was to make the public aware of the plight of the lonely, only child. 'Children, like their parents, are social beings,' Blatz wrote in a press release upon the opening of the school. 'As soon as they walk and talk they seek companionship. Too often at this age their only companions are adults and toys, i.e., dolls. Neither of these substitutes is satisfactory and if the child becomes reconciled to either, harm may be done and future maladjustment may result ... the nursery school is the solution ... The child upon the eve of realizing his social inclinations finds congenial playmates where he formerly met unresponsive toys and adults whom he does not yet understand. The give-and-take of an interesting and ever changing environment is the healthy background for building up a sane attitude towards himself and his future fellow citizens. The training in habits of recreation, application, affection, understanding and emotional stability – makes it possible for the child to avoid temper tantrums, shyness, discouragement, sulkiness, nervousness and other indications of a misdirected infancy.'[16] Frances Johnson in *Chatelaine* magazine put it more succinctly: 'Now with small families the rule, and the only child common, the nursery school offers opportunity for the child to attain proper adjustment to the world at an early age and so supplies the basis for success in adult life.'[17]

The nursery did nothing intentionally to draw fire, but inevitably public attention was riveted on the novelty of St George's School. For example, at an early staff meeting, Goodeve complained that she was presented with a problem when she was invited out to tea and then called upon to make some comments about the school. It was general policy that all lectures should be approved by the staff as a whole and an outline of the address put on file to prevent misunderstandings, but, in such circumstances as Goodeve's social dilemma, the staff decided that 'such an address should be general and that no details of the school which could be controversial or subject to study should be mentioned.'[18] Requests to visit the school came thick and fast, from President Falconer's wish to see in detail what the school was doing[19] to a request from the School of Missions to provide observation and instruction for 'two married ladies,' both of them returned missionaries, who had been giving lectures on the training of Indian infants in India.[20]

The general policy became that of allowing a visit upon written request, but only one observation to a person was permitted unless the observer was enrolled in the parent education leaders' group. As it was impossible on 'cursory inspection to gain any impression of the work being done,' Blatz asked for sample material to be assembled so that insight could be given into the type of scientific data being collected in the school.[21] Those starting a nursery or play-group found Blatz and his staff quite prepared to co-operate, even if it meant having a conference to tell what kind of equipment they had, or sending Della Dingle to the new school for a few days to help start the project.[22]

Gradually programs and policies began to shake into place. At the beginning of the second academic year (and the first complete year for the nursery), it was decided that the capacity for the school would be set lower, at sixteen, aiming at approximately equal numbers of boys and girls from ages two to four-and-a-half with no one starting after the age of three. Fees would be based on the cost of the food, which would amount to thirty-five dollars a year or one dollar a week, and the school would follow the university calendar.

Della Dingle, at Blatz's urging, established a new method of opening that had the children 'staggered' to enter the nursery. 'Some of the children,' Dingle said, 'especially the older ones, are not being very careful of the way they do things. I would like to have two or three children for about two days to train them, and then have another three come in and train them separately.' The most important areas to learn were the dressing and undressing and the washroom, and Blatz asked her to work out a plan for the first two days of taking two or three children through these routines, with the other staff observing her techniques and helping from time to time. On the third day three more children would be brought in, and the staff would start on its rotating timetable. He suggested that the staff meet each day after school to discuss the relative merits and problems of the opening arrangements.[23]

The staff timetable, prepared by Bott and Dingle, was a logistical masterpiece covering every situation in the nursery day, with Dingle and Goodeve as the constant factors and at least two other people in or out of the school as their regular duties allowed. Mrs Bott was in the school every morning for an hour and a half, Blatz unscheduled but frequent; another staff member, Miss Keens, hovered somewhere between staff and student, for she had been awarded a Rockefeller Memorial fellowship to receive training in child study and worked in the school while taking university classes. Reba Cohen fell into the staff quite by accident after enrolling in the first parents' group. Her child was having temper tantrums, and under Mrs Bott's guidance she kept a chart of every emotional episode that occurred for five weeks. At the end of it all Blatz said, 'None of us knows more about this than you do,' and invited her to join his little band. She started as secretary of the parents' group, then led a group and worked in the school part time. She sent her own child to the nursery despite the neighbours' assertions that she was queer to send a baby to school, that they had never heard of anything so ridiculous, and that, besides, she was becoming a social climber.[24]

The mothers assisted in the school almost right from the start, spending a regular hour or two there each week to learn a particular routine and then being called upon to stay right through the school day whenever the staff was short-handed.[25] Even though the mothers might be there to see for themselves, Blatz wanted a more decisive way of co-ordinating information between home and school, so that any problems could be handled consistently. Someone suggested sending a note of what had happened in school and asking the parents to report to Miss Dingle, but Bott, a little older than the others and a parent himself, wisely commented that this could come as a shock. Furthermore he was concerned that the mothers might ask Miss Dingle questions she might not be able to answer, and he thought Blatz should be consulted first. The arrangement was made that Blatz would be available three mornings a week to discuss such cases with Miss Dingle and the mothers.[26] A few months later Blatz worked out some routine forms about the children to give information on 'what had transpired during the week, how long they slept, how they played, how they got along at mealtime, etc.'[27]

The nursery planning always had an eye on how everyone, adult and child, coped with every situation. In one of the earliest meetings Blatz called attention to the fact that at lunch that day in the nursery there had been 'eleven children and seven adults, which with second helpings necessitated 72 trips for the maid back and forth from the kitchen, after which the maid was pretty well tired out.' The solution to be tried was that a staff member who had no duty assigned immediately after lunch should help to serve the children.[28] A few months later they tried having the children serve themselves, but by October the exercise had gone full cycle with a report that this took practically as long as with adults serving; the maid's time was three-quarters of an hour longer; it was very difficult for the younger children, indeed for any of them in such congested quarters, and the decision was to go back to having the maid, Margaret, serve.[29]

Some other early changes in the planning came about simply because of the realities of Canadian winters and the need to bundle up against the bitterness. Without the convenience of warm, light-weight garments such as we have today, children's clothing of 1925 was not only difficult to manage but was usually applied in layers to provide sufficient warmth. It was helpful when mothers started to work in the school, because they could be assigned afternoon duty to give extra help in dressing children still in the throes of waking from their afternoon naps. That helped, but it was just a beginning. One mother complained, quite justifiably, that her child was returning home in wet clothes. Bott had typically ingenious suggestions for constructing little drying racks in front of the radiators, or, alternatively, hanging the clothes from the ceiling, above a boiler inverted over a gas plate, which would radiate the heat. On a more practical level, the clothing itself was suspected, and fur coats were declared *non grata* as almost impossible to dry. However, Mrs Bott had discovered a very modern and highly satisfactory suit for Elizabeth that kept a child quite snug and dry, so she was asked to demonstrate this prototypical snow-suit for the mothers at the next nursery group meeting.[30] The real moment of epiphany came, however, when it was discovered that by having the children go straight outdoors to play when they arrived in the morning, one entire dressing-undressing routine could be cut from the day. It was Blatz's idea, although it was pushed by a suggestion from the deputy officer of health for Toronto, who felt that the timetable did not have sufficient emphasis on outdoor activity and fresh air, and that three-quarters of an hour, or even an hour, would be much less time than children spent outdoors at home. Blatz said he was perfectly in sympathy with the suggestion and, although the children usually went outside for a total of at least an hour a day during two playtimes, the outdoor play could be moved to first thing in the morning to ensure even more playground time. A parallel plan could be made for active indoor play in rainy weather, to keep the timetable consistent.[31]

Undressing and dressing just once a day, instead of twice, was the logical and efficient way to halve the time spent struggling with winter clothing and allow the time and effort to be put to more productive use as outdoor play. This sequence of the nursery day, with vigorous outdoor play starting the morning, followed by quieter indoor pursuits, remained essentially the same for all Blatz nursery programs and became the accepted plan followed in the first Ontario day-care legislation of 1947.

Fresh air and exercise, even indoors, were Blatz's solution to the behaviour problems exhibited by a little boy 'from the only broken home in the school.' Blatz reported that he refused to drink his milk at school unless he wanted, and was extremely attached to his mother, who indulged him. The mother was making a determined effort to regulate his habits, but she was living in her parents' home and the child was not allowed to make a noise when his elderly grandfather was resting or sleeping. All the little boy had to do if he wanted something was to start an uproar and he would get his way. Blatz found there was a room on the third floor, however, well away from grandparental territory, and suggested that if the boy became obstreperous he could be dressed in outdoor clothes and taken to play up there with the windows wide open. In the more simple matter of drinking milk at school they would give him smaller quantities and get him to start by tackling just that amount.[32]

Another little boy (Peter) was considered by his mother to be 'overstimulated' in school. He was restless at naptime, and the family maid advised Dingle that the teachers should be harsh with him when he did not sleep. There was a great deal of adult stimulation at home, and Peter simply seemed to be making the best out of his time with the other children, Blatz thought. The whole question of over-stimulation merited serious attention, however. If a child was going to be over-stimulated by being with children of his own age, he would have to make the adjustment some time and it would be a question of whether it were better to make it at two or at five. Perhaps St George's School should make a study of it. To help Peter, Bott suggested that a screen might be provided to divide a portion of the playroom to allow Peter to concentrate on one or two companions and not be distracted by everyone he saw. Blatz reported another problem: Peter was so ravenous when he went to lunch that he ate two of everything and eight rusks. There might be some relation between his diet and over-stimulation, Bott thought, because if a child were so hungry he would be sure to be restless. Blatz would interview the mother and report.[33] Although no

direct record remains of Blatz's report to the staff on his meeting with
the mother, there is almost no doubt that the nursery was helpful in
getting Peter settled. Two years later, in the minutes of a staff meeting
there is a brief mention that Peter, by then four years old, gave the
nursery school 'an interesting talk on steel and heat.'[34]

With feeding problems, Blatz generally advised letting the child
eat, or not, by placing the food before her and 'if she wants it she can
help herself, if not let her go without.'[35] It was not always easy to make
such a studied display of nonchalance when the usual medical advice
to parents of the time was to see that their children were stuffed full of
everything that might be good for them. Blatz made it easier to appear
unconcerned by coupling his advice with instructions that would divert
parental attention from how much or how little was consumed. The
parents were put to keeping records of mealtimes that they took to the
school for discussion. This kept them too busy to coax or cajole at
mealtimes.

One of the earliest record forms was developed at the school to
supply further information and guidance to parents in observing special feeding problems. It was followed in quick succession by nursery
school records of sleep, mealtimes, the length of time spent outdoors,
how long the children took to dress after using the toilet or to put their
toys away, the nurse's record of each child's behaviour during the daily
medical inspection, the findings of the nurse's examination and whether
the child was accepted or not for school that day, and a daily report to
parents dealing with the mothers' questions about their children during
school hours. In emotional situations any member of the staff who
witnessed the episode was expected to write an individual account of
the matter before discussing it with other observers.

These early records were refined in detail over the years, but in
their basic form so little was changed that they remained an essential
part of the longitudinal research at St George's School. Blatz looked
on them as a way of studying the routine adjustment processes of
children in relatively controlled situations. He was emphatic that the
records were not designed simply to accumulate data or to seek out
specific norms of behaviour, but rather to assist in understanding
processes of individual adjustment.[36]

He started his research with the hypothesis that three areas of
function were significant in human adjustment: the appetites, the
emotions, and the attitudes. He listed hunger, thirst, rest, elimination,
sex, and change as the six organic appetites, all of them having a

physiological need to be satisfied and all of them giving rise to conscious motivation with peripheral wants and goals that vary from person to person. The first five appetites were generally accepted as fundamental human motives and, although his Chicago teacher, Harvey Carr, had already listed most of them as the forces directing what we do, the appetite for change was Blatz's addition. He incorporated this appetite for change and activity into his earliest system of function, considering it basic to the development of interests. Later it was tied to his ideas on learning, and later still it provided the energy for the shifting balances in his security theory. Among the emotions he ranked fear and anger as the two basics, both acting as strong driving forces, though not necessarily in a negative way. While in their extreme form these emotions can prove destructive, in a milder degree they can be stimulating. Anger used effectively can be exhilarating, he thought, and a limited degree of fear can be experienced as adventure.

The attitudes he defined as approach and withdrawal, which would develop as likes or dislikes and further define the person's adjustment.[37]

Having labelled these sources of physiological function and psychological action, Blatz had an initial structure for his longitudinal research. It was designed to follow people through all the stages of life, developing and changing with them.

The first children in the study had been registered at birth in order to attend the nursery at two years. It was a condition for attending the school that for three consecutive days of each month, the mothers were to make records of their infants' adjustment to the appetites and emotions as well as their developing attitudes. The information required was very detailed and objective, concentrating on observable behaviour rather than on drawing inferences. For example, the instructions to parents for recording non-compliant incidents was as follows:

> Any resistance or objection made by the child at any time during the three day period should be noted with full details: Describe the behaviour of the child in objective terms, e.g., crying, whimpering, screaming, kicking, stiffening, running away, slapping, etc. – not in indefinite and interpretative terms such as complaining, protesting, irritable, etc. Note treatment or care (or lack of treatment) e.g., lifted, changed, left alone, ignored, etc. Show how child reacted to treatment – stopped immediately or gradually, began playing, etc. Note how long objection lasted.[38]

The observations entailed a minute-by-minute account of the parent's (or other adult's) attention, care, and action and of the infant's responses and spontaneous acts. Interaction between adult and infant was clearly delineated, as were social contacts with other people in the house. Routine care was to be described in full, but parents were cautioned not to allow the recording to interfere in any way with the child's daily care or schedule.

The continuous record form meant three very busy days, for with even the youngest baby, every cry, coo, sneeze, smile, whimper, or wail was recorded on long sheets of paper showing the hour of the day and the place, who was with the child, who cared for him, and how. The morning bathing-feeding-changing time was to be recorded as a series of separate activities and the infant's behaviour noted in each instance. Records of emotional disturbances were to include a note on the preceding situation, the people present, the child's behaviour, the treatment or lack of treatment during the episode (such as whether he was picked up, changed, nursed, left alone, ignored), the person administering treatment, and the child's reaction. Along with the obvious time, place, people on hand, and contents of the meal, the special eating records listed whether any foods were refused and what help or reminders were given at the mealtime. Elimination records noted every time the baby wet or soiled his clothes or managed to use the toilet. As well as the records kept for these three days a month, the parents were also asked to make a verbatim record of all the sounds and words uttered by their children during fifteen consecutive minutes each week. (If silence happened to descend, they were to try again later.) The child was to be in his customary surroundings, either alone or with a brother or sister and, if his parents were present, they were to avoid promoting conversation. The parents were given simple and precise instructions for noting the circumstances and were taught a phonetic notation system of using English words, wherever possible, to explain vowel sounds.[39] Each month parents were to make a developmental record of changes and any problems observed in the children's general health, teething, motor development, new sounds or words, sleep, play, bowel and bladder control, co-operation with adults, changes in feeding, changes in daily routine, immunization, illness, accidents, findings and recommendations of the child's own physician, and any 'mannerisms' such as thumb- or finger-sucking, nail-biting, masturbating, twitching, blinking, stuttering, or stammering.[40]

A number of parents were keen enough to volunteer to keep additional informal notebooks of events that occurred between the record-ing cycles. These diaries allowed mothers the pleasure of describing the steps taken or the word spoken without the frustration of having to wait for the next official recording days. All the records were chan-nelled through the parent education staff, who gave assistance to the mothers with any problems that arose either in the record keeping or in child management.

Upon entering the nursery school, each child was given a research number to be used throughout the years of the longitudinal study. Today, these files are locked in the Thomas Fisher Library at the University of Toronto, and the identity of these 'Blatz Babies,' as they became known (some of whom are now old-age pensioners), is further protected by maintaining the secured files by numbers rather than by names in all but the most extraordinary circumstances.[41]

Nursery school records followed the parents' infant records in the sequence of the longitudinal study. There were no more regular reports required from home once the child was in school, though the parents participated in some of the nursery studies. The nursery records were based on observed behaviour and selected to show the children's prog-ress in their ability to help themselves, to make independent efforts, and to indicate their attitudes to routines, to their social sur-roundings, and to adult direction. The research was entirely based on careful record keeping in the controlled nursery school environment, and even the first outside study (an anthropometric analysis of physical growth under the Department of Anatomy) fit the same general de-scription. Blatz emphasized that 'the child is not "experimented with" in the sense that some critics dread ... the children themselves take very kindly to such enquiries and care is taken to prevent overstim-ulation and fatigue.'[42]

The fact that every person involved in research was also expected to be familiar with the nursery and its children helped to ensure that research studies were kept free of stress and integrated with the overall objectives of the St George's School. Of these, the research and the laboratory school were two legs of the child-study tripod, lending sub-stance and support to the third, and all-important, purpose of educat-ing parents. The earliest classes got under way almost immediately for the parents of children enrolled in the nursery, with the mothers organized into groups in the parent education division to discuss the problems they met in handling the children at home. By study, discus-sion, and reading of the literature of child study, the mothers in these groups were 'working to make themselves more intelligent in the guidance of their children's lives.'[43] Parent education for interested members of the general public began in earnest a few months later after Sidonie Gruenberg, president of the Child Study Association of America, travelled from New York to address a meeting of Toronto parents. Almost immediately two groups of parents began to meet with Blatz and Helen Bott on alternate Friday afternoons for study and discussion.

'The object of this work will be two-fold,' Blatz wrote in a press release. 'First, to learn from parents those things which they are best able to find cut by reason of their intimate contacts with their children, secondly to help parents to formulate sound principles of training and apply these principles in their homes ... Mothers who will take the trouble to learn to observe their children can supply material from which general principles of child training may be formed. They will thus serve not only themselves but a wide circle of parents.' Parent education would be of mutual benefit to the researchers and to the public, with parents supplying material of interest to scientific workers and the scientific workers bringing first aid to the families.[44]

The general public disapproved of parent education at first, although not nearly as strongly as it disapproved of nursery education. It seemed ridiculous that mothers would seek to be taught what they were expected to know by instinct. It was, however, a little easier to tolerate (or ignore) the idea of groups of women gathering to discuss a matter of concern to hearth and home than it was to withstand the threatening sight of groups of little children gathering beyond the confines and concerns of hearth and home. Parent education began to gain acceptance, and before long women read: 'In this scientific age hit or miss methods in anything from raising poultry to building a radio are frowned upon as ignorant and wasteful. Even the raising of babies has eventually become reduced to a science ... and science is now gravely turning her attention to the mental and social adjustment of the child to see if a decrease cannot be made in the appalling number of misfit adults for which society has to suffer and care.'[45] And, turning to another journal, they were told: 'Intelligent parents realize that they need training for the most important job in life, that they cannot afford to approach this all-absorbing problem of child training without adequate preparation and they are eagerly grasping the opportunities offered in the training courses.'[46] While the *Star Weekly* asked rhetorically, 'Who so ignorant then as to claim that mothers will not welcome any findings of science in the realm of character and personality, just as they have in the fields of health. Nobody realizes more than they do that the changing conditions of living demand changing methods if our boys and girls are to adjust adequately to the complex modern society of to-day.'[47]

Within a few months the initial two courses had multiplied to six. Demand for new groups became so great that the St George's School had neither staff nor space to accommodate them, and so turned to training parent education leaders to conduct groups for an ever-widening community of interest.

Today, however, professionally structured parent education classes have nearly disappeared. Perhaps it is because today's parents have more knowledge available to them from other sources, or because their confidence in their own judgment has been enhanced by a wider public awareness of the needs of children. Perhaps parents are more relaxed and realistic about child raising than parents of the 1920s and 1930s, who were intent on the alchemical quest of trying to make the behaviour of future generations as good as gold. It is possible, too, that today's parents consider parent education an unwelcome form of external control that would violate their rights to privacy and self-determination.

There is certainly a strong contemporary argument to support the latter view, particularly among feminist-revisionist writers who criticize parent education for usurping the rights of parents (and of mothers in particular), claiming that it was designed to erode confidence in natural ways of child rearing. Blatz and his parent education colleagues have been painted for this portrait as grim cradle-snatchers and stern prophets of efficiency, determined to undermine self-assurance and plotting to wedge otherwise well-rounded parents into slots that were uncomfortably square.[48]

There is another argument, however, which holds that people will listen only to the messages they are ready and willing to hear. According to this line of reasoning, it would have been virtually impossible to interest parents in new ways of child raising unless parent education held some satisfaction, significance, or useful purpose in the parents' lives. Lawrence Frank, musing on the early days of the child study movement has commented that some of the schedules and rigid routines emphasized in the 1920s were eagerly embraced by women who otherwise felt they were being ground down by the never-ending demands of child care. Thus, recommendations for four-hourly feedings and systematic toilet training and 'permission' to put the baby to bed in its own crib and at a definite bedtime were greeted as welcome routines of escape from the all-consuming ties of traditional maternal practices.

Furthermore, child study often resolved a conflict for mothers who had received an education and who might have felt it would be wasted by staying at home, living the lives of their grandmothers. Parent education classes, with their observations, assignments, and book reports, proved engrossing and challenging in themselves, with the added reassurance that such studies could do nothing but enhance family life. Enrolment in the courses became a way to make motherhood a stimulating challenge and to enliven domestic life by making it an enterprise of efficiency and merit.[49]

As Nellie Chant, one of the first parent education leaders, wrote in her recollections, the earliest groups at St George's School were made up of 'alert, interested, highly intelligent women with a very real interest in the problems and responsibilities of family life.'[50]

Blatz led some of these groups, particularly in the evenings; as well, every meeting was recorded verbatim and carefully scrutinized and analysed afterwards, so that he and his staff were able to discuss problems that might arise. In a staff meeting regarding concrete difficulties that the mothers brought to the parent education staff, 'Dr Blatz said that the thing to do is not to suggest a remedy for the particular trouble but to get the mothers to question their own technique, to go back and analyze the case from the first beginnings; these analyses to be written out and handed in for the consideration of the staff.'[51] Later programs were based on the problems recurring in the meetings, and gradually the courses developed into an orderly sequence of topics. Any acute problems were referred to Blatz for his guidance as a clinician.

The emphasis in the groups was on helping the mothers develop more enlightened ways of viewing children 'and one was led to think of things differently, and to make some analysis of causes and gain more understanding of human behaviour.'[52] Without a unifying theory and without a syllabus or even a developed sequence of subjects for parent education classes, Blatz and his staff decided to base the leaders' study on psychology itself. Because it would be hopeless to try to give a proper course on the subject in such a short time as the allotted ten weeks, Blatz suggested as an alternative the selection of ten topics that could be divided among various lecturers, with each class including a systematic presentation with time for discussion. The topics included neurology, three lectures on motivation (which included instinct and emotion), two on learning and habit formation, two on knowledge, perception, imagination, and reasoning, and one each on volition and character formation.[53] After that the students would be on their own to gather the practical application from their own experience, from studying, and from discussion with the St George's staff. Formation of the leaders' training group made it urgent to start a library of books and journals to be kept in the building for staff and the growing group of students. Gradually, too, as the courses continued, the content shifted towards discussion of research in child development, and the students spent longer in the nursery both observing and working with the children.

Soon staff members of various social agencies became aware of the usefulness of parent education to their work, and asked St George's School to provide classes specifically for them. Again, the child study staff was too small to cover the demand; furthermore, although the St George's School was acquiring a growing knowledge of child development, it was not focused on specific social work problems. A plan was worked out to add training in parent education leadership to social workers' existing professional skills by organizing a course for social workers. They would study at the St George's School one day a week for two academic years in a course that was both practical and theoretical. They spent the mornings at the school attending a series of lectures on the content of child study and the practice of parent education, along with systematic observations in the nursery school and intensive use of the child study library. During the first year they observed a parent education group in session, and in their second year they led a study group in their own agency with the help and supervision of someone from the St George's School. There were no formal qualifications for admission: the applicants simply were sponsored by the organizations that would benefit from their training, and, although the courses were primarily designed for social workers, they often included representatives from the Home and School organization and church organizations as well.[54]

As the nursery school developed and the research grew, both helped parent education to take on a more definite form. Although each individual class varied in style and in the proportion of lecture to discussion according to the personality of its leader and the interests of the group, the content was refined into a set of topics that gave the framework for a series of courses. Eventually, parents could enrol year after year for classes on pre-school learning, the school-age child, discipline, adolescence, and family relationships. Blatz kept in close touch with the questions that arose, gave special help where needed, and usually made at least one stellar appearance at each St George's School group.

The research was taking shape, and Blatz and his colleagues were beginning to be able to apply some of the early observations to the understanding of children at school and at home. Blatz himself was in and out of the nursery, very much aware of its children and their parents, just as the world outside was becoming aware of him.

In the first thirty years of the century, the population of Toronto doubled. Most middle-class families were smaller than a generation or two before, however, and health care was such that parents could usually expect their children to live to grow up. It was now less risky for parents to become fond of their babies and to make long-term plans for them. The nests may not have been as full, but they were safer, and mothers managed to be just as busy. Most of them willingly diverted the time it would have taken to raise ten or fifteen children to concentrate full attention on their little families of two or three or four.

Blatz brought parents the message they were ready to hear. Raising children takes knowledge and skill; it is an occupation that needs to be learned. And learning to bring up a baby according to Blatz's system was an exciting adventure, for there was always something to do and something to discover. There were records to keep, meetings to attend, and books to read. In the parent education classes the mothers were not simply told what to think or feel or do; instead, they worked their way towards solutions under the guidance of a professional leader. The framework of ideas seemed to make practical sense and allowed them to approach new problems with confidence. Blatz himself was charismatic, witty, often surprising, and his self-assurance was reassuring. He was both sophisticated and approachable and seemed the antithesis of the current stereotype of the sombre school official. The more parents saw of him, the more they wanted their children to be part of the picture.

The nursery school kept its enrolment possibilities quiet but the word spread, and within a year or two the waiting list to become a Blatz baby had grown to unmanageable lengths.

The Blatz era was under way.

# 4 Fame without Fortune

In the mid-1920s child study and psychology expanded like a great bubbling yeast. Universities borrowed staff and ideas from each other, pinching off pieces of the starter to set out new programs or to revitalize the old. By 1927, Psychology at the University of Toronto was well on the rise and looked very tempting to other universities hungry for well-qualified young faculty. Blatz's St George's School for child study was gaining public acceptance for both its nursery and its parent education programs, its research was taking shape, and Psychology itself was now a department with a strong staff largely gathered and maintained by the Canadian National Committee for Mental Hygiene.

'Our investment in the Department of Psychology, University of Toronto has been worthwhile,' Clarence Hincks wrote in his unpublished autobiography. 'It made possible the bringing together [of] perhaps the most able staff of any similar department in North America and included men such as E.A. Bott, William Blatz, Sperrin Chant, William Line, David Ketchum, and E.D. MacPhee. On two occasions the entire group was offered double salaries, first at Yale University and secondly at the University of Chicago.'

J.D. Griffin, a psychiatrist and a former pupil of Blatz, has an addition to the story. After Yale propositioned the Psychology staff, Blatz led a little delegation to Hincks to tell of the offer, which would be hard to refuse unless Hincks helped them to earn some compensatory money. They proposed that Hincks should arrange the investment of their savings. Hincks reluctantly agreed and sent off the psychologists' money to J.W. McConnell of Montreal, president of St Lawrence Sugar and an astute financier who was also a member of the board of CNCMH. Six months later cheques arrived from Montreal for double the amount of each person's investment. They declined to cash the cheques. 'Do it again,' Blatz said to Hincks. Six months later, new cheques, representing a further multiplication, were presented, but again Blatz demanded a repeat performance. This time Hincks and McConnell refused: McConnell did not like the look of the stock market.[1] 'Fine,' said Blatz. 'Easy. We'll do it ourselves.' So the psychologists, led by Blatz, plunged into the stock market in October 1929 just in time to catch the market's rush towards the precipice.

They were among the lucky ones, however, for although they lost a little money, and although both New Haven and Chicago in the meantime had lured others with the enticing salaries once held out to them, at least their jobs at Toronto were secure. For Blatz, the university became the rallying point of his activities, but his work, his interests, and his fame spread far beyond Toronto during the next ten years. He was invited all over North America to give lectures, and his books became popular on two continents. When he spoke he attracted large audiences and usually was controversial enough to draw a press report or editorial comment the next day. He had what has been described as 'a golden personality, a success personality,'[2] and his early career saw it polished to full lustre. Wilhelm Emet Blatz, the serious young man from Hamilton who had once thought of becoming a Catholic priest but who pleased his mother by studying medicine, was transformed into Dr Blatz (William E. Blatz in his writing), the psychologist who had something to say about almost everything and who was the admired prize of the Toronto establishment. When, in 1930, a group of well-to-do people sought Blatz's help with their progressive school, he was already enough in demand that he agreed to direct the school only if everyone would do exactly as he told them. The group fell into line with Blatz's dictum, and Windy Ridge Day School grew alongside St George's nursery until the two were joined some twenty years later. It was St George's School, however, that developed the programs and Windy Ridge, with its parallel nursery and early elementary grades, that allowed a further extension and fostering of Blatz's ideas.

Within two years of the opening of St George's School, Blatz had begun to gather a staff whose members gave child study at Toronto its particular flavour and who remained Blatz's faithful disciples throughout his entire career.

Carroll (Langstaff) Davis started as a student in 1927 and remained as lecturer on nursery school practice for the little groups of graduate students who were gathering knowledge of child development along with their psychology degrees. Margaret Fletcher arrived at the same time as Davis, having written a postcard to Blatz to ask if he would consider employing her without training. He remembered her from the Hart House project, where she had studied with him and been a volunteer worker.

Della Dingle was still head teacher when Fletcher joined the nursery, but Blatz himself spent a great deal of time in the school with the children and helping to train the staff. By two years after opening the school, he was very much in control of the situation. He was definite about what everyone was to do and was able to create such complete trust in what he was doing himself that the staff accepted his word as law. In the same way that the injured veterans had fallen under his spell, crying children, lifted into Blatz's arms, would almost immediately stop sobbing. 'He had an extraordinary skill with them and he taught it to us. The first impression I remember was not to be bothering the children all the time, to let them run their own show but we were to look after them,' Fletcher recalled. 'We became very fond of the children and began to understand them with Blatz's help. And then the children became fond of us and began to trust us. There was very little trouble with the children.'[3] Blatz understood unacceptable behaviour, but he simply would not allow it. He had the knack of controlling behaviour without fussing; children had confidence in him, and older people who had suffered traumatic experiences received the same kind of reassurance.[4]

Despite the precise schedule and recording of the children's routines, the playtimes were very relaxed, with the children choosing for themselves. The staff was there to prevent homicide and suicide, as Blatz put it, but otherwise was expected to stand back and not to play with the children. Students and staff members-in-training were set to observing and recording the children's activities, which was useful in itself, but also helped them to resist the temptation to interfere with the children.

The research took a bizarre but temporary turn in the early years of Fletcher's employment. Dietitians from household science wanted to see if the colour of food would have any effect on the unsophisticated tastes of young children. They coloured fish fillets royal blue, potatoes pink, and the desserts a rainbow of colours. It made not the slightest difference to the children's appetites, though the adults had difficulty in joining them at such meals. More traditional taste tests involved trying a series of puddings made with the recently developed infants' cereal Pablum, and helping the paediatrician Dr Frederick Tisdall of the Hospital for Sick Children to find an acceptably appetizing recipe for Sunwheat biscuits.[5]

The beginning of the 1930s marked the addition of two very important elements in child study at Toronto. These were the move to larger quarters and the arrival of a young student who became Blatz's trusted deputy, Dorothy Millichamp.

Millichamp had been an assistant in the biology department but decided to change course for an MA in psychology in order to work with Blatz at the St George's School. She became one of the three students of 1931. Carroll Davis lectured to them on nursery practice, which involved sitting on the little playroom chairs and talking, for, apart from one basic book on pre-school children by Harriet Johnson (*Children in the Nursery School*, written in 1928), there seemed to be virtually nothing systematic written about nursery schools.

Dingle had been replaced by Edith Deadman (of the Home Economics College at Ohio State University), who taught the students a type of research that mainly involved observing how many buttons the children were able to fasten by themselves. The psychology MA students saw Blatz in the nursery during their practice and took his course in genetic psychology along with students in honours psychology. 'My main concern during his lectures was to keep my head down so he wouldn't ask me a question and develop an argument which you know who won.'[6]

Deadman left at the end of their first student year and Fletcher became senior member of the nursery, remaining there until her retirement some thirty years later. Millichamp herself joined the staff in 1932 as a nursery assistant and remained with Blatz throughout his career.

Millichamp was going on perfectly happily with the assistantship until the day a year or so later when Blatz told her she would be put in charge as the senior academic person working with Fletcher. She felt ill prepared, but Blatz insisted that she could do it and finally she agreed.

> This changed my role. It was typical of Bill. He called Margie in and said that I would be in charge academically but she would run the

nursery school. We asked him how we would work this out and he said, 'Work it out.' After a few months we went back and told him we couldn't work it out. He said, 'You can, and I won't tell you how.' So we gradually learned and became the best of friends working out this interesting arrangement.

Soon after he gave me the title of 'assistant director' and I began to assume responsibilities as deputy for Dr Blatz. Mrs Bott was in charge of parent education but I took over student teaching and research.[7]

In 1931, the same year that Millichamp entered as a student, the St George's School moved up St George Street into two attached houses at numbers 96 and 98, virtually doubling enrolment in the nursery but still leaving an ever-growing waiting list for parents who hoped their children would become Blatz babies.

The extra space made it possible to have separate playrooms and cloakrooms for a junior group (two- and three-year-olds) and a senior group (older threes and four-year-olds). The playrooms were furnished much as in the smaller building, but there was more to play with, for there was the growing realization that children's concentration increased when they had a wider selection of playthings. The toys and puzzles were stored individually in wooden boxes neatly ranked on low shelves and, with the proliferation of construction sets, the more elaborate materials were made available to the seniors in their own room without frustrating the younger children. There was a large dining-room, a nurse's room (where the children were admitted to school), a waiting-room for parents and visitors, and two sleeping-rooms, where the children were not divided by age. Neither were they divided by age or sex in the washroom, except for the fact that the older children, with a longer concentration span, used miniature washbasins plumbed in place, while the younger ones still seemed to need the active involvement of carrying washbowls to and fro while they filled and dumped and refilled them again at the sink. The row of miniature toilets, undivided by compartments, was a Blatz innovation that brought horrified attention. 'Do you mean that boys and girls use the same toilets?' visitors would ask. 'Why yes,' was Fletcher's enthusiastic response. 'Isn't it marvellous? Just like at home.'

Another innovation was the screened observation rooms, one of them overlooking the dining-room and washroom, the other positioned to view both playrooms. These were virtually corridors walled with fine wire mesh, and if the lights were off and the visitors were quiet, observers appeared only as blurred shadows. It was no secret to the children that there were people behind the screens, but it made the intrusion less obvious and the children could go about their day without being disturbed. The screens solved what had been a constant problem in the old building by allowing an increase of visitors and students at the nursery.

The playground was again fitted out by Bott, who created even more new equipment. Both age groups played in the garden at the same time, and although a smaller jungle gym and low armchair swings were available for the younger children, there were no attempts to divide them by age. The adults positioned themselves around the garden, each surveying a definite area or standing close to a potential hazard, but otherwise generally frozen in place and not interfering. If a child climbed too high and panicked, there was no pulling down or picking up; the adult simply helped the child stretch a tentative foot to lower rungs of the jungle gym until on familiar ground again.

By the time of the move, the adults' role had been clarified and a general approach to the nursery program was taking shape. There were two main parts to the children's day: free-choice learning and conformity learning. Learning was the key to development and adjustment in Blatz's developing theory, and the adults' responsibility was to provide an appropriate environment and to guide the children's efforts in both routines and in play. This guidance, however, had to be largely unobtrusive.[8]

Free-choice learning took place in children's play, and the adults' task was to plan a suitable combination of three factors to foster it: play space, play materials, and playmates. After that they were to remain in the background, being interested, supportive, and helpful but always only in terms of the children's choices and the children's own goals. Even the fact that the staff referred to themselves as 'adults' rather than 'teachers' reinforced this, and they further blended into the background by covering their street clothing with uniform blue smocks.

There were some minimum requirements in play, largely in matters of constructive play and concern for the rights of other children, but generally it focused on developing the children's general interest and abilities. There were neither patterns nor models to copy in the playrooms, and if the children were busy, the adults remained in the background no matter how unorthodox the use of the materials. The spirit of each playroom was the same as on the playground, namely adventure, but here the adventure was in the realm of ideas and accomplishment rather than physical challenges.

Conformity learning happened mainly in the daily routines of personal care, such as eating, sleeping, toileting, washing, and dressing. Here the children were expected to learn and to carry out the goals and procedures set for them. In Blatz's plan the formation of a habit indicated an efficient response to needs without having to waste energy on negative emotions. Even the habit itself could bring about a feeling of serenity and enjoyment of the activity. (The idea of the useful function of habits, of course, carried on from his studies at Chicago.)

'Dr Blatz believed that the *willingness* to conform in situations essential to the individual and to society was a must in the development of mental health. With emphasis on the willingness. Of course the routine requirements had to be made both interesting and satisfying – and they had to be *consistent*, a Blatz watch word.'[9]

All the routines were analysed and set into a series of efficient actions that the children usually enjoyed mastering. The washroom had always been active, but the dining-room settled into small groups at each table, with the juniors carrying their plates back from the serving table with every helping, and the seniors spooning out their own desserts at the table. Margaret (Husband) Kirkpatrick divided her time as dietitian between Windy Ridge and St George's School after completing a thesis on the food preferences of pre-school children. (Using the frequency of second servings as the best index of preference, she found that stewed foods were most favoured; creamed the least. Preference appeared for foods that were relatively bland but had a definite form, while texture was usually more important than taste.)[10]

When cumbersome coats and leggings yielded ground to the innovative snow-suits, the cloakroom routine became a marvel of speed and efficiency. Blatz designed rows of individual cupboards at child height with low hooks and a shelf for outdoor shoes and playroom slippers. Undressing or dressing was whittled down to a scant two minutes per child by resolving the task into its elements and then working out the most effective sequence of steps for its completion. The adults helped, but only as much as necessary to accomplish the job smoothly, with everything kept businesslike and no one feeling rushed. 'The degree of conformity expected is a coöperative attitude toward learning and participation in the procedure according to ability,' Blatz wrote.[11]

Conformity and non-conformity were always balanced against each other. Blatz saw 'the ideal finished product' as an adult who 'fits into the social scheme where necessary, and still indulges in individual opinions and behaviour ... so that the compromise between conformity and individualization will become increasingly more efficient and pleasant ... he has learned to accept willingly the consequences of his behaviour, to develop judgment and foresight.'[12]

This idea of accepting consequences became the core of Blatz's theory of discipline, a theory that he later shaped into his definition of security.

His plan of discipline was designed 'to *teach*, not to punish, to bribe, to reward, to cajole nor to persuade ... an attempt to teach the child to resolve the inevitable conflict between conformity to group demands and the satisfaction of individual needs. This is a compromise and, as such, is difficult but not impossible.'[13] His plan fell somewhere between the extremes of complete freedom of expression and rigid discipline. As such he tried for a balance of conformity with the recognition of individual wants.

The adult's role was to plan the requirements necessary for the child's needs in every situation, keeping them to a minimum but seeing that they were followed without fail. There were definite consequences for refusal to adhere to these limited demands, and again, consistency was the rule. The adult procedure was also outlined: if they were ready to learn, the children were given choices and encouraged to make their own decisions, either to carry through or to accept the consequences. There were no rewards and no punishments.

The learning began with consideration for the rights of other children. Removal of the child to play alone was Blatz's answer to social issues; if the children cared to belong in the group they accepted its requirements. There was to be no personal scolding or moralizing on the part of the adults. Instead the child was guided in righting the situation; doing so might involve returning another child's toy or awaiting a turn. Hitting was usually followed by the consequence of requiring the child to play alone for a while. Consequences were always to be immediate, invariable, adequate, and inevitable. If natural consequences were not apt to be immediate, or would be too much for a young child to handle, the adult could arrange for related consequences. For example, when children were throwing toys the consequence would be removal of the toy.

Over time, the children became as familiar with the requirements and the consequences as the adults, and working it all out was usually a friendly affair, though sometimes it was harder on the adult than the child. For example 'Harry' was finally given the choice of settling down or going back home for the day. This was a very infrequent consequence, but his behaviour was upsetting everyone, even himself. He chose to go home but almost immediately regretted his decision, though he still was not ready to do anything different about nursery school. Fletcher called a taxi, sat with him on her lap to take him home, and cried all the way back alone in the taxi.

Although Harry eventually settled into school, it is unlikely that today's teachers with today's knowledge would have taken such drastic measures. Looking back on the story of Harry some fifty years later, Dorothy Millichamp has commented that their blind spot in the 1930s was a failure to recognize that while they were doing their best to support the child's own efforts, they were also building a relationship. Later insight into dependent security with its acknowledgment of the depths of a child's feelings for and about adults, both positive and negative, cleared up several unknowns about child behaviour in the nursery school and altered some of their approaches. 'Certainly we would have better understood Harry's distress and temper tantrums. We would have postponed our efforts to teach until we had proved our dependability to him.'[14]

From the very beginning, certainly, the onus was on the adults to teach with care and to think through their plans for the children. St George's was still operating without a cohesive theory, however, and it was a long time before Blatz talked about the security of developing trust in someone dependable. The major effort in the early days was to keep struggles and confrontations between adult and child to a minimum. This could be accomplished by arranging consistent and impersonal consequences. Each episode of anger or fear was given just enough attention to help the children find their own way out of it. In Blatz's view these emotions were a part of learning, and arose when people, faced with a problem they could not solve, experienced frustration (and hence anger) or felt the need to get away (resulting from fear). He thought of such emotions as normal and a spur to effort. 'Conflict is the beginning of all learning and, therefore, an essential part of the child's experience ... Emotion, under control, is a valuable and indispensable form of response; without this possibility of energizing one's responses, learning would be impossible ... The child should be taught how he may solve situations of conflict in a controlled and efficient manner.'[15] It was the adults' job to help the children learn to control and use their emotions to solve problems, by redirecting their attention and energy into constructive channels.

After analysing 374 emotional episodes in the nursery, one of Blatz's graduate students compiled a list of 15 specific situations that could give rise to uncontrolled emotion. These situations were: being hurt (accidentally or by another child); being cold; being startled; leaving the parent to enter school; being caught in an apparatus; unusual occurrences (such as a change in routine, accidents, etc.); routine requirements (involving an interruption of an activity, perhaps); discipline by an adult; wanting a toy used by another child; having another child take or try to take a toy or personal belonging; having another child destroy a construction; another child's refusal to let him play; another child's refusal to play the way he wanted; teasing or other personal interference; inability to complete a task.[16]

In developing their techniques of nursery education Blatz, Millichamp, and Fletcher looked at each of these and planned how the adult could be most effective in handling any of the problem situations. The discipline records, for instance, showed six possible forms of discipline for the adults to choose among. These were: having the child complete the routine alone, removing the child to play alone, removing the child to wait, having the child wait on a chair, taking the child through the routine, and having the child repair the damage.

Minutes of a staff meeting in 1929 show something of Blatz's effort to hammer into shape the nursery research records and hence to develop some systematic techniques of nursery practice. Much of the discussion centred on a definition of terms such as 'Refusal may be verbal or physical,' or 'Reluctance to comply is a form of *non-compliance*.' The resulting chart tabulated ten categories of adult and child relations and eleven ways the child might relate to the adult. (See p. 84.)

For the research, 'emotional episodes' referred only to the observable symptoms of negative and disturbed feelings, expressing fear or anger and their derivatives. (Positive feelings such as excitement and pleasure were not under regular observation.) A mental testing program was also carried out in conjunction with the information on development: the nursery children were tested at least once a year on

CHART FROM MINUTES OF STAFF MEETING

---

*ADULT RELATIONS*

CONVERSATION    Initiated
Reply

RESTRAINT    Correction: Positive Verbal
Correction: Negative Verbal
Correction: Positive Physical
Correction: Negative Physical

STIMULATION    Command
Request
Implication
Putting Through (helping child to learn)

*CHILD RELATIONS*

ASSERTION    SOCIAL
ATTENTION  – Ask Question
– Showing Work
– Revolt
– General Non-compliance
– Statement of Fact

REFUSAL  – Verbal
– Physical

NEGATION  – Reluctance to Comply
– Request for Help
– Compliance – Verbal
– Physical

Dr Blatz: Have we left anything out? It is rather interesting to see that with these categories we can include all the child's behaviour for the day, and that of the adult. This will not work with 'child to child' relationships. That will have to be worked out later.

March 20, 1929.[17]

---

the Merrill-Palmer Scale and with the Kuhlman Test and the Binet-Simon Intelligence Test. Certainly the promotion of mental growth was one of the accepted values of the nursery, and these few early intelligence tests were used as tools to assess progress towards its developments. Blatz, along with his non-hereditarian contemporaries, recognized the fallibility of the tests, of course, and used them only with other information, and more to chart progress than to identify capacity. There was not, at the time, much understanding of pre-school cognitive processes, so in the nursery free play with educational materials, and under supervision, was considered to be the best source of mental stimulation.[18]

The people who gathered for parenting classes in the 1930s were fascinated by this new world of learning in the nursery through routines and free play and interested in applying its techniques to their children's daily lives. Parent education increased in popularity, multiplying its training of group leaders and social workers for specific agencies. As the nursery at St George's School was developing a theory and practice, the parent education division, too, was beginning to articulate which methods had proved to be most useful with its classes.

The parent education staff, headed by Mrs Bott, added several new members during its first five years, among them Nellie Chant and Frances Johnson, both of whom continued in long association with Blatz. Chant's responsibilities were largely for the infant and home records as well as the supervision and evaluation of students, while Johnson concentrated on the library and on introducing students to the fast-growing literature of child study. The members of the little group were ready not only to train leaders at St George's School but also to guide the initial steps of new groups in the community. One of their first steps was to organize a demonstration parent education group and to lead the neophytes past any possible problems.

Although groups might start up quite spontaneously among parents, experience showed that while enthusiasm was essential to the success of a group, a formal affiliation with an accredited organization was needed ultimately to ensure continuity and quality. Free discussion was most likely to occur in fairly homogeneous groups of between twenty-five and thirty people whose children were approximately similar in age. The leader should have regular contacts with children if she was to maintain an experimental rather than a dogmatic attitude in regard to problems of child training, and should have sound judgment in dealing with people, and preferably have training in some allied professional field such as psychology, biology, household science or social work. A doctor with an interest in mental hygiene, a psychiatrist, psychologist, school principal or someone 'who has scientific training and experience in the adjustment of human relations' should be available for consultation and, 'if a mental hygiene clinical consultation service is available, the group leader should make contacts with it in order to refer difficult behaviour problems which she herself cannot be expected to deal with adequately.'[19] The ultimate objective was to teach parents to observe and to think problems through for themselves. Free discussion was to be encouraged, and the leaders were urged to refrain from telling the parents what to do. 'One must realize that the last word on the subject is far from said, that the parents have really worth while contributions to offer to this science in the making.'[20]

Record keeping was recommended for every group as a way to vitalize the teaching. Special records could be kept at home on such subjects as 'Sleep, Eating, Elimination, Play, etc. [to] give parents additional insight into their children, and help them in the attainment of an objective attitude towards children.'[21] Verbatim records of the discussions themselves were considered to be helpful in charting the development of the group and in preparing leaders of subsequent groups.

It was then possible to organize the leaders' program of study into theoretical courses (psychology and methods of child study), seminars (on observations, clinical case methods, group methods, and the literature of child study), and practical work in observing and leading groups, as well as in coping with special problems. The students were in contact with schools and with the extension groups at a variety of social agencies, such as Neighbourhood Workers, University Settlement, St Christopher House, Jewish Philanthropies, and the Infant's Home. These organizations had all sent social workers to St George's School in order to allow them to add parent education to their qualifications, and now were able to return the favour by helping to train further students. Blatz personally guided the students through their observations at Regal Road Public School, where he was involved in a major research project, and also introduced them to clinical case methods.[22]

Regal Road was another Mental Hygiene undertaking, financed largely by the Rockefeller Foundation but supplemented by Canadian funds and under the general umbrella of the University of Toronto. The research was quite different from that at St George's School, however; instead of studying a small number of young children in all observable aspects of their lives, the researchers looked at some 1400 elementary school children and focused on a specific area of their adjustment: problems of behaviour in school. The main deliberate difference, though, was that instead of bringing the children into the university, the researchers settled themselves right in the school. It was part of the university's effort to 'establish the most effective contact between the scientist and his complex material ... [and] to apply scientific methods to the study of those manifold settings in daily life where difficulties of human adjustment take their rise.'[23]

Regal Road Public School was in a district with a population of more than 800 families representing a wide variety of economic levels and ethnic groups in a neighbourhood that combined residential with commercial or industrial use.

Blatz's own study of the children's behaviour was joined by a parallel survey of pupil classification in relation to special cases of educational maladjustment. This was conducted by another psychology professor, E.D. MacPhee. Blatz's part of the study set out both to find whether cases of major difficulty could be identified before they became acute and how far prevention might be possible; and to 'identify psychotic trends and anticipate incipient psychoses [and] eventually to evaluate general behaviour of school-age children in terms of their success in adjustment.'[24]

Longitudinal records were to provide a picture of the long-term aspects of each child's adjustment. Following the children through their school years into adolescence and even into adult life would, Blatz hoped, allow him to see whether incidents in childhood had any significance for later behaviour. A child's immediate behaviour might present a dramatic moment, but it was meaningless unless it could be analysed and understood in relation to what preceded it or succeeded it.

Rather than imposing his own list of characteristics to be noted, Blatz decided to evolve the classifications of behaviour and terminology from the teachers' own experience and vocabulary. To this end he began a series of meetings with the staff in order to formulate a common point of view. They settled on a general definition of the misdemeanours to be studied as 'any act on the part of a child which necessitated the interruption of the teaching routine for the purpose of dealing with the pupil or pupils in question.'[25] These misdemeanours ranged widely from truancy or bullying to eating fruit in class or having untidy clothes or messy books. There was no hierarchy except in disobedience, which could be classified as petty disobedience (slow to respond or a reluctant attitude) or gross disobedience (deliberate refusal to obey commands). In all the types of misbehaviour there was often little difference between the instances under study at school and the circumstances that might bring children before the Juvenile Court. Blatz, at first, distinguished the two by using delinquency to mean grave anti-social tendencies that should warrant official action. (In later years he defined a delinquent as a person of any age who acts contrary to the approved customs of the community, whether or not these customs are incorporated into a Juvenile Court Act.)[26] Any distinctions were, of course, largely open to individual interpretation. It was usually the children who were without the support of family and friends who were considered to be more than merely disruptive and to require intervention by outside officials. Yet the behaviour could be exactly the same as that of their family-supported classmates.

The classifications changed, enlarged, were regrouped, disappeared, and blossomed under new names as the study evolved. In 1926–7 the teachers had identified some sixty-five types of behaviour, which they could chart with a specific letter and number code for each occurrence. In an unusual twist for the time, the children's identities were protected by making the symbols unintelligible to anyone who did not have the key to the code.

The Regal Road principal was keen on the study, and Blatz was able to work out a reciprocal arrangement whereby the teachers devoted a certain amount of their time to observation and record keeping while the research staff gave assistance and advice if the teachers asked for their help.

The raw data from the teachers was organized in various ways according to grades, age, mentality, and sex and was compared with other variables. Blatz acknowledged in his preliminary report that the method might still be imperfect; at least the teacher-written checklists were objective, however, and generally safeguarded against the injection of personal prejudices into the material. By making it possible to compare the records of the same children in different years, the method also allowed the teachers' preconceptions to be evaluated.[27]

Blatz continued to gather data at Regal Road from 1925 to 1933. He amassed a huge amount of information and made a few stabs at analysing it, both at the time and in a major follow-up effort after the Second World War, when approximately one-third of the original 1400 children were traced. (Richard Volpe of the Faculty of Education at the University of Toronto has more recently been engaged in contacting some of the original people in the study.)

When the study was in full swing, Blatz included several of his graduate students in the research. Elsie Stapleford recalls spending one day a week at the school, testing all morning and going over the cases at lunch with the staff, in what became an informal weekly seminar. 'Blatz was always there and he would zero in on the cases from our reports.'[28]

J.D. Griffin was involved, too. He described it as 'a tremendous project – very imaginative because Bill had a whole public school to work with and he set out in a very grandiose way – very well planned – to study all the children in a whole public school and he had money, I suppose from Rockefeller, and appointed staff.'[29]

The initial results of Blatz's research found that the misdemeanours reported in all the classrooms were most frequently restlessness or lack of application. 'One wonders,' Blatz mused, 'whether it may not point to a too rigid school curriculum. Does it not suggest the wisdom of an experimental attitude towards the curriculum and methods ... [to awaken] wholesome and spontaneous interest on the part of the children?'[30] He found, too, that the number of misdemeanours (particularly those such as uncleanliness, deceit, swearing, emotional outbreaks, timidity, irregular attendance, and stealing) fell off markedly in the higher grades, though at different rates for the various types. There were more misdemeanours reported for boys than for girls, and, although frequency was not closely related to chronological age, the number of problems seemed to peak between ages seven and nine.[31]

The Regal Road study was a highly absorbing part of Blatz's early career, but it was only one of several involvements that took a very busy Dr Blatz beyond the university campus. Along with Regal Road and the Juvenile Court, another major Blatz project outside the St George's School was at Windy Ridge Day School. It had been founded by a group of parents in 1926 as a co-operative kindergarten, and later they had added some grades and hired some teachers from the States to make it into a progressive school. By 1930 it had lost its sense of direction, and representatives of its board of management approached Blatz to ask if he could help them. He agreed, but on one condition: 'I'll take it over only if you will run it exactly as I say,' he told them, and, to strengthen his position, he refused a salary.

The school was housed in an abandoned shop on Eglinton Avenue West, but in 1930, when Blatz became director and changed its name from the Progressive School to Windy Ridge, it moved to Heath Street East where it had enough room to add a nursery and younger children. (Still later it moved to Balmoral Avenue after Blatz had raised sufficient cash to buy the larger house and extend enrolment to grade three.)

Progressive education had established itself much earlier in the United States; it was not until the 1930s that it began to gain a foothold in Canada.[32] Windy Ridge gave Blatz his own firm position on the Canadian beachhead, and he set to work with a will to advance the ideas of Dewey – ideas that he had admired from his Chicago days. He applied and adapted his experience with nursery education to the curriculum of older children. The ideas flowed. The kindergarten children worked on a loom and baked bread. There were school trips to the harbour, to art galleries, and to the train station. A school newspaper was launched, and Blatz hired a French teacher. None of this may sound out of the ordinary today, but it was wildly innovative at a time when children were expected to stay with the basics.

There was less public criticism of Windy Ridge than of St George's School, however. Carroll Davis attributes this to the fact that Windy Ridge was used by some of Toronto's wealthiest families: the Gundys (stockbrokers), the Gooderhams (distillers), the Burtons (proprietors of one of Canada's nation-wide department-store chains), and the Eatons (proprietors of the other). This world of business, finance, and society was perhaps less available to general scrutiny than the world of the academics and professionals who took their children to St George Street.

From time to time there was some resentment among the Windy Ridge people of the fact that the school they had built had disappeared to become Blatz's particular project. 'The Board was devoted to him but a little afraid at the same time.'[33] In any confrontation of board and Blatz, Blatz need only remind them that things were to be done exactly as he decreed. 'You can't fire me because you don't pay me.'

Parents' meetings were another matter. When Blatz spoke, the room was always crowded. Most of the fathers turned out, but heckled at their peril. No mother was allowed to knit while Blatz talked, for he demanded undivided attention. His talks ranged widely, from discussions of techniques of child raising to broadly philosophical topics. He expounded on his developing security theory while it was still little more than a gleam in his eye, and in another lecture, to prove his point that abilities are general and talents non-specific, he offered to learn to play the piano in a year. He met his deadline and gave the parents a reasonably competent recital.

He had an office at Windy Ridge and was there two or three times a week, loving every minute of it because he felt few constraints. Unlike St George's School, Windy Ridge did not keep records. In an effort to communicate with parents, however, Blatz had the staff send home notes with the children every day to report on their daily routines. A few months later it was discovered that the taxi driver who transported a group of children was awarding a prize to the child who slept the longest. That had to stop. In Blatz's plan, rewards were nearly as bad as punishments.

Salaries were small at Windy Ridge, so the staff tended to be people who could afford to work for little more than pocket money and the satisfaction of doing something interesting. Blatz managed to assemble a staff who were highly qualified, enjoyed their work, and were able to maintain a collegial relationship with the staff at St George's School. Enrolments were small, too (between sixty and eighty in the whole school), so that Windy Ridge also gave the teachers considerable freedom to put imagination into their work.

Windy Ridge was known for its plays and parties. Dora Mavor Moore taught a drama class at the school and produced plays that were much admired by the parents and the press. Blatz himself preferred spontaneity, and put on his own little play with the school children – a production that involved knights and swords and battles. The children loved the dashing about, although no one else could follow the action.

Margaret Findley, the school secretary, has told of a special party Lady Eaton gave for the Windy Ridge staff. A sumptuous feast was spread, and there was even a whole barrel of oysters. When he was taking his leave Blatz thanked his hostess effusively: 'That was a wonderful party, Lady Eaton.' Then dead pan, but with a twinkle in his eye, he added, 'But it was nothing to what they can do at Simpson's.'[34]

At St George's School, too, the staff was a tightly knit group, working together and partying in any time left over. According to Millichamp, there was no hierarchy or competition or encroaching on one another's territory. Each staff member had specific areas of responsibility, but all worked together in carrying out the projects that Blatz instigated. 'There were always projects; far more than we could manage. We never finished one before there was another. We could go to him for advice, but I learned to figure out how he would like a project done.'[35]

St George's developed its own rituals. There was tea each afternoon for everyone and, in accordance with Blatz's insistence that hard work should be balanced with regular relaxation, every office had an iron-framed camp cot for staff rest times. There were little jokes, too, endlessly repeated, which, as in a family, usually evoked indulgent laughter. References to the time that Blatz dared to serve lamb with raspberry jam never failed to bring laughter, for it was long before anyone had heard of lamb with raspberry vinegar as almost a culinary cliché.

Blatz was a bundle of energy. 'When a project had to be done he would throw himself into it completely and we would all follow,' Fletcher said. 'He would work all night if necessary. If we were making props for the June party he would come down all weekend and paint the props. This always got the willing co-operation of his staff.'[36] Reba Cohen agreed that no task was too small for Blatz; even if staff were just folding forms and stuffing envelopes, Blatz would be in the thick of it.[37]

Blatz's Hamilton family had always enjoyed every possible social event, with its garden parties at 'Kehr Ein,' seasonal gatherings, and annual picnics, all accompanied by hearty food, plenty to drink, enthusiastic singing, skits, and harmless practical jokes. Blatz meanwhile had learned to move easily in the more muted world of Toronto society in the 1930s, with its cigarettes, cocktails, and canapés. When relaxing with his staff and close friends, however, he could still enjoy a rollicking good time.

The staff parties were only tantalizing rumours to the first-year child-study students, but riotous realities in the second year, for by then they were part of the group. 'The parties were quite wild,' Millichamp has commented. Many of the festivities were at Mental Hygiene's headquarters. A favourite game was for four psychiatrists to toss a colleague in a blanket. At fancy dress parties, Blatz was renowned for his repeated appearances as a baby wearing a frilly bonnet and long nightgown.

Blatz usually took two or three of his staff along for the ride when he went to give a lecture out of town. 'I remember going to New York and visiting William Morrow, the publisher, and we gave a party for him when he was in Toronto and when he left he said, "Wonderful to see such a staff working so hard, so interested in their work and having such a lot of fun." '[38]

On major occasions, David Ketchum of the psychology department would set it all in rhyme to be sung to a familiar tune. He and
Blatz were both suited for centre stage, but Blatz was more often there,
and when Ketchum mentioned Blatz in verse his words usually took
on an edge.[39]

When the Blatzes were leaving for a European tour in 1930 there
was the customary uproarious party at Mental Hygiene's headquarters,
and Ketchum's farewell song ran to seventeen verses, some of which
follow.

> Within very few years our bright William has passed
> Step by step up the ladder – he sure rises fast!
> And it's only the cynics, a poor jealous lot,
> Who insist that air rises because it is hot.
>
> The whole of Toronto is scared stiff of Bill,
> For he's known far and wide as a man with a will;
> And the Bursar who queried his travelling accounts
> Soon felt grateful that Bill did not give him the bounce.
>
> And now he is leaving to voyage afar
> In the lands where you still can take drinks at the bar;
> And it cheers us to know, as we long for him here
> There'll be no enuresis in Europe next year.

A hearty chorus followed each verse:

> So fill up your glasses and drink with a will
> To our brilliant, aggressive and versatile Bill!
> His views and his stories are far from polite
> And his ways are peculiar ... but Bill is ALL RIGHT![40]

The tour, sponsored by the Laura Spelman Rockefeller Memorial
fund, was specifically to allow Blatz to look at nurseries in the United
Kingdom and Europe. Blatz, his wife, and their daughter, Gery, set off
with Dr and Mrs Harry Spaulding from Mental Hygiene. The little
group visited England, France, Austria, and Germany; Mrs Blatz and
Gery then stayed in Munich with Mrs Spaulding while Blatz and
Spaulding visited Russia. Travel in Russia was an unusual adventure
for Canadians in 1930, and upon his return Blatz's comments on

Russian life received rapt attention in Toronto, which was beginning to feel the effects of hard times in the economy.

'In Russia we have 150,000,000 people working for an unselfish goal (they are working for one another and for the state) and what we fear is that we shall have to become more unselfish,' he told the Fabius Club.

'Picture a young man 24, and his wife, 20, with two children and another one coming, living in two rooms, on three dollars a week, with no recreation and scarcely enough to eat. Picture below them another family, with six children, with less to live on and wondering why they should rear children to a world which offers little prospect of a happier lot. That picture ... is not Russia but Toronto.'

The Russian system of education Blatz said he considered to be the most ideal ever foreseen or anticipated by any state, while for monetary rewards Russia had substituted an increased social status. 'Their incentive is the satisfaction for effort expended towards a common weal. The unselfish interests of the state have been substituted for the selfish interests of self and family.'[41]

The trip to Europe had been further enlivened when Mrs Spaulding tossed her wedding ring into the ocean as they left port and turned her attention to Blatz. The Blatz marriage at the time was not doing as well as other Blatz efforts, and although a separation had already been considered, the Blatzes wanted Gery to grow up in a two-parent family. They were good enough parents and friends to sustain the agreement. The Blatz-Spaulding entanglement was soon over, although the friendships were preserved; many years later, when a divorce became feasible, Mrs Blatz was to marry Dr Spaulding.

Gery's remembrances of her childhood are of travelling with her parents to the places where her father lectured, and of sitting with both parents while they listened to Edgar Bergen or the Saturday opera or while she did her homework. 'It [the homework] was never done for me but whenever I asked a question I always got an answer, and my most vivid recollections of both of them was that their knowledge was really profound. I had great confidence that if I asked how to spell something, or where a country was, they always knew.'

She added that she thinks her father brought her up according to his theories. 'I was never spanked. I was isolated and sent to my room. I enjoyed my room, but I didn't like being sent away from everyone else at the dinner table. I can't ever remember being told that I had to do something. I remember asking permission and usually got it. I never remember anything as unfair.'[42]

An only child, Gery grew up to be competent, considerate, and responsible. Her father sewed for her, did much of the cooking, and let her make her own decisions. Long after she was married and her own two children were in nursery school, she herself became a pre-school teacher.

But there were two other 'Blatz children' who were always in trouble. It was said that these 'Bad Blatz Boys' sawed the legs off dining-tables and poured ink on oriental carpets. Someone had it for a fact that they pulled down the curtain rods and cut up the curtains for tents. Someone else heard that they threw stones at the living-room window. They had even been seen to dance a jig on the piano. They were the despair of their teachers and were expelled from Upper Canada College. They were rude, destructive, disobedient, difficult – and totally a figment of the public's imagination.

No one was ever sure how the stories about the Bad Blatz Boys started. A mention of Dr Blatz or his ideas could bring a growl from a cynic. 'Just look at how he brought up his own children. He might have a lot of fancy ideas, but his own boys have turned out to be no good at all.' To mention that Blatz had only one child, a pleasant little girl, was not always enough to satisfy the public's appetite for scandal. Perhaps Blatz had been forced to send his boys away somewhere to save face, it was hinted darkly.

The stories persisted throughout Blatz's life, and as he became better known his detractors seemed to have even more need of these oblique criticisms.

Blatz's public persona grew along with his publications and the attention they brought. He published three books in quick succession: on parent education, on children's social adjustment, and on nursery education. At the same time he was busy turning out papers and pamphlets and making speeches all over North America.

The first book, *Parents and the Pre-School Child*, which he wrote with Mrs Bott in 1928, made a major contribution to the cause of parent education. It outlined the St George's School approach to the subject in detail. The first of its three parts was addressed to both parents and professional workers, the second directly to parents; the third part showed how records kept by mothers could be used to help them to learn about their children. The whole aim of the book was 'to point out ways and means of avoiding the pitfalls that lie in the way of every normal child in the course of his social adjustments.'[43]

The ten chapters in Part II were especially arranged for use by parent education groups so that one topic could be selected for each meeting; if, as was customary, meetings were held once a fortnight, the ten chapters would represent a year's work. The chapters covered the appetites and the formation of habits in eating, sleeping, and elimination; they also dealt with play, sex education, the emotions, attitudes, fears, and temper tantrums. Each chapter included an outline to promote discussion, a guide to further reading, a selection of the questions parents most frequently asked on these subjects, and a summary of some of the observations or suggestions group members had made about their own children. At the end of every chapter was a case history, dealing with a related problem that had required clinical consultation with Blatz. Although the book's emphasis was on avoiding difficulties, the case histories were included in order to show how the principles that were used for therapy could also be used for prevention. Each case history gave a statement of the problem, noted the child's chronological and mental ages, IQ, developmental history, attitudes, and habit training, and described the discipline in the home. A general diagnosis was made, recommendations were given, and progress reports and comments from the parents' home records were included. All the cases showed definite improvement.

Part III presented samples of the forms and record charts needed to show a child's progress. The forms were 'so arranged that they could be used by the average mother who is intelligently interested.'[44]

The early chapters in the book were more theoretical than practical in relating principles of mental hygiene to child study and parent education. Blatz was insistent that the material should be absorbed by parents as necessary background to making reasoned judgments on daily matters of child rearing.

The book was readily accepted by J.M. Dent and Co. for publication in Toronto and London and was forwarded to William Morrow and Co. of New York for consideration of an American edition. Although the Child Study Association of America reported favourably on Blatz's manuscript, Morrow had a problem with the first part of the book in particular, thinking it might be too much for the average parent to understand.

> I feel very strongly that the book is so valuable that it ought to be presented in a way that would gain the widest circulation for your views ... Is it possible for you to consider some rearrangement of the

book – some difference in presentation that would help parents apprehend more readily the important message the book contains for them? I am very keen to have parents read more sound books on education, and to take more active interest in educational problems. If they do, the reforms that you advocate will come more quickly ... Just think how much more good would be accomplished by a book that parents could grasp quickly, and which they would talk about, one to the other, and pass the recommendation along.[45]

Blatz wrote immediately to say that, as the Child Study Association of America had indicated in its report, the book was not of the popular type and that it was precisely Blatz's intention that it should not be. He declared that the market was flooded with books on child study that were worse than useless for promoting serious work in parent education, while at the same time there were multitudes of wide-awake, reflective parents who were ready for solid material requiring effort and concentration. The book had already been revised several times in the light of experience with parents. It was designed to be used by parents with qualified group leaders, and he considered it effective for such use. 'It is most essential at this stage, we think, to try to raise the standards of work in Child Study and it is to parents who are ready for this honest effort that we appeal.' He closed with the comment (a veiled threat?) that if Morrow had no further use for the copy he would appreciate having it back shortly as it was his only draft.[46]

Morrow replied that he needed a few more days to make up his mind because his wife was now reading the manuscript and was likely to have some suggestions.[47] Five days later Morrow capitulated. He wrote to Blatz to say that it was too good a book to pass by and that his wife said it was just the very book that would be practically a Bible to her if she had another youngster to bring up. He would be proud to have the book on his list. Furthermore, he had seen an announcement that Blatz would be in New York for meetings of the Child Study Association, so perhaps they could talk at that time.[48]

A telegram from Blatz and an invitation to lunch with Mr and Mrs Morrow marked the beginning of a friendly association that saw all the books produced by Blatz in his lifetime published in the United States by Morrow and his successors.

The book was well reviewed and *Parents Magazine* awarded it one of its three annual prizes for the best books for parents. Even behavioural psychologist John B. Watson waxed enthusiastic about it.

'It is so sanely and so clearly written. The material is very, very good and the attitude of the authors is beyond criticism ... of all the books which have been coming out on children the last few years, I think this is the best.'[49]

Blatz had promised Morrow to revise *Parents and the Pre-School Child* in the light of criticisms and comments upon its first edition, but the book had such an enthusiastic reception that it stood unchanged; instead, he and Mrs Bott added a companion volume with a different orientation. *The Management of Young Children* was published less than two years later by McClelland and Stewart in Toronto and William Morrow in New York. Again the book was designed as a text for parent education classes, giving outlines, reading lists, illustrations from group discussions, and, in some instances, clinical case histories. Its focus, however, was more on social adjustment than on the establishment of habits to control appetites and emotions. The central theme was how parents could manage their children so that they would grow up learning how to live with others.

It was unashamedly a philosophy of child training rather than a scientific treatise. 'Child Study is still a young science,' Blatz wrote, 'and while its easier and more obvious aspects have been fairly well charted the more complicated questions of social relations, the development of personality, etc., are only beginning to be approached in any thoroughgoing fashion. Meanwhile parents are living in the midst of situations which can ill afford to wait till authoritative pronouncements are available for their solution.'[50]

The book was designed to make practical use of what was already known about how parents could provide experiences to help their children learn to live with others. Mistakes would be expected, and the learning would never be complete.

Here Blatz closed the door on the magical perfectability that psychology in the 1920s had seemed to promise. He observed that one of the common misconceptions in the popular attitude to child training was that it could be possible to produce a perfect child, faultless in morals and conduct. A second misconception followed from the first: that the training of children must consist largely in trying to detect symptoms of maladjustment, each to be treated by a specific formula. He dismissed this as the 'patent medicine scheme of child training.'[51]

Before publication of the American edition, William Morrow wrote to Blatz as follows: 'I think you will want to decide whether or not you should let the *Parents Magazine* publish chapters from the new book.

We will acquiesce cheerfully in any decision you may make, though we should prefer to see only selected chapters in the Magazine rather than the whole volume.'[52]

In fact, although *Parents* published only excerpts in this case, it was usually an enthusiastic purveyor of Blatz's words and wisdom. The magazine had been launched as a voice of child study and parent education with covert support from the Laura Spelman Rockefeller Memorial, which channelled funds to its aid indirectly through, in turn, Columbia, Iowa, Minnesota, and Yale universities. (The story of these undercover operations is outlined by Stephen Schlossman in the June 1979 Proceedings of the Rockefeller Archive Center.)[53] Blatz's first article in *Parents* was a test for fathers, published under the heading: 'Are you fit to be a Father?' It was followed by articles of advice on dealing with anger and fear, cultivating truthfulness, training a child to take responsibility, the happy family, first steps in character building, and a child's choice of friends.

Blatz also enjoyed the attentions of such solid professional publications as the *Yearbook of the National Society for the Study of Education* (where he reviewed studies of emotional and social development) and Murchison's *Handbook of Child Psychology* (where his chapter on the physiological appetites was given equal weight with chapters by such researchers as Margaret Mead, Kurt Lewin, Lewis Terman, and Jean Piaget).

In between the popular and the academic were the articles he wrote for *Childhood Education, Progressive Education, Child Welfare, University of Iowa Bulletins*, and, with great frequency, *Child Study Magazine*. He also wrote chapters on behaviour problems of children and the play life of the child for a Toronto paediatrician's book on child care,[54] and contributed an essay to William J. Perlman's critique of the movies.[55] A reviewer of the latter identified Blatz's chapter as 'by all standards the best and most convincing in the volume' and 'worth the price of the entire book.'[56]

Closer to home, Blatz started the University of Toronto Child Development Monograph series in 1933, which published eighteen issues in its seven-year lifespan. This series provided a vehicle for circulating the research findings of Blatz and the child study staff; it overlapped with and was eventually replaced by the *Bulletin of the Institute of Child Study*.

In all, Blatz published some thirty-five pamphlets and articles between 1930 and 1935, though an exact count is difficult, for much of his effort was turned towards the ephemeral world of popular magazines. He has been roundly criticized for failing to test his mettle by submitting more to professional journals. Certainly he lost interest in experimental psychology almost immediately after his student days, choosing to concentrate instead on longitudinal research and on developing techniques and theories to serve his daily work. He found he had a great deal to say, and he was in such a hurry to say it that he did not bother with the rigorous documentation required by learned journals. During the Depression years, moreover, with money scarce both for research and for university salaries, there was a strong incentive to concentrate on commercial success. Blatz quickly became adept at writing and speaking in a style that appealed to the general public and helped to make child study a subject of popular interest. This, of course, fulfilled the Lawrence Frank – Laura Spelman Rockefeller ambition to educate parents to improve child life, and furthermore turned around Beardsley Ruml's earlier lukewarm assessment of Blatz.

Initially the Laura Spelman Rockefeller Memorial had higher hopes for Montreal than Toronto; as it happened, however, the program at McGill foundered while Blatz prospered. McGill had got off to a strong start with a paediatrician at the helm, accompanied by two psychologists from the University of Toronto, J. Winfred Bridges and the second of his five wives, Katherine M. Banham Bridges. The latter published her research on the social and emotional development of pre-school children; apart from her book, however, the McGill project produced very little other research in child development. The Bridges went their ways shortly afterwards, and in 1930 Carroll (Langstaff) Davis, then a junior instructor at the St George's School in Toronto, was sent to McGill in an attempt to keep the sister school – and particularly its nursery – afloat. There was no one at McGill with the energy or drive of Blatz to take hold, however, and so she turned her own attention to enjoying her work with the children. When representatives of the Rockefeller Memorial paid the school a surprise visit and asked about the research, she gave an honest answer. There was none. Soon afterwards, the Laura Spelman Rockefeller Memorial fund abandoned the Montreal project, although a group of parents salvaged enough from the nursery to continue it on their own and even to add elementary grades. They called it the St George's School of Montreal.[57]

The public attention that Blatz brought to the St George's School in Toronto led the Rockefeller officials to renew their grants without hesitation. After the publication of his first book, Blatz was sought after as a speaker, for he was popular enough to fill Eaton's College Street auditorium on a weekday afternoon, or Massey Hall in the evening. By 1930 he was on the lecture circuit – touring the western provinces, then New York and Indiana, Ohio, Michigan, and Illinois, Virginia, Nebraska, and California. He taught summer school in Iowa, Oregon, Chicago, Harvard, and Hawaii; he spoke on CBC and NBC radio, and he was the featured speaker at conferences for parents and teachers on mental hygiene, nursery education, and camping. At the end of one of his first public addresses, a discerning listener asked him a profound question: 'Dr Blatz, have you ever been a mother?'[58] He claimed that he never forgot it (though it didn't faze him). He held his audiences spellbound. He was now the stand-up entertainer his family had half-expected him to be. His listeners might be startled or offended one moment, convulsed with laughter the next. He liked to keep them a little off-balance and thinking every minute. He wrote his lecture notes on scraps of paper just shortly beforehand and always looked absolutely calm and collected. It was not as easy on him as it seemed, however. He told his close colleagues that it was hard work, that he would be so drenched with sweat after a speech that his suit jackets often needed to be relined. The Dr Blatz the audience saw was totally in control: a little man, dressed always in a three-piece suit, with a bow-tie, his hair receding, his waistline rounding, his face inscrutable behind the tooth-brush moustache and circular glasses, saying outrageous and infuriating things to tease his audience into a reaction.

Nellie Chant remembers one discussion during which a woman with the satisfied air of having found a problem Blatz would not be able to solve easily rose to propound a question. 'Now Dr Blatz,' she said, 'if my little girl sets out to test my patience in every way she can, then what can I do?' Quick as a flash, Blatz said, 'That's easy, you just pass the test.' There was laughter, but he did not leave her deflated and went on to discuss what might lie behind the child's behaviour.[59]

The audiences collected Blatz aphorisms and anecdotes. He suggested that every child should be given a BA at birth that would be taken away when he began to learn. He declared that every marriage is always a mixed marriage. He wondered why certificates were required for teaching, for erecting buildings, and before qualification as a medical practitioner, when for parenthood there was no legal requirement other than an ancient ceremony. He declared that there were two great causes for unhappiness in the world – Christianity and the family. He suggested that the charming child was to be pitied more than admired, because such a child learns to cope by charm and not by developing interests and skills. He offered to refund the admission price to anyone in the audience who had not told a lie in the last week. When asked to identify the most important years of a person's life, he named the last ten.

Perhaps Blatz's most significant speech during this period was that given to the Eighth Annual Iowa Conference on Child Development and Parent Education in 1934. The address, published later, was the first written statement of Blatz's theory of human security.

In the early nursery days Blatz's actions and techniques had been governed by situations as they arose. A few years later he pinned together his framework of physiological needs, motives, and emotions; it still lacked a unifying structure, however. Blatz and Sperrin Chant discussed the way in which learning led to independence and from that evolved the beginning of the concept of security. From time to time Blatz had mentioned the developing idea to students and parent groups.

At the conference the ostensible topic was 'Human Needs and How They Are Satisfied;' but, in an attempt to strike at the root of social living and its first principle, Blatz chose to go beyond it to a discussion of physiological needs. The fundamental human need was security. He gave a simple statement of the basics of a theory that was to become increasingly complex, sophisticated, and multi-layered, and that he continued to rework until just before he died. He saw it as an evolving theory rather than one that could ever be called complete. In this first statement, in 1934, the definition of security is the same as in his last statement thirty years later. Some of the terminology is different, however (there is at first a disturbing use of the word 'conflict,' for example, where later he talked about 'selecting' and 'making choices'). The structure of the theory is much simpler in the first version than in later versions, and it also lacks an explanation of the dynamics of growth and change.

'The secure individual,' Blatz wrote, 'is one who when presented with a problem chooses an alternative and then is willing to accept the consequences.' Security, as distinct from safety, could be achieved either through the mechanism of dependence, where someone else assumes the responsibility, or through learning to be independent. Independence would be the eventual goal, with dependence a state that should be outgrown as the person matured.

The increased emphasis Blatz put on active learning and making choices removed him entirely from any lingering accusations of affiliation with Watson and the behaviourists. Blatz said that learning was the most important phenomenon for the psychologist to study. It was learning that brought security, for as soon as a person learns to do something his security increases in that area. Learning is born out of the conflict of making choices, and without this kind of conflict there would be no learning. We should foster the conflict associated with making choices, and in doing so must always present the child with the alternatives and their solution, Blatz said. He gave considerable weight to compromise at this stage as a way of satisfying needs and conforming to social rules. The search for security would be in four major areas: in the person's life work, leisure interests, overall purpose, and social affiliations. Adjustment would vary from one area to another, Blatz wrote, and ideally people should be able to compensate in any one of these areas for a lack in any of the others, so that when a crisis happens they will be able to cope.

Blatz continued to develop the security theory and to present it in slightly different forms over the years, but this early thinking on the subject gave him a structure for more practical matters. The nursery theory, for instance, was formulated in *Nursery Education: Theory and Practice*[60] and illustrated further with a children's book of photographs of St George's School that he wrote with the school secretary, Marjory Poppleton.[61]

The next challenge he was to encounter would give Blatz a further chance to expound his theories, to organize an almost ideal nursery, and to demonstrate to a watching world the techniques and values of nursery education.

# 5 In the Dionne Nursery

The aspect of Blatz's many-faceted career that most attracted contemporary public attention and retrospective criticism was his involvement with the Dionne quintuplets. He was the force that guided their pre-school training and education for nearly three years. At the same time he undertook a vigorous program of research, a program that, although incomplete, resulted in two books and an international symposium on the children's development. His work with the Dionne quintuplets gave world exposure to the ideas that he had been developing at the St George's School. Furthermore, it was an opportunity to put his theories to two major tests: planning a twenty-four-hour-a-day program and working with children whose background was very different from that of children in his Toronto schools.

The winter of 1933–4 was unusually cold and further shadowed by unsettled events in Europe, the deepening Depression, and increasing unemployment. That spring, however, in a simple northern Ontario farmhouse, an extraordinary event took place that seemed like an affirmation of hope: Mrs Oliva Dionne gave birth to five little girls, all apparently alike, all obviously frail, but all – if tenuously – alive. Almost as if a star shone over Callander, wise men from the south soon began to find their way there.

News of the birth of the babies travelled far and fast. Allan Roy Dafoe, the doctor on the scene at the babies' birth, quickly became a folk hero. He managed to keep the babies alive during the first few days by a combination of common sense and guesswork, and his resources were soon bolstered by the advice of his younger brother, William, a Toronto paediatrician, and by such contributions as an incubator and a supply of mothers' milk.

When it appeared that the babies might indeed survive, the public's interest and curiosity mounted. Promoters approached the father with proposals for exhibiting the babies, but the Ontario government intervened to assume guardianship instead.[1]

The first concern of the guardians of the quintuplets was with the babies' physical care. As Blatz described it later, it was 'a period of suspense about their survival and the hazards of premature birth and primitive facilities for care.' In the first year the major focus was on their survival and health, but when they passed the age limit reached by all previous quintuplets it became apparent that they were 'no longer merely a successful experiment in modern medical care but had emerged as five separate individuals.'[2] There could be 'only one thought in their Guardians' minds: whatever their training is to be, it shall insure the dignity of human life.'[3]

It was Blatz who set up the program for the babies' early years.

William Dafoe was an old football friend of William Blatz. They had been at the University of Toronto together, and now Dafoe was a fashionable Toronto doctor while Blatz was a well-known child psychologist. The St George's School for Child Study was eight years old at the time. Although still highly controversial in its methods, the school was beginning to become popular with the more avant-garde members of the academic and medical communities. It seemed logical for Bill Dafoe to consult Bill Blatz on behalf of his brother, and Blatz quickly fell into the semi-official role of educational consultant and researcher for the quints.[4]

The opportunity for research was unique. Studies with identical twins were beginning to shed some light on the relative influences of genetic make-up versus the influences of environment and experience. Since the five little girls were in all probability identical, any differences in their development would have to be the result of environment rather than heredity. Here was a perfect opportunity to study the influences of nature and nurture with five ways of cross-checking.

At the same time it was probably equally important to Blatz to have an opportunity to elaborate and test his plan of child rearing. The quintuplets would be living in what was virtually a full-time nursery school. Unlike most institutions caring for the very young, the quintuplets' nursery suffered from no serious shortage of money.

The quints could be provided with a physical environment completely planned to Blatz's ideal standards and staffed with adults whose only concern would be the optimum development of their charges. Whereas the St George's School program had evolved in response to Blatz's developing theories, here was a chance to lay out the whole Blatz plan from the start. With such an ideal opportunity to demonstrate his ideas to the world, Blatz was content to undertake the work without a contract and without a salary. He continued to be employed by the university, of course, but the Dionne project did not involve Ned Bott or the psychology department as such, and it marked one of the first steps in the eventual independence of child study from psychology.

In the early 1930s psychology was still the golden-haired child of the idealists. Although Blatz himself had already dismissed the notion of raising perfect children, public sentiment still clung to the hope that, if all available remedies were applied to a problem and there were no contradictory influences, it should be possible to raise exemplary members of the human race. Success in producing even one such exemplary person should provide the key to improving all of humanity. In this case there was a chance of producing not just one but five better people. Indeed, it was not long before the quintuplets were being seen as super-children. A visitor to their nursery described them as 'little bits of perfection.'[5] In 1937 the *New York Times Magazine* noted that, 'Every aid that scientifically controlled environment can offer the quintuplets toward becoming perfect human beings certainly they have had. Taken from their humble home as scrawny, weak and premature babies, for three years they have been brought up in a sunshine-flooded nursery, specially devised, from sleeping porch to concrete wading pool, to make them healthy, agile and intelligent.'[6]

Blatz's hopes for the children were more realistic than idealistic, but he still had optimistic aims for their adjustment. In *The Five Sisters* he set forth his three general goals and guidelines for the work he planned to accomplish with the children.

The Dionnes, Blatz said, represented childhood *per se* to a world hungry for knowledge of these particular children. People everywhere would be scrutinizing the children's plan of training. This created an opportunity to demonstrate to the world how care and effort during childhood could lead to a happily adjusted adult and to encourage people to apply this knowledge to other children. This was Blatz's first goal.

The second goal was to foster the children's individuality and to regulate their lives so as to allow them to appreciate the fullness of living and to make individual choices of vocation. It was hoped that some day each of these children would, in her own right, present to the world some aspect of human achievement that would bring her acclaim, not just as one of the group of Dionne quintuplets, but as Yvonne Dionne, Annette Dionne, and so forth.

The third goal related to their religious and cultural heritage. It was a non-specific promise. No details were mentioned, but it was Blatz's aim, he declared, that the girls' training would enable them to appreciate fully the responsibilities of their heritage as 'representatives of a great race and a revered religion.'[7]

More than fifty years later we may judge for ourselves how far these goals came to be realized. Certainly the world did scrutinize the children's plan of training and avidly devour every word written about the details of their lives. Blatz continued to write on child rearing for popular publications and to draw large audiences for his public speeches, and there is no doubt that his association with the quintuplets further widened his audience. Dafoe, the simple country doctor, wrote a newspaper column on child care and a *Guidebook for Mothers* that strongly echoed Blatz's theories and applications. How well the plan of pre-school education succeeded is more problematic, for the quintuplets were raised according to Blatz for only a few years. It is hard to tell what had the most long-term effect, the Blatz-style full-time nursery school or the later influences of the Dionne farmhouse.

In the 1930s the public seemed to feel that it owned the quints. If the babies caught a cold or one of them fell from a swing, there would be cries of, 'What are you doing to our babies?'[8] Today, although the three surviving quintuplets purposely live outside the limelight, the press lurks around the corner ready and eager to describe a new event in their lives and to engage in more retrospection about them. A popular book depicting them as participants in a 'thirties melodrama' has been adapted for television. Another book describing their lives as a 'Canadian tragedy' is on the news-stands. The public still avidly devours any news about these three middle-aged women who are perpetually remembered as part of the group of five babies. The debate about what should or should not have been done in the ensuing years continues today. We still have a proprietary interest, it seems.

Certainly the quintuplets' lives have been far from tranquil, although the three surviving sisters seem to have made adjustments to their adult worlds. In their book *We Were Five*, they recall the time in the nursery as their happiest years.

On the second point, the development of individuality, once again there are no clear-cut answers. Certainly Blatz looked to personality differences as evidence of the importance of environment over heredity, and he worked on encouraging individual interests and initiatives. But these efforts were not enough and were begun too late to answer the eventual criticism that the children should have led very separate lives right from the beginning. Today the usual practice in multiple births is to raise the children with a strong emphasis on individuality, providing from the earliest years different clothing, different schools, and different experiences. In the 1930s it would have been considered perverse to separate such charming look-alikes.

Indeed the very fact that the Ontario government had set aside a trust fund for the quints' well-being and education posed a dilemma. The government fed the fund with one hand while it fostered a North Bay and Callander tourist boom with the other. It is unlikely that public pressure would have allowed extreme manifestations of physical and social individuality. Tourists, who came from far and wide, expected to see the children dressed alike and engaged in similar activities. Their individuality was maintained only through a sort of colour-coding, by which all the girls wore identical outfits, but each had her own special colour. If differences had been carried any further than this, the public would not have stood for it.

Blatz's long-term plan was for the quints to be educated in a new school with their siblings and neighbouring children; again, however, the implementation of educational decisions was taken out of Blatz's hands before the children reached school age. It is also important to note that, when they returned to the Dionne family household, the quintuplets remained a group apart – almost a family within a family. Had they been raised as five virtually unrelated individuals it might have helped them to integrate more comfortably with their other siblings. However, they would have lost a major source of comfort in alien surroundings: the solace of each other's company. Today's thinking on twins has partially reversed the idea of individuality at all costs, for it is now recognized that the emotional bonds between twins is highly significant to them and that it can be highly traumatic for them to be separated from each other.

It was on the third point that Blatz's involvement with the quintuplets foundered. Blatz started his work with the quintuplets in April

1935, when they were eleven months old. His plans for educating them were unfinished, however, and his research on the differences in their developing personalities remained untested, for he was ousted after less than three years. The point at issue in his dismissal was the one of fostering French culture and the Roman Catholic religion. Although the children spoke French for most of the day, he had added some English in an attempt to encourage bilingualism. Moreover, Blatz's early personal piety had given way to serious doubt about his own boyhood faith, and he was no longer a practising Catholic. Although he set aside time for the children's prayers in their daily routine, he resisted the idea of having religious pictures and a miniature chapel in their playroom. Moreover, his emphasis on the need for learning to make one's own decisions was sharply at odds with the way girls were usually raised in northern Ontario at the time. Blatz always put a high value on non-conformity within the limits of safety. In the best Blatz nursery tradition, the children were encouraged to express their own ideas with play materials and were given the choice of what they would undertake in their play. The traits of meekness, piety, and obedience were not considered as important as learning to choose and to be creative. In 1938 Blatz wrote prophetically that 'to have required absolute obedience ... would have placed the children at the mercy of later exploitation.'[9]

Blatz's first goal of demonstrating to the world a successful plan of raising children, involved applying the principles he had developed at the St George's School to a twenty-four-hour-a-day program. 'The unusual circumstances of their multiple birth does not in any way affect the plan of training,' he wrote. 'It merely complicates its administration.'[10] It was absolutely essential to have a consistent and rational plan of training, says Dorothy Millichamp, who worked with the quintuplets as Blatz's research assistant. A busy parent might be able to cope effectively with a single child, or even with twins, by making moment-to-moment decisions, but quintuplets were a different story. Here were five young children who could all be of one mind about what they wanted or did not want. Breaking into the tight-knit group of the five could be enough to fray the temper of even the most patient adult. Furthermore, there were a variety of adults in the children's lives. If all had different expectations and methods, the children could become quite confused and upset. A consistent plan was needed, one that could be thought through and followed by all the people working with the children. In this way some sort of stability might be achieved.

Along with the plan would go a careful keeping of records. Certainly the records were an important part of the research, but they were also part of staff development. They provided an opportunity for the adults to analyse their own actions, to compare notes, to discuss problems, and to make plans. The plan would involve practice in making decisions and would leave no room for adult coercion by scolding or by spanking.[11]

In setting up his program Blatz made explicit plans for the quints' physical environment – plans that involved turning the Dafoe hospital into a nursery school. He reorganized the interior of the recently completed building and designed a playground. Progress in inculcating routine habits in the children was carefully charted, and Blatz drew up schedules to rotate the nursing staff with his teachers from the St George's School.

When Blatz first became involved with the quints, public interest had become stressful for both the nurses and the babies. Endless crowds of people were arriving at the hospital determined to see the children, and there seemed to be no way of denying them access. A method would have to be found to let the world look at the children without putting them on show in a way that would dominate their lives. At this point Bill Dafoe sought Blatz's help on behalf of his brother, Allan Roy Dafoe.

Blatz set about at once to create a playground that was partially surrounded by the kind of one-way screens already in use at the St George's School. The main feature of the design was a corridor with fine wire mesh along one side. When the corridor was darkened, observers could see and hear the children in the daylit playground. The presence of observers was not kept secret from the children; they could see the shadowy figures of lines of adults and hear their voices behind the wire netting. But the arrangement did allow them to play without being unduly disturbed by the thousands of visitors who came to see them. (As well as the observation playground there was a private playground where the children could play out of the public eye.)

'The screened playground was such an unusual feature and answered so many of Dafoe's problems that it helped Blatz to convince Dafoe that something was needed beyond straight hospital care,' says Dorothy Millichamp.[12]

The next step was to try to get down to the children's level and to give them a chance to become more active in their own lives. In both play and routines the children tended to wait for adults to initiate an activity; then they would start to do everything at once and all together. Before Blatz, for example, the babies generally stood about in play-pens waiting to be fed; then, after quite passively accepting a spoonful or two, they would dart to the other side of the play-pen, out of reach. Blatz ordered five high chairs, cut the legs down, and arranged them in a semi-circle, so that one nurse could supervise while the babies fed themselves. The high dressing-counters where the nurses had bundled inert children into their clothes were replaced with individual cupboards and low hangers so the children could learn to dress themselves. The five potty chairs where the quintuplets tended to do little more than sit and play were replaced with two child-sized toilets. Now they could take turns and learn responsibility for their own needs.[13]

In play, the five children also tended to act in unison. Wherever one went the others were almost sure to follow, and when one started to play with something the others would want to join the game. Their play itself was quite passive, however. They expected the nurses to do a good deal of the entertaining – and to entertain them as a group, at that.

The first problem was to replace imitation with individual initiative. But progress was slow. One of Blatz's first suggestions was to send the children indoors from the playground one by one. In the St George's School this gave an unhurried opportunity for individual child-adult interaction, yet when Blatz tried it with the Dionne sisters it worked quite differently. When one was leaving the playground the other four immediately stopped what they were doing to line up while waving and chorusing, 'Goodbye.'[14]

Rearranging space, providing equipment, and specifying staff responsibilities seemed to be major priorities. As the hospital had originally been designed, there was very little room for play, either indoors or out. More space was needed. The children's toys included a plethora of stuffed animals, wind-up toys, and a few balls, but little to challenge them or keep them busy on their own. They needed more appropriate things to do.

The nurses were without a schedule of duties and found themselves on hand virtually all day and every day. They could predict neither the peak times, when all hands would be needed, nor the lulls, when they could have had a break. The nurses tended to become so involved with the children that they were reluctant to take time away from the action and go off duty. Consequently they were getting overtired and over-anxious about their responsibilities. Obviously their working hours and duties needed to be clearly defined.

Blatz tackled the reorganization of space, the equipment, and the schedules all at the same time. The plans were largely implemented by Dorothy Millichamp.

The Dafoe hospital had been built to meet the medical needs of five infants so frail that their very survival was in doubt. It served its purpose well for the infant years, but the space needed rearranging for the children's pre-school education. One of the first steps was to build a separate staff house. Thus the space formerly occupied by the nurses' rooms was turned over to the children's use, and the nurses had an opportunity to spend their off-duty hours well away from the nursery.[15]

In Blatz's new set-up, the staff dining-room became the children's, and the nurses' two-bedroom wing was redesigned to make three rooms: an infirmary, a small additional playroom, and a room where a child needing time out from the group could play alone. The children's bathroom was enlarged to incorporate a cupboard and some unused hall space. The bathroom then had room for small-scale plumbing rather than potty chairs.

This meant that there was now a separate setting for each nursery procedure – washing, toileting, sleeping, eating, group play, quiet play, and isolation for illness or 'unacceptable behaviour.' Furthermore the children's quarters were separated from staff living quarters, with only one interior entrance to the children's area.

Separate cupboards, tagged with each child's picture symbol, and movable screens to go between the beds, just as at the St George's School, gave new privacy and individuality to the children's bedroom. The porch made an auxiliary sleeping area and was equipped with small hooded beds, storm windows, and sleeping bags.

Two playrooms, one large and one small, were furnished with nursery school materials: small tables and chairs, toy cupboards, pegboards, colour cones, beads, toy animals, hammer toys, picture books, painting easels, blocks, plasticine, and art supplies.

The outdoor observation playground, in Millichamp's words, was 'surrounded on three sides by a U-shaped covered hallway with windows looking out into the playground. The inside is arranged in tiers to allow for three rows of observers. Windows equipped with one-way screens prevent people being seen from the playground. An inner fence prevents children from approaching windows. People enter and leave by doors opening out beyond main hospital fences.'[16]

All the equipment (a sand-box, a wading pool, a cement runway for wheel toys, a jungle gym, and a block box for large hollow blocks) was placed within the inner fence of the playground. After the observation periods the gates could be opened onto a further strip of lawn and garden where the children could play well away from the eyes of all but their caretakers.

In the washroom routines, facilities were deliberately limited to two toilets and two washbasins, in order to stress individuality. The children could not be led off to these routines *en masse*; instead the nurses would have to be aware of each child's individual needs. In play, however, there was sufficient material to go around and five of every major item (kiddy cars, tricycles, wheelbarrows, toboggans, doll carriages). The duplicate play equipment also fostered individuality, for the children did not have to compete or share and take turns while still too young to do so willingly. Ensuring that each child had her own possessions encouraged the children to play co-operatively rather than anxiously and competitively with one another.

Blatz's earliest reports noted that the routines were confused and inconsistent, with the nurses becoming disorganized and rushed, while play was largely on the adult's initiative, not the children's. In the ensuing months the major problem was to disentangle the two and establish nursery school procedures. Blatz and Millichamp set about this by drawing up timetables delineating specific responsibilities for the staff and detailed plans for the children (and more subtly, by re-arranging rooms and ordering appropriate equipment).

Scheduling activities for the quintuplets and their caregivers presented particular problems. First of all they had to be on a twenty-four-hour-a-day program that would combine the characteristics of both a school and a home. Second, although the nurses had all been sent to the St George's School for an introductory training program, their pre-school experience was very limited. While adults who were highly experienced in working with lively young children could be relatively flexible and innovative in their daily plans, and could follow a sequence rather than a clock, those with less training would need more guidance. A timetable specifying precise activities and staff duties was therefore set up to help serve as a curriculum. Moreover, since nurses and nursery school teachers have very different objectives in their work, it is difficult to turn one into the other. Teachers must often stand back in order to foster independence and self-help. There is little in a nurse's training to encourage this. Nurses are, in fact, generally taught to interact with a patient and not to hold off while the patient struggles with something new or makes mistakes. They are taught, for instance, to take responsibility for looking after the needs of sick children. Ordinarily the emphasis in nursing is not on helping children learn to go to the bathroom on their own, eat on their own, wash and dress themselves, and play on their own. Yet this is what the nurses-turned-teachers in Blatz's Dionne pre-school were now expected to do. In order to give the quintuplets any degree of freedom, it was necessary to assign the nurses quite specific tasks and places; otherwise they tended to hover and take over from the children. A clear timetable, carefully planned and followed, gave a sort of 'ad hoc' training to the nurses in the Dafoe hospital.[17]

A third major problem in scheduling for the quintuplets was the fact that the public was obsessed with them. It was clear to Blatz that if the children were to have anything like a normal life, their days had to have a definite sequence and order. But at the same time plans had to be made for the public to view them. The outside world's hunger for a constant supply of reports and pictures of the little girls appeared insatiable. In regular photographing sessions the emphasis was on spontaneity, so such sessions could usually fit quite naturally into the children's day. News-reel features and full-length movies were a different matter, however. Most of the time the cameras would be satisfied with nothing fewer than the full five children. 'The moving picture staff most cooperative and willing to adjust but no understanding of the situation [of] either nurses or children.'[18] There would be bright lights and a crowd of a dozen or so adults all coaxing, cajoling, and directing the children to follow the script. Blatz planned the integration of the children's routine with limited movie-making hours at well-spaced intervals and had to stand firm against encroachments. He also had to stand against pressure from above, for all this publicity was pushed by members of the Ontario government who saw the quintuplet business as an important boost for the province's mid-Depression economy. Their second birthday party was broadcast on CBC radio, and one of their guardians, David Croll, minister of public welfare in the provincial Liberal government, announced that the children's newest contracts with Twentieth-Century Fox films would bring their wealth to half a million dollars. 'Indeed, the Midas touch that seems to lie in the chubby hands of five two-year-old girls [is] known clear around the world ... [they are] the Province's natural resource and the community's gold mine.'[19]

World attention led to another kind of problem in planning for the quintuplets: their physical security. Two years before the quints were born, the world had been shocked by the kidnapping of the Lindbergh baby. The son of the pilot-hero had been stolen from his bed and never seen alive again. By the 1990s we have grown cautious about exposing potential kidnap targets to contact with the general public no matter what the time of day or night. In the mid-1930s the concern was that the Lindbergh crime might be duplicated, so the caution was much more specific. There seemed to be little worry about the twice-daily playground observations. No one seemed concerned that the children were separated from strangers only by a mosquito mesh; as long as it was daylight and there were people around, all seemed safe. The fear was, rather, that someone might break into the nursery at night and take the babies from their beds. Staff had to be on the alert all night. Anne Harris (now Mrs Blatz) recalls being on exchange duty from Windy Ridge when a kidnapping threat came that meant she had to sleep with a gun under her pillow.[20] The staff, along with the children, were locked inside the hospital compound at night and had to be let in and out by guards. Living in something that approached a state of siege was highly stressful and gave another reason for Blatz to insist that the staff should take time for rest and recreation, well away from their responsibilities.

The nursery timetables themselves were very precise in their schedules. Blatz described them as having 'two main objects in view: first, that the five children should be handled efficiently by the nurses, without too much adult interference, and secondly that the children themselves might readily learn what was expected of them.'[21]

The early morning schedule in September 1936, for example, when the girls were a little over two is shown in the table on page 116. A revised schedule a few months later organized the nurses' responsibilities even further. It gave each nurse a morning to sleep late, and, in rotation, a mid-morning hour for hospital duties and record keeping. In a letter addressed to nurses Jacqueline Noel and Claire Tremblay, Millichamp wrote: 'Dr Blatz is sending Dr Dafoe a schedule over which we have spent considerable time ... to get the schedule in proper working order is the most important job we have at the moment. In fact, on it hangs the keeping of Miss O'Shaughnessy and in fact your own jobs, so follow this closely for the next two weeks, will you? We will

| Time | Routine | Organization | Nurse on duty |
|------|---------|--------------|---------------|
| 6:30 | Out of bed<br>Toilet<br>Codliver oil<br>and orange juice | – group routine<br>– group routine<br>– sitting on floor<br>in playroom | 2 nurses<br>2 nurses<br>1 nurse |
| 7:00 | Play | – free | Nurse at<br>breakfast |
| 7:30 | Undressed<br>Bathed<br>Dressed<br>Ear, nose, hair<br>(to playroom)<br>Toilet | – individual routine | 2 nurses |
| 8:10 | Bibs on<br>To dining room | – in playroom<br>group routine | 2 nurses |
| 8:15 | Breakfast | – in dining room<br>2 groups<br>first serving<br>self-service | 2 nurses<br>serving<br>Alternate<br>at table |
| 8:45 | Toilet (other play)<br>Dressing (play) | – individual routine | 1 nurse |
| 9:45 | To playground | – one or two groups | 2 nurses |

discuss changes when we come up. It will be up to each one of you to make it possible and insist on the other taking her time.'[22] (As it happened, Noel and Tremblay did lose their jobs, with far-reaching consequences for Blatz's programs with the quintuplets.)

The major routines in the children's day were eating, washing, mid-day relaxation, dressing, toileting, and getting ready for bed. All three nurses were usually needed for these peak times to allow the children individual attention. In September 1936, the nurses were advised that they could eliminate the children's current scrambling at the door and impatient crying for attention by planning in advance exactly how to proceed. For instance, if one child was to go off to get washed or dressed, the nurses should decide beforehand exactly which one it should be. If there was crying, the nurses should wait for this to stop before going on with the routine, and if crying was continuous the child should be removed from the others. Certainly a physical struggle should be avoided. In fact, Blatz said, the children should be handled very little during the routine in order to increase their own skill in helping themselves and taking responsibility.

The nurses were advised to make each routine consistent in every step and sufficiently simple so that the children would also grow accustomed to taking 'turns' ('c'est ton tour'). They were to deal separately with each item of care and were warned never to overlook the fact that the child is a complete individual, acting towards the environment as a child, and not simply a bundle of functions, organs, and systems.[23]

Detailed records were kept of all routines. A look at planning for mealtimes is indicative of the kind of program that evolved. In May 1936 (when the quints were two) Blatz and Millichamp noted that the children were locked in a battle with the nurses. The nurses were so anxious for the children to get sufficient nourishment that they were feeding them almost completely. The children were refusing food, and in fact were becoming so emotional about it that they took any opportunity to fling their dinners around the room. The end of the meal was described as 'hectic,' with the children pushing away their remaining food, running around, and sobbing. Blatz recommended that the nurses try to adopt an unconcerned attitude, giving small enough servings that the children could be expected to finish them, and making matters more interesting by encouraging the children's participation in feeding themselves.[24]

In September's report it is noted that the children were still mostly being fed by the nurses in the night nursery. The little girls were inattentive, frequently refusing their food and throwing temper tantrums. Blatz decided that they were old enough to graduate from high chairs to a nursery-school-type dining-room with tables and chairs and a serving counter where the children could help themselves to dessert and put away their own dishes. Between-meal drinks of water and milk were made into routine requirements, with the children expected to 'accept the drinking of a regular amount.'[25]

Two months later there was a little more order in the mealtimes. The children put on their bibs in the playroom and went into the dining-room one by one. The meal itself was relatively peaceful and organized, but behaviour would deteriorate until, by the end of the mealtime, the children would be out of control. Although the little girls were noted to have developed more skill in the mechanics of eating, the nurses were still 'doing considerable feeding.' The soup course seemed to complicate the mealtime and lessen the amount of solid food the children ate. At the same time they were 'overfond of desserts.' Blatz recommended that the first helping of dinner be made a little larger and that soup be served only with the second helping of solid food. To control confusion at the end of the meal, the tempo should be slowed. As well, a separate table was set up to the side for isolating any one of the girls who was causing a disturbance. Again the nurses were asked to let the children learn to feed themselves.[26]

In January, the problems of lack of interest in the first course and the confusion at meal's end were tackled. The dessert and biscuits were kept out of the room, and thus out of sight, until at least two of the children had finished the main course. A note of 23 January 1936 says simply:

Finishing routine organized:
– child puts napkin in basket
– gets tray – clears dishes
– sits down – fingers rinsed – bib removed
– goes out when directed.[27]

In February the routine was further reorganized. The children entered the dining-room in little groups. The first two were settled before an adult brought in the others. 'The first serving should be an amount which children will eat (usually) without urging ... no urging for second servings should be given but might be made more interesting by placing serving dish on children's table ... if only one dinner is eaten – only two servings of dessert should be given (this should help to prevent habitual filling up with dessert),' and the child not wanting more dinner should wait a while for dessert in order to avoid the rush towards dessert time at the start of the meal.[28]

And what did they eat? A memo of 28 August 1937, when the quints were three years and three months old, notes their diet. It consisted of cod-liver oil, acidophilus milk (pasteurized milk with dormant bacteria added to make it more digestible), plus Pablum, gruel, cream cheese, eggs, bacon, liver, macaroni and cheese, peas, corn soup, asparagus, string beans, beets, spinach, and potatoes for their main courses. They also drank orange juice and milk and ate raw and cooked apples, bananas, fresh strawberries and raspberries, prunes, and apple sauce. Desserts were jelly, tapioca, custard, caramel pudding, and floating island, and the accompanying 'biscuits' (or their equivalent) were Sunwheat cookies, graham crackers, arrowroots, brown bread, date and oatmeal squares, or angel cake.[29] During Blatz's time in the nursery it was a point of pride that the quintuplets had never tasted candy, and it was not until their fourth birthday party that they tasted ice cream.[30]

Blatz and Millichamp steadily reorganized the other routines as well, and in much the same way. In the beginning, washing involved a struggle between a nurse and an inattentive, wriggling child. A few months later the routine was broken into a series of precise stages, and by November 1936 it was noted that the children were becoming efficient in helping themselves. There was quick progress in dressing also: a note made in November 1936 recorded that the children's 'attention was not on the procedure'; a note two months later indicated that the children were showing interest and self-help.[31]

In systematizing the toilet procedure, Blatz and Millichamp asked the nurses not to take the children to the toilet as a group but, instead, to set up individually prescribed times for each one of the five. A memo of 6 November 1936 advises: 'use judgment as to taking to toilet (when child asks; better to have wet self than to establish a game).' The nurses were further instructed to insist that the children sit on the toilet, even if for a 'very short interval,' and to see that they got off after success or after four to five minutes.[32] Again, by two months later there had been considerable change. All were using the larger toilets, accepting the routine, and managing their own clothes. At two years and eight months it could be noted that bladder control was progressing but bowel elimination was uncontrolled. A month later, in a reorganization of the routines, the nurses were instructed to see that 'bowel movements be assured at morning routine' and suppositories be avoided at evening routine.[33]

Today, after several decades of permissive toilet training, one may wonder how such adult regulation of children's toileting could possibly be called 'self-help.' It would not be acceptable by today's child-rearing methods. It must be remembered, though, that it was a big change from earlier methods, for it was not accompanied by stress and shame. Toileting was treated very matter-of-factly by Blatz and his staff, with the emphasis on efficient ways to satisfy physical needs. The main purpose in planning a toilet time and procedure was to avoid interruptions and discomfort in the important free playtimes. Habit training was carefully built by a series of precise learning stages in order to avoid a power struggle. A nurse's report of 25 November 1936 notes three items about one of the quintuplets:

- she consented nicely to get suppository
- she made correct sign of the cross
- she can pull zipper up and down

The afternoon rest and mid-morning lie-down-to-relax times presented few problems, but bedtime itself was less easily managed. The nurses' daily records tell something of the story. Records of 30 March 1936, when the quints were just under two, show, for example, that although only five children were involved, with all the running around and jumping in and out of bed that took place that evening, in actual fact the nurses performed the equivalent of tucking seventy-one children into bed.[34]

Spanking was out. Patience coupled with firmness was the order of the day. Blatz and Millichamp instructed the nurses simply to lay the children down each time they stood up and, if the disturbance continued, to separate them. Plans for bedtime were based on the premise that sleep itself could obviously not be required, but that rest and relaxation should be expected.

Eight months later there were still problems. The worst of the bedtime dashing about had ceased, but the children were 'playing, thumping, etc. and vocalizing in response to one another.' They refused to have their sleeping blankets fastened, and the nurses were not insisting that the children lie down.[35]

Blatz and Millichamp suggested that the nurses use nursery school teaching procedures such as direction, assistance, and restraint. If a child was particularly obstreperous, it was recommended that she be kept away from the others for the night, with a nurse nearby to give 'personal teaching' about settling down. Presumably this personal teaching would involve the nursery routine of requiring that a child learn to lie down peacefully, and the adult would quietly and tactfully resettle the child as many times as needed until this requirement was met.

A report in early January from the nurses saw the bedtime routine improving,[36] but in late January, after Millichamp had been in residence in the nursery, she found the children still restless and noisy, taking up to an hour to settle down. She recommended that the bedroom be cooled off and the children covered and pinned in their sleeping bags with the adult using teaching techniques to help the children relax and lie quietly.[37]

The plan of learning in the routines was standard Blatz of the time, and thus a world hungry for details of the daily lives of the quintuplets could get a clear message about the importance of fostering regularity of habits, consistency of requirements, and growing independence in meeting one's needs. Most of the information was disseminated from press reports, films, and news-reels. Blatz's book *The Five Sisters*, published in 1938, also gave his detailed rationale for developing routine procedures. The public's fascination with the quintuplets gave him a powerful vehicle for spreading the word about his methods.

To learn about the Blatz approach to pre-school play, however, the visiting public could make direct observations for themselves of the children's time outdoors.

In addition to organizing space, providing equipment, and scheduling times for different types of play (indoors or out, free or controlled), Blatz put a great deal of thought into planning for the progressive development of imagination and individuality. After the routine business of the children's daily lives had been accommodated, Blatz estimated that three or four hours of the day would be left for play.

Ordinarily, outdoor play could have elements of both freedom and control, but with the climate of northern Ontario limiting time outdoors, Blatz used the playground mainly as a place for the children to express exuberance and develop confidence. Outdoor play would provide an opportunity for adventure, he wrote: 'Danger situations such as climbing, tumbling, sliding and falling can be deliberately arranged so as to guard against serious accidents and yet give the children a feeling of enterprise and adventure.'[38] Supervision should be unobtrusive, with the adult's responsibility 'to prevent suicide and homicide.'[39]

In most of the outdoor time, the quintuplets were scheduled to be on view to the public, so the observation playground was supplemented with the private garden Blatz had planned, where there would be no spectators to complain about the children's occasional tumble or scrape.

Indoors it was possible to plan for both kinds of play. There was a large playroom with a toy cupboard and a fully equipped dolls' centre for dramatic play. The other playroom was for more directed activities, with the emphasis on working individually.

A third small room was set aside as a carpentry workshop for precisely structured teaching about the safe and efficient use of tools. The girls worked there daily, two at a time with a teacher, and used good quality hammers and saws. (This was in accord with Blatz's consistent refusal to link play materials with definitions of sex roles. Children at the St George's School were encouraged to play with what they liked; carpentry was offered to girls as a matter of course, in the same way that doll play and housekeeping were enjoyed by the boys. It was quite out of keeping with French-Canadian child-rearing practices of the time to break down the traditional male-female roles in this manner. It must have become another source of irritation for the girls' father to see them headed in a different direction from his other children.)

Blatz was aware of the need to introduce the children to the arts, and there was a conscientious effort to expose them to French culture, but these choices were made by English Canadians. In most families the home is the place where the standards of aesthetic appreciation are set, while formal education is usually directed towards the acquisition of specific skills. In the quintuplets' situation, on the other hand, the 'Guardians had not only to set up a scheme for teaching the rudimentary skills but also to supply the home atmosphere for learning.'[40] Consequently there was a particular emphasis on music, art, and stories in the Dionne nursery. In music, for instance, the girls had a piano, percussion instruments, records, and a 'Victrola,' and sang or danced to French and French-Canadian folk tunes.

Notes from the St George's School staff show the development of plans for play, starting when the quints reached two. They found at first that there was no specific planning for play, and the nurses, with no regular routine, were hovering over the children as they played, giving almost constant attention and help. The children were showing very little interest in the materials; when they did show interest they simply screamed if they could not cope with something. As well as ordering pre-school equipment for indoors and out, Blatz and Millichamp further defined the playtimes, alternating an hour of free play outdoors with fifteen or twenty minutes of organized play, and for the indoor time providing half an hour of quiet organized play before lunch and supper. The nurses' timetable arranged for them to alternate their supervision. They were given a chance to show the children how they could use materials, but this opportunity was limited to the short 'organized playtimes.' Otherwise they were instructed not to interfere with the children's play and to ignore episodes of screaming.

Four months later, in September 1936, it was noted that free play inside was 'non-constructive' (in fact, the children were hurling the toys around) and the equipment itself was meagre. Millichamp ordered tables and chairs, along with new construction toys, and kept these for use in specific playtimes. Outdoors there was very little purposeful activity, and the children were constantly seeking adult attention. Again, the nurses were asked to leave the children to their own devices and to busy themselves with something else while the children played. But they found it difficult to do so, and the problem persisted.

In November of that year playtime procedures were further defined in an attempt to establish a balance between free play and adult-directed play, both outside and inside. During free play, the nurses were asked to leave and keep an eye on the activities from another room entirely. In supervised quiet play, the nurses could be on hand to help the children settle at tables with 'constructive play equipment' and to guide them in putting one toy away before taking another, but otherwise the children were to be allowed to choose for themselves. For ten or fifteen minutes of the morning the nurses were allowed to become involved with stories and music, organizing play, or simply playing with and entertaining the children.

The first two kinds of play, free play and quiet table play, were standard in nursery school, as were music and stories; but entertainment as such was not part of the usual pre-school program. This was left for home. As the Dionnes' program encompassed the full day, however, there were extra times early in the morning and after the evening bath when each child spent a while alone with a nurse for a special story or conversation.[41] A subsequent memorandum urged the nurses to 'utilize periods of individual attention to stimulate talking.'[42] On the other hand, the bedtime story itself was to be read or told by the adult and the children taught to listen rather than to participate at that time. It was designated as a particularly suitable opportunity for religious stories.[43]

Blatz noted that twins can be retarded in their language development by as much as four to eight months, and do not catch up with single children until about the fifth year. The quintuplets were exactly as far behind as twins would be expected to be.

The February 1937 program plans put an emphasis on language

learning, an emphasis that coincided with a new jump in the quintuplets' acquisition of speech. It was not until the end of their third year that their spoken language took an extraordinary spurt.[44]

Although Blatz was always adamant about keeping routines business-like (for example, his instructions were to limit conversation during routines to directions and brief mentions of the material and activity in progress), playtime itself was meant to be a different matter. A report by Margaret Fletcher on one of her visits to Callander a few months later noted that one of the nurses appeared to be overly stern. The play periods the nurse organized were too controlled. No talking or freedom other than in choice of materials was allowed.[45] This was contrary to Blatz's overall plan for child rearing.

As well as gaining knowledge about Blatz's approach to routines and play, the world at large was also learning about his method of discipline in raising the quintuplets. The attendant publicity through film, the written word, and viewings of the five sisters at play gave an opportunity for Blatz to emphasize that he regarded his theory of discipline as a theory of teaching and not a scheme of punishment.

When a child's behaviour upset the other children, the consequence was to have the child play alone for a while. This was standard nursery school procedure at the St George's School and carried a message that Blatz hoped would reach parents and persuade them that spanking children was neither necessary nor acceptable. He set up a little room where a child could go to be alone or be asked to stay by herself for a while. It was equipped with a table, chairs, toys, and books and designed to be a quiet but pleasant place. Blatz called it an isolation room. The press called it a gaol. Blatz countered with a photograph in his book of a smiling Marie, captioned, 'Isolation: the sole consequence of unacceptable behaviour. Marie, in common with her sisters, has never experienced the use of fear as a method of discipline.'[46]

Although the press may have (perhaps purposely) misunderstood the point of the isolation room, the fact was constantly before the public that the quintuplets were being raised according to the most modern ideas in child training. It was a source of wonder to see the babies flourishing under the best kind of care. Public attention was drawn to the way the quintuplets seemed to lead a well-regulated, healthy, and apparently happy life in their pre-school years.

It was resounding proof to Blatz and his followers that the St

George's School program had wider application, and it was evident to much of the general population that the new ways of raising children could produce serenely confident and competent youngsters. Nevertheless, these were not the ideals of French-speaking Roman Catholic families in northern Ontario, and already Oliva Dionne was beginning to rally support in his struggle against the invaders from the south. Blatz's confidence was running high, however. Unaware that his days with the Dionnes were numbered, he prepared to present his work to the North American professional community.

# 6 Studying the Five Sisters

The research conference that Blatz called in the autumn of 1937 was intended as an interim evaluation of the programs designed for the quintuplets and the children's progress therein. It involved some three hundred educators, physicians, and psychologists, who were all eager both to share their expertise in child rearing and to learn more about the particular circumstances of the quintuplets' life history. It was to be one of a series of consultations and conferences. As it happened, it was the only one.

The main thrust of Blatz's research was to show how the quintuplets, genetically identical, would each develop her own individuality. As such, it would be a clear demonstration of the influences of environment, which, although similar for the five children, would inevitably differ in its details and social interactions. Although public sentiment would not have peaceably allowed the separate upbringing of these identical quintuplets, Blatz's plans for the girls in their twenty-four-hour-a-day nursery emphasized both individual attention and developing independence.

The research itself largely focused on how the quintuplets were growing to differ from one another. Reports of their development were published at the time of the October 1937 conference and appeared as six monographs in the University of Toronto Child Development series. Blatz was the senior author of five of the reports: those on the quintuplets' mental growth, early social development, development of self-discipline, routine training, and early development of spoken language.

Two members of the university's biology department published the biological study of the children. The monographs were bound as *Collected Studies on the Dionne Quintuplets* and published in 1937. The same basic material was presented less formally and published the following year as *The Five Sisters: A Study in Psychology*. It brought a five-page illustrated book review in *Life* magazine, which called it 'an absorbing scientific analysis of the personality and behaviour of the Quins.'[1]

Publication of the first book marked what was, in fact, the culmination of Blatz's research with the quintuplets. By the following spring he was no longer involved in their upbringing.

During his years in the double job of educational consultant and researcher, Blatz had developed a system of observation and record keeping that allowed him to study most aspects of the quints' daily lives. It also involved considerable measuring and public reporting of which child's test scores were running highest or lowest. The research, however, was coupled with cautions about the limitations of the tests. Blatz looked on the tests as a measure of achievement (and thus an indication of what might be learned in later years), but never a measurement of intelligence as such.[2] Blatz's work with the quints took place before the days of defined codes of ethics in research. There were no external guidelines pushing him when he declared of his own accord that the studies should not be allowed to dominate the children's lives. Research was fitted into the children's ordinary activities, and the nursery school routine had a higher priority than the research. It is also to Blatz's credit that he ignored a suggestion from the first annual congress of radiology at Chicago that the quintuplets might help the science of heredity materially by being subjected to complete X-ray examinations.[3]

Blatz's initial involvement with the quintuplets coincided both with the new guardianship (David Croll, Judge J.A. Valin of Sudbury, Allan Dafoe, and Oliva Dionne) and with the enlargement of the hospital. In the first eight months he laid the groundwork for his research, and in January 1936 he called together a research committee consisting of faculty from the universities of Toronto, Chicago, and Minnesota, as well as the Iowa Child Welfare Research Station and the General Education Board of New York (represented by Lawrence Frank). Dafoe was in heady company and out of his depth on this committee, but scrupulous care was taken to make it appear that all initiatives came from him. Millichamp recalls that Blatz was keenly interested in planning for the children and excited about the research, yet he played his role as Dafoe's supporter with an easy sociability and deference for the country doctor's opinions. Minutes of the first research committee meeting show Dafoe as requesting that scientific recording of the children be undertaken and that scientists from the United States be invited to participate.[4] The committee was headed by Dr C.H. Judd of the Department of Education at the University of Chicago, and its work culminated in the First International Conference on the Dionne Quintuplets of October 1937.

The most important aspect of the early research was to establish the biological relationship of the five sisters. After an examination of handprints, footprints, facial features, tooth formation, hair whorls, growth measurements, and photographs of the quintuplets, John MacArthur and Norma Ford, both of the biology department at the University of Toronto, concluded that in all probability the children were identical quintuplets of monozygotic origin. The single cell probably underwent several divisions, leaving Yvonne and Annette as the strongest of the five, with Emilie and Marie, smaller than the others, somewhat lagging in development and probably the result of a later cell division.[5] (Emilie and Marie both died young, Emilie at age twenty-one during an epileptic seizure in July 1954, and Marie, apparently of a stroke, in 1970.)

Blatz's own work focused on the development of personality differences. 'Never before in the history of human genetics have five identical children been born into circumstances where the opportunity not only may be but must be provided for following their growth and development under controlled conditions,' he wrote.[6] The rationale for his program of research was to consider the children's progress from four aspects: motor, language, adaptive, and personal-social.[7]

The nurses were made responsible for the day-to-day recording of adjustment to routines, of early vocalization (both by taking notes and by using the phonograph), of the children's use of play materials, and of social contacts, emotional episodes, and behaviour requiring adult intervention. For much of this the nurses used virtually the same forms as had been developed for the St George's School. The nurses' records were analysed by Blatz and his staff, who then integrated them with specific psychological tests and plotted learning curves. (These recordings of activities and reactions were minutely detailed. There are, for instance, notes on the children's use of right or left hand. The criterion used was to observe which hand they used when they started a meal and to record the number of times the left hand was used. Emilie, for example, used her left hand about one-third of the time, Cecile occasionally, and the others almost never.)

The reactions of the children to various situations were recorded in order to show similarities and differences in the development of each child's individual personality.[8] Since the babies were at least two months premature, they were starting with a major developmental handicap. Rather than compare their growth in detail to that of full-term babies (for even the use of statistical correlates to correct for prematurity could be misleading), Blatz decided to concentrate his comparisons within the group of five, giving norms only as a general guideline. No intelligence quotients as such were given, because he felt that they would be misleading.[9]

A test was given roughly every two months to all five children using three basic test forms: the Gesell, the Kuhlman, and the Merrill-Palmer (Stutsman). Although the children's scores stayed within close range of one another, there were persistent differences in their rankings. Yvonne was consistently highest in achievement; Cecile and Annette alternated for second place; Emilie sometimes equalled but never ranked above Annette or Cecile; and Marie was invariably in fifth place.[10] The children showed an accelerated growth compared to that of other children, with Marie's rate of acceleration less than the other four, perhaps because she was the most physically lagging.[11]

Because of the children's prematurity they were handicapped in their early performances on tests of motor development, language skill, and adaptive behaviour. However, personal and social skills, which have relatively little to do with actual physical development, were acquired more rapidly than other skills.[12]

Motor development (indicating the organization of muscle groups) lagged in all the children, but most of them had caught up with the general population by the age of three. In language development the picture was much the same. Blatz viewed language as a tool of civilization that assists in social interaction and is dependent for its development on opportunities to practise and to use it. He recognized two kinds of language, both of which can convey meaning: the spoken word, and gestures.[13] The quintuplets (as is characteristic in multiple births) developed a system of gestures that was so efficient that it was partially responsible for their delayed speech. Their spoken language was also late in developing because of their prematurity and the fact that they were surrounded day and night by adults who constantly anticipated their needs. A fourth factor was the lack of adult pressure to establish their identity through the way they talked. As quintuplets they were unique already: people marvelled at the fact that there were five of them, and there was no need to look for any other source of wonder, such as how well they might speak. The quints' lag in language almost certainly lowered their total scores on mental tests, 'presenting a picture of mental retardation that may be spurious,' Blatz noted.[14]

Again, the unique circumstances of the children's birth influenced their development of adaptive skills, which in turn was reflected in their test performance. In Blatz's system children learn in order to adapt to changes in their environment. Both their power of reasoning and stability of judgment depend on their skill at learning to adapt.[15] Again, most early exploratory experiences depend upon physical involvement. The quints' lag in motor development delayed some of these adaptive skills. In one instance, however, their unusual environment allowed them to function precociously. One of the pre-school tasks in the tests of adaptation involved opening and closing a door. As doors played an important part in the quints' lives, they were able to perform this task earlier than most other children.[16] Blatz took the position that most tests for the development of personal and social skills would be difficult to select because of the varied customs of different communities. As these are so diverse, the tests usually do little more than examine artificial behaviour chosen to fit a particular pattern of social life. The Gesell tests for social skills, on the other hand, involved such activities as reacting to the reflection in a mirror, explaining pictures, recounting experiences to others, and giving names or responding to inflection of voice. These have relatively little to do with physical development, and the quints' tests showed that they acquired these personal-social skills earlier than other skills.[17]

Blatz attributed the quints' slow development in the early years to a combination of prematurity, inheritance, and an environment that lacked the stimulation that comes from being with other, older children.[18] Their close biological identity was due to their common inheritance, but there were enough variations in their records to show that environmental influences played a large role in their mental development.[19] The more they responded differently to situations, the more different each one's environment grew; this in turn called for further differences in their responses. The differences grew faster the more they practised them. Yvonne, initially the most advanced, became increasingly competent, while Marie, the smallest, remained in the role of the baby. It was more the dynamics of the situation than the static aspects of environment that led to the differences,[20] but the planned environment itself played a major role in unleashing the quints' mental development from the effects of prematurity. Although there were differences among them, as a group, their progress was steadily upwards, and in the pre-school years they gained ground on their contemporaries. This acceleration Blatz attributed to their carefully organized pre-school education. In 1939, after Blatz's research had ceased, he was nevertheless able to make a confident declaration at the annual conference of the Progressive Education Association that the Dionnes were proving to science that environment is more important than heredity. 'Physically and mentally they are above par. Environment has made them what they are. And we are blessed to have such a fascinating experiment. It will be of inestimable use to science.'[21]

In the first eight months of his involvement with the quintuplets, before the research committee was established and before the hospital was turned into a nursery school, Blatz was virtually alone in organizing and conducting research. At the first meeting of the research advisory committee, he was able to present a report of his research to date and obtain the sanction of the committee to continue. In actual fact he still kept the research almost entirely under his control. He invited those present at the meeting to consider themselves an advisory board with power to add members from other fields as needed. It was also decided that the research 'should be conducted for a time as has been done to date, namely, by the staff of St George's School.' Any additional researchers would be registered as assistants at the school. All research proposals would be submitted to Dafoe for his approval, and research would be published only through channels approved by the committee. Furthermore the existence of the committee would be withheld from public knowledge until it was ready to present its first research findings. Then, and only then, any materials released could be drawn upon by any members of the committee.[22]

The committee suggested at its first meeting that additional emphasis be placed on measures of mental development, physiology, locomotor ability and physical control, verbalization, adjustment to routine, and measurements of manipulation of material. Suggestions for new fields of research included the Dionne family history, an anthropological study of the children's community, a test for measuring the children's reaction to musical tones, and measurements of drawing ability, colour discrimination, and sense acuity. The committee's research ideas included full use of contemporary technology: photographs, phonographs, moving pictures, Dictaphones, and, at the suggestion of Dr G.D. Stoddard of Iowa, 'ex-ray' photographs.[23]

The committee, although vowing to be guided by Dafoe, nevertheless gave him a strong push towards establishing a plan for the children. The committee 'advised that Dr Dafoe be impressed with the importance of early planning of an educational programme.'[24] Blatz already had the situation well in hand, however, announcing that he had a French-speaking nurse who was undergoing teacher training at the St George's School in preparation for working in the quints' new nursery school. (It was in the September following the meeting, when the quintuplets were twenty-eight months old, that their infant nursery was restructured as a full-time nursery school.)

Shortly after the first committee meeting Lawrence Frank wrote to Blatz with a research suggestion:

> The thing that appeals to me as probably the most interesting possibility, with the minimum of difficulties, would be a plan whereby a daily photographic record would be made of the kinds of play activities of each of the quints when using the blocks and other small easily manipulated toys. This suggestion is based upon the work of Erik Homburger at Harvard and also at Yale, where he is getting extraordinary indications of personality development in kinds of structures young children build with blocks and toys. If you could get their constructions recorded photographically and dated, I think Homburger would be willing to give the time to interpreting these records, which would become highly significant because they would be made on a group of children undergoing presumably the same regimen of care and training and with greater or less identity of heredity.

(Erik Homburger later changed his name to Erik Erikson and went on to develop a theory of growth and development, outlined in *Childhood and Society*, which he published in 1950.)

The major conference on the quintuplets was scheduled for the spring of 1937, and intervening research committee meetings continued to emphasize the need for making no announcement of work in progress until after the conference.

The conference was postponed from spring until fall and eventually was held at the Royal York Hotel in Toronto on 30 and 31 October

1937. Initially two hundred invitations were sent to 'leading authorities on child psychology and behaviourism,' and other people were invited upon the recommendation of those included in this initial group. Invitations were mailed on the special Dionne Quintuplet Guardianship stationery. The letterhead was emblazoned with a map of Ontario and a large star showing Callander as its focal point. The rest of Canada was presented as an amorphous mass. An orange and gilt drawing of a maple leaf bore a portrait of a baby's face in each of the five leaf lobes. The quints and Callander and Canada were the centre of the world's attention.

At the conference, the Honourable H.A. Bruce, lieutenant-governor of Ontario, a member of the board of governors of the university and a friend of Blatz, welcomed the delegates to a day of papers and discussions based largely on Blatz's research along with the Ford and MacArthur biological studies and William Dafoe's paper on the physical welfare of the quintuplets. (The Dafoe paper was published in the next month's issue of the *Canadian Medical Association Journal*, November 1937. On publication Allan Roy Dafoe, OBE, MD, of Callander, Ontario, was listed as senior author, with his Toronto brother, William A. Dafoe, MB, FRCS(C), MCOG (Eng.), in the secondary position.) The sessions were attended by 189 people and 247 were at the banquet, which was followed by Allan Roy Dafoe's presentation, 'The Life of the Quints,' illustrated by moving pictures.[25]

The highlight of the conference was the second day's visit to the Dionne nursery. Blatz engaged a special train to take 243 delegates to Callander (a not-surprising increase in numbers over those who had attended the formal sessions). The same arrangements for viewing the children from behind the screens prevailed for the scholars as for the public, but they had a longer look and an explanation of Blatz's plans for the quintuplets. The message about child raising came through so clearly that a delegate from the United States Department of the Interior, Office of Education, wrote to Blatz suggesting an exhibition room to help the average visitor see the possibility of utilizing the ideas that had been 'demonstrated so excellently.' Visitors would be able to go there (after observing the children) to see diagrams, posters, sample menus, clothing, and pictures explaining the reason for some of the procedures followed in the nursery.[26]

Interest in the pre-school program reinforced Blatz's first goal of demonstrating the possibilities of a salutary environment in early childhood education. The second goal, of studying the development of each girl's individual personality, was already being pursued in his research. The conference ended its proceedings with a resolution, which, in effect, amounted to a vote of confidence in Blatz's research program. The resolution spoke of the soundness of the work already accomplished, saying that it was making 'a contribution of distinct and lasting value not only to the development of the Dionne Quintuplets themselves but to the welfare of all children.' It spoke of the high-mindedness of the researchers in keeping the children's welfare uppermost, and urged that every effort be made to continue and augment a program of research under the same happy auspices and also to expand the educational program so as to offer the quintuplets the greatest opportunities for a normal physical, educational, and social development.[27]

This strong statement of support for Blatz's work was timely, for already the clouds were beginning to gather. Four months later he would be removed from the position of researcher and educational consultant for the quintuplets.

The reasons for Blatz's fall from grace centred on two closely related issues: the quintuplet's relationship with their family, and the question of the children's integration with the French-speaking Roman Catholic community. When Blatz had set forth his three goals for the children's upbringing (to serve as an example of child-raising practices, to observe the development of individuality, and to foster their cultural identity), his third stated aim was perhaps more expedient than realistic. He was on fairly sure ground with both his pre-school educational theory and his research endeavours, but for the third goal he had few clear-cut plans. One suspects that on seeing the armada approach he may have set about hoisting his flags with a claim that the territory was already under control. In fact he wrote *The Five Sisters* just as his research-education empire was crumbling.

After the children had, in Blatz's words, escaped unscathed from the early threat of careers in World's Fair concessions, they were placed under the guardianship of the Crown through the Ontario government. Mr Dionne was named a member of the guardianship group, but policy decisions about the quintuplets were thenceforth made in committee. The guardians controlled the children's business affairs and all matters pertaining to their estate. Their income came from contracts for motion pictures and photographs as well as from endorsements of products used in the home. 'By an Order-in-council of the Dominion Government the use of the words Quins, Quints or Quintuplets and their French equivalents is forbidden for advertising purposes without the permission of the Guardians.' By late 1937, half a million dollars was held in trust for the quintuplets. The capital was invested in government securities and the income used to meet the quintuplets' expenses of approximately $1800 per month.[28]

These expenses of close to $22,000 per year included salaries for nurses, guards, and housekeeping staff, and the cost of the upkeep of the buildings as well as of the girls' direct care. (The Dominion Bureau of Statistics – Statistics Canada – reported that the average annual wage in Ontario in 1931 was $1,005.) Although the Dionne family finances were brightened a little by the public attention given to the quintuplets, there was a considerable difference between the way life was lived in the hospital and the way it was lived across the street at the family farm.

'What about the other five Dionnes?' asked Mary Dougherty in the *Pictorial Review* at the end of their first year.[29] She referred to the five living brothers and sisters of the quints: Ernest (born in 1926), Rose (1928), Thérèse (1929), Daniel (1932), and Pauline (1933). A sixth child, Leo, had died. The two groups of siblings lived across the street from each other and worlds apart. Dougherty perceived the other children as more puzzled than envious, but wondered if they might not in time become the victims of inferiority complexes. Certainly at the quintuplets' first Christmas, gifts for the babies poured in from all over the world. Several donors, in misguided attempts to smother any sparks of sibling rivalry, remembered the older children as well, presenting them with sets of the most popular toy of Christmas 1934 – a little basket jammed tight with five bisque baby-doll quintuplets.

Blatz marvelled at the fact that for the first time in history five children were growing up in the restricted social atmosphere of multiple contemporary siblings.[30] A note written in May 1936 mentions that Dr Blatz had advised that the older brothers and sisters be allowed to visit the nursery;[31] in fact, however, any unannounced visits were apt to meet with resistance from the nurses.

The parents' role was not defined as such. Mrs Dionne seemed to be, along with the nurses, only one of a group of several alternate mothers. In their autobiography the quintuplets describe their mother as little more than a visitor. 'We knew there was one visitor, who came across the road to see us, whom the nurses taught us to call *Maman*.'[32] There were occasional skirmishes involving Mr Dionne in particular ('Dionne climbed under the fence,' notes a staff memorandum dated

May 1936), but Mrs Dionne's presence was generally encouraged. A memorandum of 7 November 1936, following the residence of Harris and Millichamp while one of the nurses was away, reads:

> *Family Contacts* –
>     September seventh, 3:30 to 5:00 p.m.: Father, mother, Rose and —— [name missing] remained with children, assisting at routine. Activity usually in form of entertaining or cuddling – no constructive play – children accept readily.
>     September eighth Mother and —— participated in outside play, in dressing, indoor play and remained during lunch. A.H. [Anne Harris] and D.A.M. [Dorothy Millichamp] left alone with children. Visit may have been to reconnoitre – Mother carried through routines without too great disturbance and did not interfere with meal except when Emilie used left hand.

Margaret Fletcher says in a taped interview that she went to the Dionne nursery for three weeks, ostensibly to prepare a Christmas radio broadcast featuring the quints. Blatz particularly asked her, though, to see if she could help Mrs Dionne to be a little happier. Fletcher says: 'The father wanted money and the mother didn't know if she was coming or going. She was getting pushed around. I made friends with her. We sang every night. Family sing-songs. Mrs Dionne came over every evening to be with the quints. When she came over, the nurses had instructions to let her be in charge. Dr Blatz told them to be sure to let her do things for the quints – to feel that she was their mother. But the nurses had difficulty letting her do it.'

On the other hand there is a note that one of the nurses opposed Dafoe in favour of the family. 'Dafoe had wished the family to be ordered not to kiss the children. J. Noel refused,' reads a memorandum of 4 January 1936. The doctor's edict was probably justified, for at the time the children in the farmhouse all had colds and intestinal upsets. However, the situation had deteriorated to the point where such confrontations were not unusual, with the nurses defending their nursery territory from both family and doctors.

On another occasion the same nurse noted that the children 'do not cry or make any fuss when parents are leaving now. Does not either look at the house and call for her parents since we gave more individual attention, about one month.'[33]

Public opinion in English-speaking Canada tended to judge Dionne rather severely. In her article on the Dionne family, Mary Dougherty comments that:

> The father has stopped working upon his farm, feeling perhaps that he has already done his required duty as a citizen and a parent. Is he justified in believing that the world now owes him a living – better than that: a luxurious living? For the time being he and his family are receiving government money on which to live without the necessity of their usual work.
>
> Should Ovila [sic] Dionne be urged, for his own good, to continue pretty much as he has always lived, as his father and grandfather lived before him, as all the Dionnes would have lived now and in time to come, as simple, hardworking, honest, frugal, law-abiding men and women, who asked for no greater joys than those which God and the happiness of their little children gave them?[34]

Blatz, however, realized that when doors are once opened they cannot easily be shut again. Although in the closing pages of *The Five Sisters* he put cultural fulfilment as one of his goals, earlier in the book he was less certain of the possibility: 'Even this short period has sufficed to show that these children can never remain like their antecedents, plain-living denizens of the north country, close to the soil, close to their French-Canadian traditions and to the simple pleasures and occupations of their rock-strewn farms. Like Marie Antoinette, who, with her friends, dressed in peasant garments and played at being farmerettes within the precincts of Versailles, these children will only play at being French habitants.'[35]

At the time there was not the same public concern for preserving cultural identity that there is today, but nevertheless Blatz did seem to make a conscientious effort to foster both the learning of the French language and the development of the children's Roman Catholicism. He planned prayers and religious stories, employed Catholic nurses and a Catholic psychologist,[36] and his staff noted, under notes on language development, such items as one of the quints saying 'Jesus' four times during the 6:15 p.m. circle-time and another pointing to the Sacred Heart badge and saying the word 'coeur.'[37]

Blatz acknowledged that the guardians had a particular responsibility to foster French traditions, and to that end he arranged for a French Catholic teacher to be trained at St George's School[38] and ordered French story-books.[39] The staff was put to translating English nursery favourites into French and preparing 'French phrases arranged to provide consistency in directing the children': 'C'est le temps de jouer – se reposer – aller au lit – aller à la toilette – mettre les jouets a côté,' as well as 'c'est malheureux' and 'tu peux le faire toi-même.' The English-speaking staff received lists of equivalent French words for various furnishings, items of clothing, and toys.[40] In studying the girls' speech development, bilingual recorders made a brave attempt to identify the French sounds and record them in English. The children sang the folk tunes of French Canada, and their prayers were in French.[41]

There was no lack of outside interest in the problem of learning languages. Blatz received, for instance, an enthusiastic offer to foster the children's development in both languages from a Professor Leon Barreau of Chicago who claimed to have 'pledged for the last 25 years to give to (1) all my students (2) maximum practical knowledge (3) in minimum time. I beg the honour to demonstrate to you by actual coaching of the Dionne quintuplets how easy it is for youngsters to learn the ESSENTIALS of certain Modern Languages while being limited to TWO mental operations and no longer FOUR mental operations. I guarantee results, quick PERFECT RESULTS with the help (a) of SCIENTIFIC French books and records (b) plus my teaching of French by DISSECTION my own method now being prepared and copyrighted ... *what I have suffered to learn Modern Languages, THE DIONNE QUINTUPLETS SHOULD NOT SUFFER.'*[42]

The letter was dated a month after Blatz's dismissal and after it had been decided that the quintuplets would learn only one language: French.

Blatz had not gone far enough to satisfy either the children's father or the more conservative elements of the French-speaking Roman Catholic church. He had drawn the line on religion by refusing to allow a chapel to be built in the children's playroom, and he stood firmly for the idea that the children should learn English as well as French.

The Dionne family was bilingual. Mrs Dionne understood English, though she actually spoke only French, but Mr Dionne and the children in the farmhouse usually spoke and wrote in English. However the French language became a rallying point for another issue: custody of the quintuplets. The local church, French-language newspapers, and such societies as the French-Canadian Association of Education and the Fédération des Femmes Canadiennes-Françaises closed ranks behind Mr Dionne in his efforts to have the quintuplets returned to his care.[43]

'I may respectfully say,' wrote the president of the federation to J.V. McAree, columnist of the *Globe and Mail*, 'that, as Dr Blatz is not familiar with the French language, even if he were the most hustling Catholic, he cannot properly and thoroughly discharge the duties of directing and supervising the religious, profane and linguistic education of these children.'[44]

One of the guardians, Judge J.A. Valin, who had been educated in both French and English, countered with his opinion that it was absolutely necessary for the girls to become bilingual. 'I feel I must see that they get adequate instruction in English as well as their native tongue of French. Up to now they have spoken only in French,' he told the *Toronto Daily Star*. He added that, as long as he had a voice in the affairs of the quints, Blatz would remain as chief adviser. 'The judge is equally firm that, as advised by Dr Blatz, English instruction of the children should be continued without interruption. He does not agree that early training of the quints in the English language will interfere with their thorough knowledge of French.'[45]

The trouble came to a head over the question of which nurses and teachers were to be employed in the Dionne nursery. Even though two of the nurses had received brief training at the St George's School, their attitudes towards child raising were quite different from that of Blatz. Blatz wrote to Dafoe about the problem:

> Since last April my nurses have been reporting that Miss Tremblay is changing in her attitude towards her work. On several occasions I have reported to you that she was uncooperative, especially with reference to the teaching of English. I did not feel like insisting too much until I found out what you and Judge Valin's attitude was towards this matter. Even after I told her that the two of you were in accord I found her attitude unsympathetic.
>
> My regular records every month indicated that the children were progressing satisfactorily, but when Miss Harris was resident during September she noted and reported to me the following:
> (a) Miss T. was far too strict and the children were demanding too much of her attention. She misinterpreted this as affection and was rather pleased thereby.
> (b) Far too much attention was being directed towards the children's

own bodies. By the attitude of the nurses, N and T, which is most narrow-minded and almost pathological, children were made conscious of false modesty.

(c) Both nurses seem to feel that the children are their own special trust, for life, and resent any criticism or interference.

Although the situation does not appear extraordinarily acute at the present time I feel that we should take steps to remedy it.

When I was up Saturday I took the following steps:

(a) I told N. that there was to be no more nonsense about her attitude – that you were responsible for the children and that her job was to carry out orders.

(b) That she was responsible for Tremblay and she was being guided too much by Tremblay's fanaticism.

(c) That my nurse, Miss M. was coming up in November and was going to make a complete report on routine, discipline, atmosphere etc.

I would further ask you, Roy, to give me permission to look for further help at this time. I would recommend -

(a) That an English, French speaking Catholic of good education and good family be engaged and sent to St. George's School for at least 6 months at which time T. could be released and her place taken by this candidate.

(b) That a French-Canadian nurse, trained at a good sick children's hospital be found and given a training at St. George's and N. released in June.

(c) That O'Sh. be kept on till next fall.

(d) That the teacher rather than the nurse be put in charge of the hospital after this change is made.[46]

In early March the change-over was carried out. The two French-speaking nurses were replaced by one who spoke English and another who was French Canadian but who considered herself more at home in English.

Dionne was incensed, and the French-Canadian Association of Education demanded to meet in private with the guardians. Dionne insisted that his children should return to live with him and that their education should be planned by someone who was both Roman Catholic and a francophone.

Within six weeks of his dismissal of nurses Noel and Tremblay, Blatz himself was asked to leave in order to allow the government of

Ontario and its director of bilingual education to take over the education of the quintuplets. 'Suddenly the researchers were barred from seeing us for testing any more,' the quintuplets wrote in their autobiography. 'Their work, for whatever value it may have had, was broken off, and nothing like it was ever started again in the nursery. It seems that a new kind of wall was being built up around us, invisible yet every bit as restrictive as the high, steel-mesh fences.'[47]

And so ended an era for the quintuplets that they later described as the happiest and least-complicated years of their lives. It was a snug, secure world, they said, with an atmosphere of carefree days. Certainly the nursery atmosphere had demonstrated Blatz's plan to the world, and certainly, in retrospect, the quintuplets recall the days there as happy ones. Blatz's plans for their schooling and his research on the development of their individuality were both far from complete, however. In their book, the sisters describe their later girlhood with the family as filled with tension and a sense of being unjustly used, particularly when it came to their father's handling of their finances. They were treated by their parents not as individuals but as five who really amounted to one. Their chances to express their individuality through career choices, contrary to Blatz's hopes, seemed limited, for the girls remained ignorant of alternatives to the traditional roles of teacher, nun, or nurse.[48]

Certainly, the quintuplets would have been treated very differently today; at the time, however, there seemed to be no alternative to government intervention if the quints were even to stay alive. It would have been impossible in the earliest days for mother Dionne to look after them and father Dionne to protect them, said D.A. Millichamp in 1982.[49] Today we are more skilled in ways to strengthen the parents' own role, but much of what we know today we did not know then.

Millichamp says that the Dionne nursery was more like a child-centred boarding school than an impersonal institution. The children were surrounded by adults who were keenly interested in and concerned with their welfare. 'And we cared about them. Oh my, how we cared about them,' adds Margaret Fletcher.[50] Today more is known about parent-child interactions and the importance of permanent relationships, but at the time of the quintuplets' childhood there was no concern about the fact that the babies and parents were not able to build deep ties with each other. The quints were brought up by a collection of adults whose goal was neither to threaten nor to dominate (as distinct from the goals of many adults at the time). The emphasis was on friendly relationships, and the program was geared towards developing independence in the children. They were initially protected from grim interpersonal relationships and thus were totally unprepared for their father's domination of them.

The children probably found their primary security in each other. They were tremendously good to each other and there seemed to be no rivalry – no crying for attention – in the nursery, says Millichamp.[51] In the Dionne home, and in later years, the children have tended to form a family among themselves, as they describe in their book.

Today, the need for extended care would have been worked out by the parents and with the parents. The adversary positions of Mr Dionne and the guardians might have been avoided, and with it some of the pain the quintuplets endured in their years at home after the nursery. As well, even if the public and the press had demanded access to the details of the lives of the quintuplets, our increased understanding of children would have helped withstand the pressures to make the children's lives a public spectacle. Although Blatz himself was usually cautious about the kind of research he conducted and published, and although he turned down several proposals for intrusive types of investigation, the decisions he made were individual ones. Today's guidelines on research with human subjects would not permit the same publicity about details of the children's growth as was considered acceptable in the 1930s.

Blatz was deeply involved in his work with the children, but when it was terminated he showed no great regret. There was no looking back. He never mentioned it again. Instead he cut his contacts completely and went on with his other projects.

# 7 The Practical Counsellor

Although the Dionnes' door was closed to him, Blatz was more than ever in demand as a public speaker, his security theory was maturing, there were changes at the St George's School, he had bought a 150-acre farm at Caledon, and he was becoming known as a wise counsellor for people with problems.

By 1937 the Rockefeller funding through Mental Hygiene covered only about half the child study expenses, and the university governors appointed a special committee to consider the future of the St George's School. The decision a year later was to make child study an autonomous faculty within the University of Toronto, which would keep it under the wing of the university but invite outside financing. The St George's School for Child Study became the Institute of Child Study.

The change in organization loosened the bonds between child study and psychology. Blatz himself remained a member of the psychology department but was answerable directly to the university president. Graduate work in the nursery school continued to give credit towards a psychology MA, but the expected emphasis of the institute was to be on interdisciplinary research. (It had been the intention to involve other departments in child study right from the start of the St George's School, but this had been done very little. Now a new organization invited new proposals.)

Two factors – in addition to child study's growth and increasingly complex structure – played a part in separating child study from psychology. First, Bott's business method was 'very high to the vest,' as

Roger Myers described it, and no doubt it irked Blatz not to know what was going on. With a separated Institute of Child Study, Blatz would have his own budget to manage and his own decisions to make. The other element was the coolness growing between Blatz and his old mentor, Bott. Helen Bott had recently become involved with the Oxford Group, and it became a way of life to her, absorbing most of her interest. Blatz disapproved of her connection; Bott defended his wife; and this became a source of friction between the two old friends.[1]

Helen Bott left the staff of the institute in 1938, and Karl Bernhardt, a Canadian with a PH D from Chicago who had been teaching in the psychology department at Toronto, succeeded her as head of parent education. Bernhardt also became assistant director of the institute, along with Dorothy Millichamp, and started the quarterly *Bulletin of the Institute of Child Study*, continuing as its editor for the next twenty-six years.

Institute publications were given a further boost when Mary Northway joined the staff and became its research director. She had studied psychology at both Toronto and Cambridge, and her own formal research was in measuring the development of social relationships. She was also an enthusiastic camper and a prolific writer who turned out a number of essays and books about her wide interests.

Northway further developed the research programs in which the children from the earliest longitudinal studies were followed through their school years, and beyond, by an annual interview with parent and child. The interview was conducted informally, and a second form was prepared to give details of the child's normal day, friends and social activities, recreation, interests in reading and movies, work and allowance, home discipline, emotional upsets, ambitions, dreams, memories, physical progress, special problems, and progress in school. Reports from the children's schools were requested, but were discontinued when they proved less informative than the parents' and children's own reports of their schooling. With the youngest children, the interviews were conducted almost entirely with a parent, but as they grew older the children were asked to answer some of the questions apart from the parent, until they were old enough to give the information for themselves, with a parallel interview for their parents. Later, as the first children reached adolescence, the questionnaire was lengthened to include questions about boy-girl relationships and attitudes towards parents and siblings.[2]

In 1939 the institute received a grant from the provincial

Department of Education to provide theory and practice for students at the Toronto Teachers' College who were taking the two-year Kindergarten-Primary Specialists Course. The annual grant of $5,000 from the Department of Education often proved a life-saver in lean financial times.[3] More important, at last it gave Blatz and his theories a voice in the public school system.

During these years Blatz continued to formulate his security theory. It is indicative of the times that his early statements of the system should put a strong emphasis on the importance of independence. In charting histories of childhood it has been a common observation that parents, whether they realize it or not, bring up their children according to the way the world appears to them.[4] Even the matter of whether children are raised with thoughtful care is, in itself, a reflection of how the parents view the children's future. Where the parents' resources are scanty and their outlook pessimistic it is likely that their children's childhood will be correspondingly abbreviated and soured.

Goals and relative values also change with different circumstances. At various times we may particularly admire people who are pious, thrifty, industrious, uncomplaining, brave, simple, complex, humane, self-effacing, self-confident, ambitious, imaginative, unwavering, or flexible. Parental aspirations may focus on any of these qualities.

In one of the first sessions of most parent education groups, parents would be asked to list the goals they had for their children. Sometimes the question would be put another way: to describe the kind of adults they hoped their children would become. During the years of the Depression the people who seemed most likely to survive were those who were sturdily self-reliant and independent.

Blatz had been promoting independence since the St George's School first opened. At first this quality was stressed largely to counteract the way in which middle-class children under five were treated – as helpless babies. He encouraged self-help in personal care, taught woodwork with adult carpentry tools, showed children how they could extricate themselves if they climbed too high, and emphasized practice in making choices and decisions. Parents in the 1920s were surprised (and sometimes a little hurt) to see how well their young children could cope. Ten years later, in the lean 1930s, early independence was more acceptable and, indeed, highly regarded. Blatz's thinking about security reflected this contemporary value.

Blatz did concede that dependent security – that is, knowing that someone else will cushion the consequences – is a satisfying state of mind. When children try to maintain this comfortable state, however, their behaviour in attempting to remain dependently secure will give rise to 'sundry of the problems of child training.'[5] On the other hand, if they acquire skills leading towards independence they will become secure as a result of knowing they can deal with any consequences that may arise. 'In this way the child, as he grows up, learns that although dependent security is a satisfying state of mind, independent security is more satisfying, because not only has a motive been gratified but there has also been the experience of temporary insecurity and the emotional fillip it has engendered.'[6]

He allowed a limited state of dependence in his statement, saying that 'having sloughed off the dependent security of childhood,' it would be helpful for people to acquire a more mature form of dependency, either with a form of religion or with friends, provided that these do not become merely substitutes for the parent-child relationship. But with it he warned that 'all forms of dependent security are subject to a crisis or catastrophe. Whatever one depends upon cannot be considered perpetual ... The behaviour of a dependent individual who has suddenly lost the object upon which he was depending accounts for a great deal of so-called pathological behaviour.'[7]

Independent security, in Blatz's system, was founded upon learning, although it would be impossible for anyone to acquire sufficient skills to deal with every possible situation in life, and thus it is impossible to become entirely independently secure. Independent security should increase, however, as people continue to learn. In fact, said Blatz, 'A well-balanced individual should become more adventurous as he grows older. We have been labouring under the delusion that childhood is the time for adventure, whereas this should be the time for caution.'[8]

Although Blatz was adamant about the central role of independence in his theory, he was perfectly prepared to discuss the details and possibilities of the system with his little group of staff and students.

The institute was still small and retained something of a family atmosphere, with Blatz very much in the paternal role. Every afternoon when the children left for home the whole staff gathered for its ritual tea with brown bread and butter. Although Blatz had a permanent, tacit reservation on a particular wicker armchair and often held the floor, it was generally a time to relax before the later afternoon classes or evening parent education groups.

In 1939 Blatz bought a derelict farm just below the Caledon Hills about thirty-five miles northwest of Toronto and spent most of his spare time for the rest of his life working on the house. Apart from the heavy work of taking out and splitting old beams and building a staircase, Blatz did the carpentry himself, constructing a series of rooms radiating from the first large room at the core of the house. He was quick and skilled with tools, but would become enraged whenever the crooked corners of the original house threw off his careful measurements. His special friend, Anne Harris, and his daughter, Gery, who went out to the farm with him nearly every weekend, were largely engaged in handing him nails or fetching tools. It was the same with Blatz's cooking: he was delighted to cook all the meals, while the role of family and guests was to fetch and carry and chop and clean up afterwards.

Blatz was not interested in farming itself. He did plant a stand of young pine trees, which he said he was growing for his great-grandchildren, but he turned over the operation of the farm to his niece and her husband. He was mildly interested in the cows and teams of horses, but was irritated by chickens, while his devotion to cats allowed the barns to be overrun with kittens. It was an aphorism of Blatz's that only a secure person could like a cat.

He brought many of his professional skills to Caledon with him. The local people would consult him about their personal problems: 'My wife and I can't agree,' or 'My son isn't getting along at school; what shall I do?' There was no clinic set-up, no regular appointment time, but, just as neighbours in Hamilton had been drawn to Leo and Victoria Blatz for help, so, too, did people in Caledon seek the counsel of the younger Blatz.

In Toronto, as at Caledon, colleagues, staff and friends, the children of friends, and the parents of children in his schools sought him out when they were facing a crisis, until counselling effectively became a secondary but significant part of Blatz's main work at the university and Windy Ridge Day School. He accepted no money for these private interviews, for presumably it was reward enough if his associates began again to function effectively.

Almost without exception those who knew Blatz in another phase of his career have drawn attention to his effectiveness as a counsellor. Yet details of his work in this field are only fragmentary and indirect, for he left no major writings on the subject of counselling that could either document or defend his idiosyncratic methods. When he died, his wife carried out a promise to destroy all his clinical records, and the only remaining written evidence of his clinical work is his correspondence with patients (in this case consisting mostly of letters to Blatz and occupying only a slim file among his papers).

We are left largely with the recollections of those who knew Blatz or received his counsel. Their accounts are preserved in taped interviews that mention his skill as a therapist, although most of these commentators have been able to make only cursory attempts at analysing his methods. Dorothy Millichamp, however, who worked closely with Blatz and learned something of his approach to counselling, has been able to give more detailed observations of his techniques in her *Conversations at Caledon*. These comments by Millichamp and others are supplemented by a pamphlet arising from Blatz's later wartime lectures on morale in which may be found a brief description of his suggestions for interviewing and on-the-spot counselling.

Theory and practice were always linked in Blatz's work, with the growth of one fostering the development of the other. Just as experience and policies followed each other in nursery education, so did Blatz's counselling techniques evolve alongside his theory. His understanding of the way people faced problems would lead him to broader perceptions and, in turn, the framework of his psychological philosophy would form the basis for counselling each patient.

His earliest formal counselling was at the Juvenile Court Clinic. As at the St George's School in its earliest days, he worked at first more by a combination of common sense and knowledge of child development than from any overall plan. He usually took the early life of his people into account, not for a detailed analysis of the past but as a useful tool to help them cope with their immediate problems in their own particular way. He understood that a person who had certain kinds of childhood experiences would have related difficulties and might find one solution more difficult than another.[9]

After his first few years at the court he began to work more with disturbed adults and less with disturbed children. In an everyday situation he interacted well with children, and he could comfort a crying child almost instantly, though in later years he seemed to be uncomfortable in counselling older children directly. Indeed, by the time J.D. Griffin worked at the Juvenile Court he noticed that Blatz 'would spend a few minutes playing and talking with the kids and then he'd disappear and talk to somebody else.'

Don Atcheson, a psychiatrist who was also one of Blatz's pupils, substantiated this: 'The mornings he came down [to court] he dealt with adults, the families of disturbed kids. The attempt to orientate to people who were having marital problems was where he was absolutely excellent. But I don't remember Bill ever seeing a delinquent kid. I could talk to him about my problems with kids and I could get tremendous advice and resources but I never saw him actually deal with them.'[10]

He viewed children's behaviour problems primarily as developmental difficulties, most of them as a normal and necessary part of maturing, although some were deviations from the course of growing up. His practical approach was to help parents and teachers to understand most problems as part of learning. This approach relieved the adults' anxiety while Blatz helped them find new ways of managing.[11]

Most of the people he saw in his clinic were distressed rather than seriously ill. They were people who were facing problems in their lives, or who needed to make decisions. They often included people with marital troubles and professional concerns, or parents whose children had disabilities or handicaps, as well as those who were having difficulty in parent-child relationships. Again, he did more direct work with adults than with children, although as he helped those who were having difficulty in school he saw the children themselves, as they grew older, rather than their parents. Much of his help was very practical, such as finding useful community facilities or working out more satisfactory living arrangements. He often worked clinically with the husband and wife together, or the parent and child together, and frequently with the whole family, which could sometimes include relatives and friends.

Those who were not completely well psychologically he still viewed as well people and treated as such. He always worked from strengths rather than weaknesses and assumed that, with a little help where necessary, most people could solve their own difficulties.

Those who were more seriously ill he referred to a psychiatrist, sometimes working in the background with the psychiatrist and following up after more intensive or traditional therapy. He was adamant that he was not a psychiatrist but a medical doctor with a further degree in psychology. Although qualified to administer psychiatric drugs he seldom did so, considering them so psychologically distorting as to be useless in the long run. If drugs were absolutely necessary he would refer the patient to a colleague in psychiatry, but only as a last resort. Instead he would go a long way to assume wellness in a person.

In many cases, the fact that he usually had confidence in people's strength would be enough to carry them through the crisis.

His concept of the normal person allowed for a broad range of individual differences, and he viewed periods of emotional distress as an essential component of the process of learning.[12] (After a major illness later in his own life, he became depressed for a time and spoke of the frightening lack of interest that he suffered. He kept on with what he was doing, however, because being productively busy seemed the most effective way to fend off the despair, and eventually he pulled out of it.)[13]

Blatz's counselling techniques themselves remain something of a mystery. He never analysed his clinical approach except to say that he used his security scheme as a framework and judged how a person fitted into it. He lectured to student psychiatrists but never wrote about his techniques or developed a systematic method that could be studied or used consistently by others. His style was, instead, highly individualistic and difficult to define. It seems to have been an amalgam of the restorative spell cast by his charismatic personality and many of the elements seen in humanistic and existential psychotherapies. The psychologist Carl Williams has mentioned an intuitive capacity as being at the heart of Blatz's technique: 'He always managed to get at what it was and to do this in such a way as to preserve the self-respect of the people who were in trouble, and they felt supported and helped. People knew from their own experience that he was a pretty humane man.'[14]

Blatz refused to consider himself part of any school of therapy. Psychoanalysis was becoming particularly influential in North America by the late 1930s, but its main influence on Blatz was to encourage him to argue for the opposite of what the Freudians held most dear. As a young man he had read the entire works of Freud, but they only served to provoke him to try to prove that Freud was wrong. Blatz contended that long-term psychoanalytic therapy could be used as an unhealthy way for people to talk around problems and thus escape the realities they needed to face.[15] He dismissed the Freudian belief in the subconscious as a further excuse for avoiding responsibility.

> The very symbolism by which it is described seems to suggest electricity as a model: dynamic, powerful, dangerous, capable of some control but periodically asserting itself by violent outbreak. But other symbols too have been employed: the unconscious was submerged,

nine-tenths below the surface, like an iceberg; it lurked in the impenetrable jungle from which it could emerge as a raging lion; it leered and lusted in diabolical, primitive sexual orgies, a heritage of our Darwinian past; it taunted, tempted, and tortured like an inquisitor. There was no escape; the id was indomitable, it was supreme; the ego was a willing though shuddering and quivering victim; the super-ego was a cringing and vacillating champion at best. And so the unconscious was groomed for the unwary, the credulous, and crafty. Human beings behaved peculiarly, so a scapegoat or whipping boy had to be found; the 'unconscious' was in the offing. Once it was brought into the open (a paradox indeed), one could behave as one wished; the unconscious was in operation, and any kind of behaviour could be excused, if not explained.[16]

Although he had something in common with existentialist-humanist therapists, he had no patience with the high degree of non-directiveness inherent in their techniques. Indeed, R.G.N. Laidlaw, who studied with Blatz and later conducted research in child study, remembered Blatz as summarily dismissing Carl Rogers and his methods with the words 'Non-directive. Non-effective.'[17]

Neither was he sympathetic to the bit-by-bit shaping procedures used by behaviourist-learning theory types of psychotherapy. Although he could certainly be quite directive in his clinical work, and often made it perfectly clear which route was most sensible for a person to take, he nevertheless left the ultimate choices to the people he was counselling. No external forces were used to push the person into a pre-selected type of behaviour. If troubled people made decisions that Blatz would not have recommended, he set about helping them try to live with the result of their choices. Learning in this way to cope with consequences was the essence of his definition of mental health. Over the years, as his security theory developed, so too did his confidence in counselling.

In the last years of his life Blatz was attempting to define a system based on his idiosyncratic style of counselling, but the project was only barely started. In spite of the proliferation of clinical methods in the last few years, no present-day method comes close to his approach. Today, literally hundreds of types of therapy vie for attention. Most are variations on the recurrent themes of analysis, behaviour modification, or non-directive counselling. There are group, family, and milieu methods, flooding, focusing, or feeling therapies, and clinical techniques based on screams or shadows.[18] They are not Blatz. Blatz did not fit into any of the special schools, traditional or eccentric. If he must be considered aligned to any group, he would perhaps be closest to existentialist-humanist therapists such as Gordon Allport.

The ability to preserve the patient's self-respect through the therapist's willingness to accept the patient as someone ultimately able to take responsibility for his decisions is a basic tenet of most existential therapies, as it was of Blatz's. Another implication in existential therapy is the emphasis on *presence*, meaning that the relationship of the therapist and patient is a real one. The therapist is not merely a shadowy reflector but an alive human being who happens, at that hour, to be concerned not with his own problems but with understanding and experiencing as far as possible the world as the patient sees it.[19] Blatz, in therapy as everywhere else, was always Blatz.

Counselling showed the upset person another side of Blatz than the one the world usually saw. Blatz the tease or Blatz the persistent arguer would be replaced by someone warm and humane and supportive. For example, he had been engaged in a running argument with a Toronto dentist about thumb-sucking, yet when the dentist's own daughter needed clinical counselling it was Blatz he sent her to for help.

Roger Myers of the psychology department said that, as far back as he could remember, if any members of the psychology staff got into any kind of trouble, either personal or financial, they would nearly always go to Blatz. 'The external view of Bill was someone sharp and witty with a cruel intelligence which would stick a knife in you, for he didn't suffer fools gladly. But if you were in trouble he would change immediately into the most humane, compassionate person imaginable. He was regarded as the person you could trust to be genuinely interested in your difficulties.'[20]

Another colleague remarks: 'Bill had a great ability, which always amazed me, of being familiar with people's very intimate concerns and yet having a good relationship and friendship with them.' He brought in a number of people to the institute 'as a way of helping them – perhaps temporarily – put them on a bit of research or got them some money for a project he wanted completed. It wasn't unusual for us to have at the institute a person who was one of his patients working quite normally with us on some piece of work.'[21]

In the same way Blatz worked closely with Clarence Hincks, both as colleague and clinician. Hincks was his senior, but when Hincks suffered his cyclical bouts of depression it was usually Blatz he turned to for counsel. 'The word was that one could always count on Bill Blatz to help you.'[22]

Blatz's therapy was usually quick and incisive. It focused on identifying the problem itself, clarifying alternate courses of action, and pushing towards a speedy resolution of the difficulties. Myers assessed his style thus: 'Blatz had a direct, dominating sharp wit along with clarity and confidence. He always knew what a patient should do. Sometimes it worked miracles. Sometimes it didn't work at all.'[23]

Millichamp had the opportunity to observe him quite closely:

He would certainly listen to them [the patients]. He'd ask incisive questions, not too many. It seems that the sorted out the problem in his own mind, using the security scheme as a basis, but he always thought in terms of the individuals and how an answer could be worked out for them. While his thinking was consistent, I never remember him using the same solution twice. His solutions were in terms of rational action. Therefore they weren't always successful because he counted on a rational person thinking things through with him. Where emotion was very pressing, sometimes the individual couldn't cope with the rationality. It usually involved that they make choices and decisions of a concrete kind. They had to become ready to take the consequences of their choices, he usually described what he thought the consequences would be. Then he helped them to make these choices, decisions, or, should I say, supported them in so doing. This took time and he would often talk with them over and over again, building their assurance and strength. Sometimes a solution was financial; or perhaps how to move out from the family; or getting care in for the children – very practical outcomes.[24]

Griffin has talked of the early days at Regal Road Public School where Blatz was conducting his early research. Frequently clinical problems would arise there:

He had a phenomenal memory and knowledge of virtually every family of children in that school. How did he get to know them with so little contact? Occasionally he would see a child or mother but compared with the kind of dogged clinical exposure most of us had been used to in learning the trade of psychiatry or psychology, Bill didn't do much of that. He was always able to size up a situation so quickly and reach a solution, a resolution of difficulties, a prescription of procedures which was so obviously sound. Brilliant at times. But whether it was sound or not wasn't important – the net result was that people were tremendously relieved and very much better. They were calmed and they felt some of the warmth and stability that Bill seemed to pass out. It would catch on them. They would feel better just by talking with Bill. A cold, distant analysis of the content of the prescription might be criticized – it would be today, but that was such an unimportant thing as far as Bill was concerned. It was the man, it was the human being, the sensitivity, his way with words, his way of relating to someone that was more important than anything else. With children and parents ... that's enough.[25]

Blatz was indeed always able to establish a strong rapport between his patient and himself. Just as the force of his personality seemed to act as a healing magic with injured veterans or with otherwise inconsolably frightened children, his charisma carried over to his psychotherapy.

Letters from patients substantiate this. A medical student wrote to Blatz: 'I look to you as the most enhancing person I have ever met. I hope you think me not a foolish child because I really want you to know how grateful you have made me. You told me to make a decision about school next year ...'[26]

Whether from a truck driver or a Havergal schoolgirl, whether on embossed stationery or scraps of lined paper, whether from Ontario or farther afield, the letters and comments from those he helped conveyed much the same message: 'You might not know how deeply I appreciate you: your patience, your purpose and your kindness.'[27] Or, 'How grateful I am to you for making me face up instead of dissolving into fragments.'[28]

A letter from Blatz to one young man may serve as an example of the way Blatz related to people. The young man was attending a professional school abroad when the school required him either to undergo intensive psychoanalysis or to furnish an informed opinion to the contrary.

The evaluation is forthright but, at the same time, positive and reassuring. Blatz wrote:

At last I am able to bring myself to write what to me is an extraordinarily courageous letter. In other words I am to put myself on record as testifying that you are sane. This is not too difficult for me perhaps because I consider that the limits of normalcy are rather widely spread.

To assume that you are in perfect mental health would be absurd. As a child you were quite timid with very sensitive vasomotor reactions. You could blush or pale at the drop of a hat. This shyness and this psychological reaction you gradually controlled. You developed a hostility towards your family, particularly your father, which was a reaction against a seeming neglect but was perhaps an exaggerated but subtle direction. Your relation with your siblings was perfectly normal as far as we know. The older siblings may have been a bit possessive but there was warmth in that relationship when you were a young boy.

There were, later in your adolescence, some homosexual trends which were not too rigid and as far as I know never overtly manifested.

In short I consider that you have mental health weaknesses which is a condition common to most of us although not in the same direction.

I was shocked to think they would consider it necessary for you to be psychoanalyzed and particularly that you should have to pay for it. Counselling and guidance of an understanding sort are always indicated but I would not consider you a great risk or that your deficiencies have ever interfered with your positive assets of enthusiasm, charm and friendliness.[29]

According to Atcheson, Blatz was often criticized because of his failure to apply major psychoanalytic principles or conform to a particular school of therapy: 'Bill Blatz practiced an art rather than a science and thus it was difficult to clarify how he did it. Whatever skills I have with patients I attribute to Blatz. He was sensitive. Concerned. Humanitarian. He gave freely of himself. Yet I can't use him as a teaching model for my psychiatric residents today. I can only hope that my students may pick up some of his qualities from me.'[30] Ordinarily Blatz made little direct use of his medical training and, in fact, was 'sometimes a little more than mildly hostile to the medical model.'[31] He advised Griffin, for instance, not to waste time as a medical intern but rather to get straight to work in psychology (advice that Griffin did not take). Griffin did complete his medical studies, then went on to psychiatry, and became chairman of the Canadian

Mental Health Association, which was reorganized out of Mental Hygiene after Hincks's death. Atcheson noted that Blatz rarely consulted in an appropriate way with other disciplines. He often took a controversial position that drew angry responses from colleagues. 'He was a rugged individualist and not diplomatic in the way he used his skills in relation to other medical professionals – and I say this with kindness and regret,' Atcheson has commented.[32]

On the other hand Blatz held his medical qualifications in reserve for the occasions when it seemed necessary to probe more deeply into the problems of a particularly ill person. He made it clear to paraprofessional counsellors that medical training was the only passport to travelling far into the lives of the extremely upset or disturbed. Psychologists on his staff were encouraged to work with people who had problems, but were to stop short of the pathological. 'Blatz always said there were some things only he could do because he was a medical doctor,' said Mary Northway.[33]

Blatz's own therapy was speedy and pragmatic, usually involving four progressive stages. First he would listen to the problem, which in effect usually meant encouraging the patients to listen to themselves. Then he would probe with questions about such areas of the person's life as vocational satisfaction, avocations, relationships with friends, associates, and family, and the person's overall philosophy of life. Next he would zero in on the problem and help the person to identify the central issues. Then would come a summary of the situation. Blatz would point to the alternative courses of action, with their possible consequences, and then say: 'It's up to you what you do.'[34]

To a woman who wrote from the west coast for advice he replied: 'I am sorry that I cannot give you any concrete advice by mail ... human affections are so unpredictable. Either you want to stay with your husband and take it on the chin or leave him and go your own way. You are the one who has to make the decision.'[35]

Making informed decisions was always basic to security in Blatz's view. His colleagues recall his saying: 'Most problems and nearly all mental illnesses, whatever the books call them, result from a person's unwillingness to make a decision. All the clinician can do is to help them see what the alternatives are, what the possible consequences of their actions will be, and then leave it up to them to decide. This is the only technique I know, and it works as long as the person has insight.'[36]

Indeed 'making decisions can be fun,' he wrote later. 'There is always tension ... The feeling of accomplishment that accompanies the final push can be exhilarating and at the same time relaxing.'[37]

During the time when a person is trying to gather data upon which to base a decision, Blatz would maintain that help could be sought from outside sources, such as from counsellors. 'They are mature agents if we ask them to tell us what we might expect. They are the sources of factual material.' Counsellors may frame the situation by pointing out the advantages and disadvantages of the various courses of action, but ultimately the choice is up to the person. If counsellors were to say, 'If I were you I would do such and such,' they would be assuming some of the person's own responsibility.[38]

For example, a patient wrote: 'I write once again to you, the conscience, for advice. This remark I hastily qualify by admitting that I know perfectly well that you will, rightly, decline to actually give me advice ... '[39]

On the contrary, however, some who observed Blatz's counselling remember that he did not hold back from giving his opinion. He was concise and pragmatic, often ending his sessions with a prescription for action. Mary Wright, for instance, has evaluated his clinical style as highly directive. He would say, in effect, 'Here's what could happen if you do this or that. So here's what you are going to do.'[40]

These apparently contradictory views of Blatz's willingness or unwillingness to allow the patient freedom of choice are not entirely irreconcilable. His therapy was usually characterized by speed. He would argue with people, if necessary, and sometimes left them feeling quite deflated when he gave them a rational explanation of their trouble and told them what they would need to do to help themselves. He would point out weaknesses that he himself accepted wholly in them, but that they could not as easily face in themselves. They might find it too uncomfortable to think of themselves with new insight, though Blatz was totally uncritical and still could respect them as upstanding people.

Very frequently he pointed out the essential thing that needed to be done and, following from this, what they had been avoiding. This could evoke tremendous conflict, for although they had been uncertain before, when Blatz pointed out the real issue they might be reluctant to tackle it.[41]

When Blatz appeared to be advocating a particular course of action, it was perhaps largely due to his essential practicality and confidence in his own judgments. When one set of consequences seemed clearly the most sensible, he could not resist tagging his own preference with an extra emphasis. The person would be left free to choose, it is true, but with a charismatic person like Blatz solidly backing his own favourite course of action, it would be difficult not to pick the winner.

In common with other humanistic therapists, Blatz worked towards developing positive mental health. Whereas Freudian therapy is based on a theory of mental disturbance and behaviour therapists work towards the absence of undesired behaviour, humanistic therapy places the emphasis upon developing an understanding of psychological health.[42] Many therapists of this type, particularly existentialists such as Allport, used such terms as 'self-actualizing' or 'becoming.' Carl Rogers, in the late 1950s, began to write of the fully functioning person. Blatz chose the concept of *security* as the central guiding principle, referring to mental health as a positive condition and not just the absence of disease.[43]

Blatz's picture of mental health develops new and additional facets in various stages of a person's life. In the first stages are strong ties with family; later comes the development of interests, then the acceptance of routine requirements, and, eventually, the development of a code of behaviour. Developmentally these stages appear in chronological sequence, but in the adult these four make up a large portion of the actions in a person's life. Adults are usually involved in social relations, in familial and extra-familial intimacies, in groups of an immediate or community nature, in such interests as hobbies, and in a job or profession. As well, they have formed ideas about such factors as authority, justice, and purpose in life. Everyone varies from time to time, and situation to situation, in the form of security or insecurity they show in relation to each of these areas.[44]

Blatz's questions in therapy focused on developing a picture of the person's adjustment in all these areas of life. The person was always considered in context. When a problem area became apparent, the emphasis would be on establishing some kind of harmony between the person and his environment. The patient would be expected to be active and in control of his decisions. Often it was a matter of attempting to establish stability through a self-arranged structure of times and places and developing enthusiasm through new hobbies and interests. 'I am trying to get more routine *and* interests in my life to prevent a recurrence,' one patient wrote.[45] Another recalled Blatz's advice to cut her work hours during convalescence in order to allow plenty of time for relaxation through the pursuit of leisure interests. For a colleague in a state of exhaustion the message came through quite clearly: she was to shorten her workday and establish priorities to make certain that her attention was given only to the most significant tasks. The rest could wait.

For some patients the focus of attention was on interpersonal relationships, such as 'the problems that concern some of the old questions that crop up in marriages – ones that need talking over with wise but not prejudicial seniors.'[46]

'Psychiatrists ... have invented innumerable names and nomenclature for ... states of disability and then proceeded to cure them more or less successfully, largely because in many cases, if not interfered with too much the condition is self-limiting.'[47] In the final analysis, though, Blatz considered the curing of people with mental illness very much an art and refused to label or develop a systematic method of psychotherapy. He was always highly intuitive, Millichamp comments. Whatever ancillary devices might be employed, the impact of the personality of the 'curer' (the existential therapists referred to it as 'presence') was still a highly significant factor, Blatz wrote in an article on 'Curing and Preventing' for the institute *Bulletin*.

Today the people whom Blatz counselled remember just that: a charismatic, sensitive person who could help people frame their problems and find solutions but whose methods defied systematic analysis or replication by others.

In 1939, war was approaching and Blatz frequently was engaged in trying to help people sort out their feelings about their role in it. He began work on *Hostages to Peace*, written as a series of letters to his cousin and her family in the United States. His mother, Victoria, was eighty-three when the war began, and it was the sixth war during her lifetime in which someone close to her was involved. 'I cannot think of anything more tragic than a memory such as this,' Blatz wrote.[48]

Blatz outlined his plan of child raising, discussing needs, appetites, emotions, choices, and consequences in terms of preparing people to live in a democracy. The plan was designed first to protect children 'against the unnecessary and hence avoidable consequences of the state of war, and secondly [to] raise a generation of children who would so arrange their own social customs that war would be eliminated as a device for solving problems.'[49] Anger and fear, he said, are easily turned to hatred of whole groups of people – those who happened to be born in another part of the world – and mislabelled patriotism when they really reflect only prejudice. He thought emotion might be more sensibly expended in the direction of enthusiasm for one's ideas and their defence.

He devoted several pages to the security theory under the title 'The Beginning of Wisdom.' Security, he declared boldly, was the only healthy goal in life, while safety was dangerous. Although insecurity made for progress, if people did not accept its challenges, they would need to adopt some form of compensation. 'These compensatory mechanisms are the root of all social turbulences, of which war is the most disgraceful and unnecessary.'[50]

By developing a pattern of behaviour with security as its goal, Blatz predicted that children, even in war or the war zone, should be able to cope with the horror and destruction of bombing without serious mental harm. The example of the parents and the general morale of the community would make the difference. He fell to musing about the recent removal of some million and a half people from target areas in Britain to what were presumed to be areas of refuge in other parts of the country. If the evacuation of children in England was carried on calmly and efficiently then probably no harm would follow. But if it were an 'inefficient social pilgrimage' with confusion and undue emotional excitement, it might be more harmful than bombing.[51] (Very recently one of the survivors of the upheaval of wartime, Ben Wicks, traced the after-effects of that social pilgrimage on the lives of young British children in his book *No Time to Wave Goodbye*. It was just as Blatz foresaw: for a few children the organization worked well enough and little apparent harm followed. But for countless others the confusion and emotional distress were, in their way, more damaging to the children than enemy air raids might have been.)[52] For Blatz the surroundings of a child during and after a crisis would be more significant than the character of the crisis itself. Even in war, he wrote, sanity is possible. The most important effort, however, should be directed towards 'training our children to avoid war. It may take three generations to accomplish this task, but after all, one of our aims in living is to afford our children, through intelligent education, an opportunity for a fuller life than we ourselves enjoy.'[53]

He ended the book prophetically enough with these words: 'We are at war – and I may have urgent duties to perform.' As indeed he did.

# 8 The Nursery Overseas

The years of the Second World War were busy ones for Blatz. He was active both at home and abroad. This time he was not rejected for service outside Canada. Quite the contrary: he was invited to do a special job for Canada to assist Britain's war effort. At the same time, in Canada he provided the expertise for organizing day nurseries for the children of factory workers. He also completed the last two major publications of his lifetime. (His next book [after *Hostages to Peace*], a definitive statement of his theory and overall philosophy, was published posthumously some twenty years later.) In fact his publication history mirrored other aspects of his public career, reaching its productive peak during the war years and then simmering quietly for the next two decades.

At the beginning of the war, Blatz was still largely regarded as an outrageous, youngish rebel. At forty-three he was working at full energy and was very much embroiled in whatever was new and controversial. During the war he was in the thick of current concerns: military morale, wartime day-care in the United Kingdom and Canada, and post-war planning. He was known as 'Doctor Blatz,' a sensible and responsible citizen, still innovative and witty and an excellent person to communicate important messages. He could still surprise and shock, but he no longer needed to do so to gain attention, for usually he already had an audience. His accomplishments were solid ones, useful and innovative in themselves, but also a verification of his theories and earlier work.

As Canada's major expert in organizing the lives of children, Blatz was invited to play a special wartime role overseas on behalf of Canada: at the specific request of Canada's high commissioner in the United Kingdom, the Honourable Vincent Massey, Blatz was sent to Great Britain in 1942 as an adviser on child care as part of Canada's contribution to the war effort. Blatz and his colleagues who formed the Canadian Children's Services (CCS) saw their overall task as helping the adjustment of young children to the particular problems of wartime. Blatz's own responsibility was to set up a training centre for day-care supervisors. In turn they would fan out to set up day nurseries for the children of war workers. Along the way Blatz gave lectures on morale and counselling methods to Canadian troops training in Britain and also found time for a series of BBC broadcasts on methods of child raising. His work acquired a new dimension, too, for at home in Canada he was largely responsible for the organization of wartime day nurseries, and later for drafting the post-war Ontario day-care legislation, the first in Canada.

Britain had first experienced the bombing of civilian targets towards the end of the First World War when German airplanes and Zeppelins attacked London. The experience had made such a great impression that planning for future emergencies focused on ways of avoiding the devastation of the civilian population by air bombardment. It was generally assumed that most of the population would be killed, shell-shocked, or reduced to panic during air raids. Even before the Second World War broke out, plans were made to move mothers and children from the cities to less populated areas and away from the danger of bombing. In the first days of the war, arrangements were enough advanced to evacuate a million and a half people from the cities that were most likely to become targets. It was actually a year before the bombers came,[1] and by then some of the effects of dislocation had begun to take their social and emotional toll.

In the spring of 1941 Ned Bott, who was serving with the RAF in Britain, met with the chief medical officer to the British Ministry of Health, Sir Wilson Jameson, to discuss some of the urgent problems of child care that had resulted from evacuation. Perhaps Canada could be of some help.

The first step in the plan would be to send two or three experts in mental health to assess the problems and make recommendations. These experts would study the adjustment of children in reception areas, residential settings, day nurseries, hostels, and evacuated areas. Their general aim would be to conduct research into the cause and effect of problems brought on by mass bombings and to look at the aid Canada could give in caring for children who had been forcibly evacuated from the larger cities.

It was logical to send the director of the Canadian National Committee for Mental Hygiene (as someone who would be in a position to make policy decisions), along with a prominent social worker, and, of course, Canada's own well-known expert on children. Once again Bott played a major role in shaping the direction of Blatz's life by setting aside the recent coolness that had arisen between them and suggesting that Blatz would be an essential member of the team.

In the late autumn of 1941, Blatz, Clarence Hincks, and Stuart Jaffary of the University of Toronto School of Social Work set sail for England as the only civilian passengers travelling in a convoy of fifty freighters. En route they battled a hurricane, a snowstorm, and dangerous moonlit nights when the convoy was particularly vulnerable. The only calamities they suffered, however, were a cracked rib for Blatz, gained when a piece of heavy furniture broke loose in the storm, and the loss of Hincks's valise of medical prescriptions. He had packed enough in the way of pills to guide him through the worst effects of a possible high or low in his manic-depressive disorder. The bag was lost en route and Hincks managed the trip on a combination of his own resources and Blatz's pragmatic psychiatry. Blatz used the event to reinforce the idea that Hincks could manage at least as well without the pills as with them.

When they reached London the three men set about investigating their own spheres of interest. Blatz visited day-care centres and also met with Lady Allen of Hurtwood, head of the Nursery School Association of England. Nursery schools had been established in England some thirty years before when Margaret McMillan started open-air centres in the slums of London in an effort to improve the health of pre-school children. There was already a well-developed interest in pre-school education in Great Britain, but the wartime pressures of providing day-care for the children of factory workers meant that people trained to work with children were in short supply.

It soon became evident that Canada could effectively provide three main types of support: elementary school teachers with knowledge of mental health principles to work in London schools with children who were subject to the stress of the bombing raids; psychiatric social workers to assist in the supervision of children evacuated into reception areas; and nursery school teachers from the University of Toronto who would organize and staff a training centre somewhere in England to prepare British child-care reservists to staff the emergency wartime nurseries. Canada would pay their expenses, and Britain would pay them a salary as teachers.

Thus was born the Canadian Children's Services. It was to see a wartime involvement in British schools and social work agencies, and, as Blatz's particular responsibility, the training of some 850 supervisors for day-care centres.

Hincks and Jaffary returned to Toronto in January 1942 to work out details of the plans. At the last minute Blatz was asked to stay behind to prepare a pamphlet on morale and to lecture to Canadian military officers in England on ways of maintaining and fortifying the morale of their troops. Hincks telegraphed to the university asking that Blatz be granted a further leave of absence to do this and to enter active war work.

The pamphlet on morale emphasized the need for officers to attempt to understand each man in their units, to listen carefully to their concerns, and to build up in each one a healthy attitude of self-respect. Officers should plan for the satisfaction of physiological appetites and help the soldier express fear and anger in healthy ways.

The officer's task would be twofold: to *train* his men and to *know* his men. Efficient soldiers must have both skill and morale, for skill without morale is futile, though morale with little skill has often won victories. The morale of the group is only a reflection of the morale of the individuals within it. The officer may drill his men and teach military skills, but he can only know the group by understanding the man. He learns this slowly and patiently by living with his soldiers, observing them, and protecting them. It is necessary to be aware if a man is getting little or no mail and to be alert to such danger signs as insomnia, loss of appetite, restlessness, or undue quietness. 'A man who is worried, fed-up, disgruntled, suspicious or lazy decreases the efficiency of the unit ... The junior officer should consider morale his major duty.'[2] The officer's responsibility to his men is, however, more akin to that of a parent than to that of a clinician. He can give sympathetic understanding in group and individual counselling, but if the problems are severe a trained person should be consulted.[3]

In England, too, Blatz managed to stir up little storms. The Honourable Walter Gordon, who had a distinguished career as chairman of the Royal Commission on Canada's economic prospects, was a strong Canadian nationalist, a prominent Bay Street business-man, and also a close friend of Blatz. Gordon used to delight in de-scribing how Blatz managed to shock 'a lot of the generals and brass hats' by recommending masturbation as an outlet for the soldiers' sexual frustrations. This was at a time when cold showers and vigorous exercise were the standard methods recommended for sublimating sexual appetites. 'The generals just about nearly had a fit. Of course the troops were probably doing it anyway.'[4]

When he returned to Toronto in March 1942, Blatz was kept busy lecturing on Britain and its children. The general thrust of his talks was that the British people were concentrating their efforts on the health and education of the children. Worry was recognized as a greater peril than the blitz itself, and civilian morale was boosted by the knowledge that children would be given every possible chance to de-velop their potential. The wartime state had intervened to ensure an equitable distribution of health care, food, and education. Emergency nursery schools had been set up to care for the children of the in-creasingly large number of women in war industries. Blatz would quote the British minister of labour, Ernest Bevin, as saying, 'I do not suppose anyone in this country thought, before the war, that a nursery school would be an essential part of our defence programme.' It was here that Blatz could offer Canadian assistance.[5]

'Nursery schools in bombed areas proved a failure,' he said, 'be-cause the children grew restive and noisy. Soon all such schools were moved into evacuated areas. Today [1942] the greatest number of children in any one school is 40. Under ideal conditions there should be three or four trained attendants. That would mean from 8,000 to 10,000 trained personnel are needed. Actually only from 400 to 450 are available.'[6]

The need for trained nursery workers was a challenge Canadians could help to meet, he told his audiences. As part of the Canadian Children's Services, Blatz would set up a model school for children near a large Midlands city to instruct teachers in pre-school educa-tion. As far as the training of the children themselves was concerned, there would be no change from the system in use at the Institute of Child Study, Mary Dale Moore reported in the May 1942 issue of the *University News*. 'Dr. Blatz is convinced that the training best suited to carry the individual through a normal life is also the best training to carry him through an abnormal life. The aim is to "develop in children an attitude in life that will carry them through any emergency and any responsibility." '

The London *Times* had reported in January that Blatz would return to England with two to three hundred Canadian nurses specifically trained in child psychology.[7] In fact, Blatz initially restricted his choice to three of his closest colleagues in the pre-school field and two of his former students. The colleagues were Margaret Fletcher, Dorothy Millichamp, and Anne Harris, who had all worked with him in the quintuplets' nursery. They were joined by former students Mary McFarland, director of the Manor Road Nursery School in Toronto, and Mary Wright from the staff of the Protestant Children's Village in Ottawa.

Wright was a graduate student in psychology who had become fascinated by the institute's nursery school. After Margaret Fletcher taught her the rudiments of working with children, Wright spent every spare moment of her student days in the St George's nursery. It also happened that she was a talented pianist who had the knack of following the children's lead. She was young, but her skills at developmental testing, coupled with her musical abilities, made her a strong choice for the group. Fletcher was convinced that music would be one of the most effective ways to communicate with the children and win their trust. That had been the case when the music program from the St George's School was applied to the work in the Dionne nursery; presumably it would work the same magic in the slums of Birmingham.

'The philosophy of discipline is the first thing the future assistants will learn in the course,' Blatz told the *Globe and Mail*. 'They will be taught to deal with childish fears, temper tantrums, the social development of the child, control of aggressiveness and shyness and how to influence the child's attitude towards his fellows.' The newspaper speculated that the model school would contain many of the features of the Dionne quintuplets' nursery, including a 'one-way screen' that would enable students to watch children without being seen. Training methods, no doubt, would match those used on the quints.

> The Canadian assistance, which Chuter Ede, Parliamentary Secretary of the Board of Education, said will be 'among the most valuable we shall receive' comes at a time when Britain's nursery system is being vigorously criticized.
> Lady Allen of [H]urtwood, chairman of the Emergency Nursing

Centre Committee, declared Britain's wartime nurseries are in a 'colossal muddle,' and Lord Nathan, who was pressed in the House of Lords for improvements, said he received many letters protesting about the Government's 'slothfulness' in the matter.

Many mothers are declining to take up war work because of the shortage of nurseries where they can leave their children and the lack of trained assistants. Dr. Blatz' school is expected to help remedy the situation.[8]

In May 1942, Blatz and his little group set off by train for Halifax, en route to England, with twenty-six pieces of baggage and high hopes.

The Canadian Children's Services had a job to do and, despite the raggle-taggle collection of bags and trunks and boxes that accompanied them, the members themselves looked highly business-like. Although Blatz himself was not in uniform, he was, as always, dressed in a meticulously tailored three-piece suit with a high starched collar and the inevitable bow-tie.

The women wore quasi-military dress – airforce blue suits with matching greatcoats, laced-up oxfords, gloves, pork-pie hats, and tailored white blouses left unbuttoned at the throat. In London Mrs Vincent Massey undertook to provide them all with ties from Harrod's to complete the ensemble.

The trans-Atlantic voyage was, in Blatz's words, 'uneventful, remarkably rapid, wonderfully smooth with good meals and comfortable beds.'

In Birmingham the women were billeted with the Cadbury family (of chocolate fame) in their country estate four miles from the centre of town. Blatz stayed in a local inn. (Although he and Anne Harris were 'very close to each other they were also always discreet and never did anything to embarrass the others.')[9]

The Cadburys' welcome to the Canadians was less than enthusiastic. Their country house had been pressed into wartime service to accommodate such visitors as the nursery school contingent. The Cadburys were careful to see that obligations were met, and were conscientious about providing an excellent air-raid shelter, but their responsibility did not extend as far as hospitality. Margaret Fletcher said they were the only people they met in England who remained chilly and unhelpful. The young women paid a healthy slice of their salaries for room and board, and although this brought such privileges as sitting at the grand dining-table with the Cadburys, the

Canadians were served very basic meals, while the Cadburys reserved special treats for themselves.[10]

Upon their arrival in Birmingham the Canadians were driven in corporation cars, with the chief of staff of the Department of Education and the chief architect, to catch their first glimpse of what was soon to be named Garrison Lane Nursery Training School.

> Through the centre of town, out through the blitzed areas we rode into the slums of Birmingham. Having seen it before I was not as depressed as the staff, whose faces were growing longer and longer, but, having entered the school and seen the miracle that had been wrought within the outer shell of what looked like a medieval monastery, hope was not only restored but reached a pitch that never afterwards faltered.
>
> The photographs that you will get soon, we hope, will only inadequately show what a wonderful job Mr Benslin, the architect, had done. We have seldom if ever seen a reconstruction project so successful with so unpromising a prospect to begin with. Our first comments were to the effect that we would like to take the whole thing back with us to Canada (Margaret dissenting but I think wholly on sentimental grounds). The first blush of splendour never entirely disappeared but after walking through the empty halls we began to ask about equipment.[11]

The equipment they had purchased in Toronto, sent through the Imperial Order Daughters of the Empire (IODE) to the Women's Volunteer Service, had not arrived. Mary Wright soon discovered four pianos, however, although closer scrutiny disclosed that they were all of mid-Victorian vintage. Also, the interior fittings of Garrison Lane School (which had served as an elementary school prior to the blitz) had been torn out and stored under the open sheds in the back of the playground. They were told that they could have anything they liked from this 'junk heap' of cupboards, tables, chairs, benches, desks, rulers, blackboards, ink-wells, potato slicers, maps, and other school leftovers.

> Our first reaction was one of lofty disdain but we hadn't reckoned on [the ingenuity of] Dore and Margaret. By this time the weather had turned as cold as a drip on the end of a dowager's nose and quite as damp and so we wandered through the school and found ourselves in a tower room about 8' x 10' under the eaves which had been the

previous headmasters [sic] retreat. This room had an open fire place, so we cadged some coal from the janitor (a Mr Coy in name and personality), and there we sat on rickety chairs salvaged from the junk heap and pondered. There we were, a bright little band, wondering how in Hell we were going to run a Nursery School without equipment. This late, cold, damp, dreary Saturday afternoon was the nadir of our trip.

In the first few days they were almost in despair, but Monday dawned all too soon and a period of frantic effort followed their disconsolate weekend.

First the junk heap was attacked. Through an oversight the painters had been left on the job. A pot of paint to Margaret is like a red rag to a bull. Soon out of the junk heap, which had turned into a virtual Alladin's [sic] Cave, came boxes, table drawers, cupboards, bookcases, casters, tables, chairs, all sorted out, all painted up and all reinstalled into the school from which they had been so recently ignominiously ejected. But their previous users would never have recognized them. Then, with the cooperation of the local authorities, we began to shift, shop, beg and cadge. Everything was grist to our mill. Soon equipment began to arrive, small chairs, nests of tables, dust bins, cups, towels, nail brushes. All of which had to be counted, signed in triplicate and later on entered in the book.

They met inspectors of districts, inspectors of students, inspectors of nursery classes, inspectors of British restaurants, inspectors of domestic subjects, inspectors of plumbing, and inspectors of music. 'They all came to see and remained to give. We took everything sight unseen, some when it arrived was weird and wonderful but the school began to fill up.'

They found a puzzling arrangement of transport facilities in Birmingham. On the west side of town were the homes of the well-to-do, on the east side were the slums. All tram lines radiated to the centre of town; none crossed town. Apparently people on the west side never visited those on the east side. 'From Primrose Hill a #71 tram takes you to Navigation St at which point you alight, trudge across town and take a #91 tram at Albert St, which in due course jostles you to Garrison Lane School – 55 min. with or without profanity. By taking a shorter route and some buses which no-one in Birmingham had up to now even discovered, Margaret discovered that you could do it in 65 min. I can testify to this because on one occasion she took me on a self-conducted tour, this spirit of exploration epitomizes our attitude from this point on.' (Later, through the combined efforts of Sir Wilson Jameson, the Dowager Lady Reading, His Majesty's inspector, and the senior regional officer, they were able to have a car and a ration of gasoline allotted to transport the five teachers from Primrose Hill to the school each morning.)

Blatz had been to London to meet the director of education and his staff. They were instructed that they were to give courses to child-care reserve students and later to more advanced pupils. Blatz was shown a copy of the curriculum but advised that it was still, inexplicably, a secret. Blatz was asked when they would be ready to begin. He had no idea but gave an arbitrary date of 1 July, then returned to Birmingham and informed the staff that the school's opening was set. The race was on.

There was no equipment and no sign of a library. Neither were there any nursery school children. They therefore decided that they should go to London to meet the Canadian high commissioner. 'So on Tuesday morning at 8:00 we gathered in the station to catch an 8:40 train with *five* pieces of baggage. Because the girls were in uniform we got special rates at the Park Lane. That evening Colonels Rae and Lemeseurer supplied a military escort and we attended the theatre to be entertained afterwards in their flat with a late supper. ("It is *fresh* lobster," said Dore).'

They were also entertained at the Dorchester Hotel by Mr and Mrs Vincent Massey.

> Nothing could have exceeded the warmth of their welcome, especially when Mrs Massey recognized Margaret as an old friend ... After each of the girls had modelled her uniform Mrs Massey decided that ties were in order, saying that this slight amendment was all that was needed to place these uniforms as tops in England. She was more than delighted with their trimness, cut and design.
>
> As none of us had our clothes coupons there was a great scurrying and planning and it was only after Mr Ignatiev [*sic*: George Ignatieff] had used the high prestige of the Commissioner's office and an exquisite use of his inimitable diplomacy, that coupons appeared in the offing and Harrod's were persuaded to part with five ties for the trifling sum of £1 / 10 / 6. Margaret, waiting in Harrod's for the

coupons to be delivered from Canada House, spent her time riding up and down on the escalators. She says it was the most restful half hour she spent in England, to date.

In the afternoon the high spot of their visit to London occurred: their official reception by the Canadian high commissioner, with photographers and press in attendance. In his lofty office, Mr and Mrs Massey and Blatz with his five teachers gathered on a chesterfield and were photographed, then clustered about the globe for a more informal shot. Then Mr Massey said, 'Admit the press' and in walked twenty-five journalists. The parliamentary under-secretary for education, acting for Mr Butler, read a prepared statement giving high praise to Hincks's efforts in helping Britain in its hour of need. Blatz gave the reply. Then Sir Wilson and the high commissioner commented briefly, before the questions began about Canada and child study and plans for nursery day-care in wartime Britain. It was an impressive and stimulating ceremony, enough to buoy up their spirits for Birmingham and what awaited them there.

One pleasant surprise was the discovery that at last their lost trunks had miraculously appeared.

The next morning Blatz and Millichamp started to interview parents and children who had been sent to them by the headmistress of Tilton Road School. Garrison Lane was an administrative appendage of Tilton Road, which they had visited prior to the London excursion. It was one of the group of schools whose nursery and infant classes they continued to visit in the midst of their duties at Garrison Lane.

> While this interviewing was going on Margaret, Anne and the Marys were acting as janitors, painters, dress makers, nav[v]ies, plumbers, chars, all over the school. Anne was snatching chairs from under the mothers and substituting those that had been painted, Margaret was discovered completely under the junk pile and the two Marys were turning tin saucers, inkwells etc. into sand box toys.
>
> This went on for two days, Sunday dawned, our equipment hadn't come, no symbols for the children's cupboards were available in all of Birmingham. We all turned in to make 120 pictures, with Anne filling in my artistic outlines. In the meantime the first timetable was born. Monday morning the temperature rose (I am not referring to the weather), more mothers, more children, more junk, more scrubbing, more arranging and more confusion. Drawers from old cupboards

painted green were our outdoor blocks, a consignment of two slides,
three wagons and a truck were sent by His Majesty's Inspector having
been manufactured in the manual training class under his jurisdiction. The sand box had been designed but hadn't appeared, 'the
garden' was a wide treeless expanse of pavement opening directly
upon the street and with a hundred-ton reserve coal heap at one side
– the junk heap forming a fitting background in the rear.

July 1st loomed in the immediate future.

Twenty children were scheduled to appear at 9:00 Wednesday
morning – our equipment hadn't arrived and so I went to Mr Cousens
and obtained an order on the Midland Educational Supply Co to see
what we could glean from their depleted stock. Tuesday morning at
10:00 Margaret, Anne and I shopped from cellar to attic, from counter
and walls, in two hours, leaving behind us one saleslady with bronchi-
tis in neurotic despair and one sales manager in utter bewilderment.
We left the store with a suitcase in my arms, Anne hidden behind a
huge package and Margaret clearing the way with a hobby horse, and
we still had time for 'elevenses' at Barrows Emporium.

That afternoon we arranged the school and a curious quiet per-
vaded the atmosphere, we were all thinking of what the morrow was
to bring. Here we were, a group of Canadians in a British slum, to be
sure we had seen the parents and the children, but some of our
interviews did very little to assuage our apprehension. Friendlyness
and a spirit of cooperation were manifested; poverty, grimyness and a
curious submissiveness were all too evident.

On Wednesday, 1 July 1942, the doors were opened to the first
training school staffed entirely by Canadians in the British Isles. The
first to arrive was Mrs Yapp, with Alan, aged two, and Gwyneth, his
sister, aged three-and-a-half.

Bright smiling faces somewhat obscured by Mother Earth and a little
awed by the bright surroundings, the illimitable space and the bright
(to them) array of toys. The entry was a good omen because as the
others arrived, tears and shrieks alternated with grim silence and
pathetic tears – the routine was begun.

Through the French doors into the garden trooped the group,
immediately to disappear like quick-silver into every nook
and cranny, every gate was explored, every door opened. Where is
Eileen? Where is George or Brian? Who is that disappearing down

the man-hole? How many are there, I have only got eleven?

For once the time table was ignored. 'Let's get them in,' said Margaret. Fortunately the count tallied, the doors closed and the construction squad roped in a part of the playground with an ash can, two pole vaulting standards and a bench as posts.

The news had apparently gone far and wide, in the midst of soothing Margaret, changing Alan, rescuing Edith, the visitors began to arrive – Inspectors, Supervisors, the electrician, Public Health officials and Lady Reading. Furthermore to add to the intensity of the day, just as the children were saying grace, the sirens started with their agonized screech. Everyone was calm. 'Carry on,' was the watchword. (We learned later that this was the practise.) By the way there is a well equipped air raid shelter in the building.

One expedient rearrangement of the routine did not mean giving up a principle. The school carried on, through Lunch where perhaps for the first time in their lives most of these children sat down to eat; through sleeping, where for the first time these children slept in a bed alone; through the washroom, where for the first time these children were in a bathroom which was under the same roof under which they lived, through outdoor play with a sentry at every standard; through tea which in their homes was only 'a piece' and through to 6:30 when the last child was sorted out and delivered to its parent. I don't think a N.S. [nursery school] staff has ever accomplished a task so successfully as I witnessed that day. I have never been so proud of a group, nor has there ever been as eloquent a justification for the choice of staff for this venture.

An exhausted group gathered in the waiting room and heaved a sigh of relief, not only because of a day well spent but it was apparent that children are the same whether in Toronto or Birmingham and that the methods of Child Training are universal.

Eight more children arrived Thursday morning and eight more Friday. The Canadians were amazed at how quickly the children adjusted to the serenity of nursery techniques.

The staff were working like clock work, the system worked, routine settled in, visitors kept coming in a steady stream, the Supervisors of N.S. under Margaret's watchful eye violated every principle of child training. Mary W. at the untuned piano was magnificent. I thought she was playing the *Reel of Tullock*, but the children were singing,

> *Baa Baa Black Sheep.* One of the workmen was astonished when he
> claimed to recognize the *Third Internationale.* But this problem was
> only transitory because on Friday appeared the most friendly piano
> tuner, who not only tuned the pianos but took over the playroom. Alan
> was just saved from being strangled by the strings below.

In the meantime Blatz and the teachers plundered the junk pile
for twenty old school desks and arranged them around the playground
to create a 'fence' more stable than the rope barrier, which had been
carried away several times by the wind. There was further excitement
when a parent, a neighbour of one of the absentees of the day, casually
remarked that she believed the sick child had been brought down with
diphtheria. Blatz immediately phoned the medical officer of health,
and the school doctor arrived during naptime. She was quite astonished when Blatz refused to awaken the children to have their throats
swabbed. 'Never before had a nursery school authority defied the on-
slaught of health,' Blatz wrote in triumph.

> She returned later with the piano tuner, the one operated in the
> playroom and the other in the washroom. We were agreeably sur-
> prised to discover that Dr Beaumont swabbed the throats of all the
> children in a half hour with a technique and exhibition of human
> understanding of children that we have never seen bettered.
>   The parents, in the meanwhile, waited for their children in the
> waiting room. The piano tuner still tuned in the playroom and the
> electrician was knocking a hole through an 18" wall to make an outlet
> for our iron. In the midst of this in walked Lady Reading with some
> Regional Officers and HM Inspector. After this we knew that nothing
> could phase [*sic*] us.

The weekend was a further scramble, for Monday was to see the
opening of the training school. Interviews with the education department and the health department elicited the information that forty
child-care reserve students were to appear at the door on Monday
morning at 9:30. The children and their Canadian teachers were reasonably well settled in the school, but there were no library books, no
chairs, and no course outlines for the students.

Saturday and Sunday were spent in revising the curriculum. In
its secret document the Board of Education had included one hour on
anatomy, one hour on physiology, one hour on infectious diseases, and

one on the chemistry of nutrition. Blatz managed to persuade Sir Wilson that this might be over-ambitious, and they substituted ten hours of systematic child psychology instead.

The forty students were divided into five groups of eight; each group observed through the screens for part of every routine, while the other groups participated in the activities. Lectures were given by Blatz and Millichamp from 1:15 to 2:45, and each member of the staff in turn conducted a seminar for each group separately from 4:00 to 4:30. They had been given a list of those whose applications for training had been accepted and were a little dismayed to find not only a range of chronological age from nineteen to fifty-three but also of education (from indeterminate to secondary school leaving).

All day Sunday the Canadians concocted signs to post around the school in an effort to help the new students find their way about. Monday morning some of the students were on the doorstep before the staff arrived. Blatz and Harris, with thumbtacks, scurried through the school posting the signs. At 9:30 Blatz and Millichamp met the group for the first time. The chairs had still not arrived, and the blackboards had been recently so well renovated that it was impossible to write on them. However, what the group perhaps lacked in formal training and chic they made up in zeal, interest, and appreciation, Blatz told Hincks.

The staff received word that all the swabs had been negative for diphtheria, but Blatz took advantage of the apparent crisis to get from each parent a signed statement allowing each child to be immunized against it. This was no routine accomplishment, because such preventive measures were still often regarded with suspicion.

Blatz wrote further:

> Even in this short time the children were learning Canadian and we were learning Birminghamese. One of the mothers came to the door and I asked her for whom she was calling and, after three repetitions, all I could understand was, 'Aged Robinson,' and I came in and asked Mary McF. for this child. After going through the list we decided it might be 'Edith Plumpton,' and it was.
>
> If the children asked us questions we usually assented by saying, 'Yes, yes' without understanding and then watched to see what they would do. Margaret went through this formula with one child, during music circle, and noticed the child had wandered off to return shortly. She didn't know what had happened. After, in the seminar, one of the

students asked Margaret if she permitted vulgarisms, Margaret said she had forgotten the incident, what was it? The student replied that the child had asked, 'Please teacher, can I piddle?' Margaret passed it off in masterful manner by stating that in a new environment we permitted old associations for a few times at least!! On another occasion I was sitting in the Senior Playroom at 3:30 and seeing the milk tray approaching said, 'Here comes the milk.' Immediately Gwyneth said 'willeefitchmemoog' and dashed out of the door with me after her, when I discovered that she in a helpful spirit went to bring her mug from the washroom to the playroom. She was a little astonished to find we had mugs in both places and that she was entitled to both.

All the students had spent some time in day nurseries or residential nurseries, and there were several aspects of Blatz's system of child care that drew their comments. Above all they were impressed by the insistence on serenity, and with it the adherence to the routine of the day, so that, once the children learned, they were secure in their adjustment. Among other points that interested them were the quiet but pleasant atmosphere at meals, the relative ease of creating an atmosphere conducive to sleep in the afternoon, and the rest period before dinner. They were surprised at how the playrooms were arranged to reduce adult interference by keeping the children so busy that adult entertainment was unnecessary. (This was the area that the Canadians found to be the most difficult in training adults, just as had been the case in the Dionne nursery.) The students also commented on the fact that the routine in the washroom was business-like and discouraged play. Two other points they noted were the replacement of sentiment by discipline and understanding and the total elimination of corporal punishment of any sort.

Blatz sent the list of students' comments to Hincks with the addition of two observations of his own:

First, English N.S. training is heavily loaded with sentiment, often nauseating e.g. at one N.S. we visited the head teacher asked in a high piping voice, 'Who's going to be my little gnome and who's going to be my little spider and who is going to be my little aspidistra?' Secondly, perhaps following on the first, is their insensate emphasis that 'children love flowers.' The only attention we have paid to this cultural myth is that, in so far as you can't grow flowers in concrete,

we asked for a flower bed and when they asked for the size we said
40 x 30 feet which astonished them a bit until we suggested that
we were going to put our jungle gym on a little turf (English for sod)
and that a little turf would enhan[c]e the beauty of the flowers in
the border.

Within a week or two the routine of the school had settled down,
the full quota of children had been registered, and attendance was in
the neighbourhood of thirty-two to thirty-five a day. The students had
entered into the spirit of the course and were responding with an
alacrity that exceeded the hopes of Blatz and his teachers.

The staff had been working from 8:30 a.m. to 6:30 p.m., as well as
evenings and weekends, organizing, arranging, discussing, and planning. After they had caught their breath, they realized two things.
First, that they had to study the background of the children and their
parents; second, that their immediate concern was the physical state
of the children.

It was by design that Blatz had selected Garrison Lane from the
number of schools offered to him on his first wartime trip to England.
'It was my intention that we could demonstrate the success of our
venture in one of the most unpropitious areas in all England,' he explained to Hincks.

English slums are peculiar and indigenous. The very architecture
smacks of the thoughtlessness and heartlessness of mid-Victorian
industrialism, succeeding generations have lived in physical surroundings that defy description. The blitz fortunately has obliterated
some, the reclaiming of these prior to the war was to my mind only a
half hearted gesture of expiation. We intend to make a complete social
survey of the families attending the school. I need only mention one at
this point. Two of the children, brother and sister, were so obviously
infested that before other than expedient measures could be adopted
Doctor Beaumont and myself visited the home. The family consisted
of the grandfather, mother and father and three children under five.
They live in three rooms in a blitz block of slum houses. The kitchen
and dining room combined are on one side of a bricked paved court,
slimy with refuse, across the court are two bedrooms, in the lower
floor of a partly blitz section but which must have, prior to the war
been very little different. The grandfather sleeps in a small anti
chamber [sic] and all five of the others sleep in a double bed and a

small cot. There is no room for other furniture, the windows are
boarded up, one can only see by artificial light. The sanitary facilities
are across the court 40' away. In rainy weather the sewage oozes up
from an open drain outside the kitchen. It was obvious, with the
sleeping arrangements as they were, infestation could only be coped
with by a general cleansing. This was done by the mother reporting at
the school, after hours, and the nurse staying overtime and applying
the requisite remedies. This aspect of our work was one which we had
approached with a good deal of apprehension. We were not unaware
that we would meet with members of our nominal role who had not
applied for admission. One lives and learns. The poignant appeal of
these children who, but by the grace of economic destiny, would be
attending St George's School makes itself felt.

Strange as it may seem the first days of school were spent by the
staff in building up a friendly and solid relationship without any
thought of contamination. Holding the children in their arms,
combing their hair, attending to their physical wants without the
least feeling of hesitation or disgust. Even [when] on the first Friday
the nurse announced undoubted signs of head lice, scabies and nits, I
didn't notice a shudder in the staff. To be sure there were some jocular
interpretations of the odd itching which in Canada would pass
unnoticed, but the consuming urge was rather that we should do
everything that we could, to alleviate a condition, which even after
three generations, could not be other than uncomfortable.

I wish I could bring back to Canada a sample of the underwear
which these children wear. In its present state it would have to be
hermetically sealed, if we were to wash them, they would fall to pieces
for lack of cohesive union.

Lady Reading stepped into the breach although wholly unofficially.
[W]e have now arranged for two complete sets of clothing for each
child which as soon as it is at hand will drape a thoroughly scrubbed
child, which scrubbing will be included as a routine once a week in
Margaret's magic time tables.

I wish to stress the statement I made above. Whether it is because
of a happy choice of staff or whether because knowledge makes one
strong, I can only attest that the inclination is towards alleviation
and not escape. Just yesterday 40 new smocks were delivered to the
school. It was as if each member of the staff had been presented with
a new fur coat.

Another factor in the choice of Garrison Lane was that a year previously the northern section of the building had been converted into a wartime restaurant. The manager of the restaurant took a special interest in the school. Through the inspector of domestic subjects in the Board of Education who arranged the menus for nursery classes and nursery schools, Blatz arranged to take on as an additional member of staff a woman who was anxious to have her child in the school. She was designated to look after the transport of food down the hall into the school. Fletcher worked out a plan by which the forty children could be fed, according to approved menus, with the least confusion. This included five members of the staff and eight students. The parents were charged fourpence for dinner, twopence for tea, and a penny for milk. This was the only charge the parents paid and was much less than even the cost of the food. The midday meal along with two-thirds of a pint of milk was almost sufficient to meet daily caloric needs and full vitamin requirements. Later in the year cod-liver oil and vitamin C were added.

When the first training course was well under way, Blatz was off to lecture at the University of Manchester and at a special course for nursery teachers at Edinburgh. The staff carried on. Near the end of their weeks at Garrison Lane, the whole group of forty students was invited to tea at the school and they made a display of one of their course projects. Each student had to make one piece of nursery school play equipment from raw material that had been found, not purchased. This was because, with the dearth of equipment, these students would soon have to launch their own schools with a little ingenuity and a junk pile, just as had so recently been the case at Garrison Lane.

# 9 Day-care Begins at Home

Once the children were settled in, the training courses for nursery supervisors quickened their pace. The second course was for forty matrons, all trained nurses, who were to be placed in charge of various war nurseries. The authorities were very anxious for them to take a refresher course, Blatz reported to Hincks. 'It was thought by this means that they would be more sympathetic to psychological aspects of their jobs. The "refresher" is a euphemism, because none of them had ever taken a course in Child Psychology before. This course was to be the first attempt at reconciling health and education.'[1]

On a typical day in the nursery the routine was conducted almost exactly as it was at St George's School in Toronto. The children arrived at about 8:30, although most of them stayed through tea-time when their mothers worked late. Blatz lectured at 10:00 and again at 1:00. Millichamp taught from 2:00 until 3:00, and Fletcher took seminars with the students after that. Between these class hours some of the students would observe, some would work in the school, and others would read about child development.

'We were interested in spreading the gospel of cleanliness,' Blatz wrote to Hincks on 14 August. They had been sent a supply of new clothes through the women's volunteer services but hesitated to put them on the children without adding a new routine to the school day. Consequently eight children every morning were soaked in suds from top to toe. 'Apparently they never had been in a bathtub before and from the struggles of two, I am sure that they thought, "The bitches are going to droon us." The result is now that we have more blondes than we had before.

'I may say that this procedure was not entirely altruistic. Because some of the children's inhabitants had left for more comfortable and opulent quarters. Anne counted twenty-one bites, Margaret seven, Mary W. three and myself one,' he told Hincks.[2]

At the first parent education meeting, twenty-five mothers appeared along with one father. Blatz talked to them about the school and what they were trying to do, arranging for a weekly meeting on Thursday nights. The response was even more enthusiastic than they had anticipated, he reported happily. At the second meeting Blatz discussed the sleeping routine, its importance, and how the school could help the mothers in 'laying down good habits of rest.' One comment that came back to him through the visiting nurse he found particularly gratifying: 'I like that bloke. He talks to us as if we knew something.'[3]

When the daylight-saving wartime hour was removed, bringing blackout earlier in the afternoon, meetings had to be discontinued until spring. (They were reinstated later by the staff after Blatz and the first contingent of teachers returned to Canada.) Blatz found a welcome response from the first meeting: 'The parents are eager and the results are shown in the children – earlier to bed, and cleaner!'[4]

Garrison Lane received applications from all over England from people wanting to take one of the courses, but it was difficult to arrange billets for them in Birmingham because the city was considered a danger area. It had been heavily bombed the year before and had suffered major fire damage, but now, despite the city's strategic importance in the armaments industry, all had been quiet for the last year. Blatz complained to the Department of Health that, in light of this, it seemed no longer necessary to control access to the city. That very night he changed his mind.

'At one-thirty in the morning, on a bright moonlight night, the sirens sounded in earnest and we were subjected to our first blitz.' Looking at it as the Chicago functional psychologist that he was, he added, 'It is impossible to give in detail one's introspections. I myself was frightened, physiologically as well as consciously.'

He wrote to Hincks about it:

I can only say that sitting in the shelter and hearing the bombs and the flack nearer and further away, is an experience that having come through it safely, one might consider it an exciting memory but one is not anxious to have it repeated. The all-clear sounded at three-thirty. I have never enjoyed a sound more nor had a cup of tea ever tasted the same.

That morning when we arrived at school we found that an incendiary had come through the roof and burned through the floor of the Rookery, that I described in our last letter, and that the French doors of the junior playroom had burst their fastenings outwards. There was a very poor attendance and we took a list of the absentees and Mary W., Anne and I visited as many as we could find and discovered that none of them had actually been blitzed.

We saw the results of the bombing, however, which will remain an indelible memory. What impressed us most was the quiet calm of the people and the stubborn efficiency with which they were repairing their homes.

That afternoon the children slept, some of them until five o'clock, parents obviously grateful for the serenity of the nursery school.

The next day we made it a point to collect our gas masks which up to this time, because of the pressure of our work, we had thought not urgent.

The next day the architects appeared and we arranged for the building of a brick wall to cut off a portion of the playground for storing coal and discussed the position of the central oval and the flower garden.

Wednesday was Anne's birthday which we celebrated by a dinner at the Queen's Pub and that night was the second blitz, which to us was more terrifying than the first. Halfway through was a lull, Mr. Shapiro who is a warden took me to see an adjacent shelter where I stayed until the all-clear. The calm and the patience and the stoicism manifested by all, even the children, is a tribute to English character.

At the Cadbury home is an excellent shelter and as Mr Cadbury is very conscientious about his menage, I felt far more at ease concerning the staff than I had on Monday night. I can understand to a slight degree what it means to have people for whom you are responsible not with you during a raid. I can understand the feelings of fathers and mothers away from home by multiplying my anxiety by 'n.' However the all-clear always sounds and 'the cup of tea that refreshes' was again enjoyed. The next morning at school we had to rope off part of the playground because many of the tiles on the roof had been loosened.[5]

Having graduated the hospital matrons, the staff started anew with forty more students, all of whom had already spent six months in nursery school and were to be offered an advanced course. During that time Blatz and Millichamp also lectured at Oxford and Cambridge. Blatz met Anna Freud on one of his tours but was not impressed: 'I was very pleased to find that our mental hygiene, which stresses prophylaxis, made a far better impression [on the audience] than the psychoanalytic school as expounded by Anna Freud,' he wrote to Hincks.[6]

The American-born Lady Astor was the member of Parliament for Plymouth (Sutton), an active feminist and interested in a variety of war efforts. She was a strong supporter of nursery education and invited Blatz to spend the weekend at her country house in order to discuss his program of child care in wartime England. He was enchanted by this weekend visit to Clivedon, a visit he described as one of the highlights of his time in England.

Once settled in his room Blatz looked through its tall windows onto the park and 'caught sight of a short, stocky figure walking along the stone-paved esplanade that fronts the building. I saw plus-fours of rather ancient vintage and long woollen stockings turned down at the top, and a beard. I thought, "That looks like Bernard Shaw," and dismissed it.'[7]

At tea-time he discovered that it was indeed Shaw, visiting Clivedon to celebrate his birthday with the Astors, as he did every year. Dinner was a formal meal, though Blatz commented that, as Lord and Lady Astor did not serve liquor in their home, and Shaw was a teetotaller, the other ten guests were also of the same persuasion for the evening.

At dinner Blatz was seated next to Shaw and was impressed with his eighty-seven-year-old youthfulness. He went so far as to liken Shaw to an enthusiastic adolescent with the wisdom of Solomon.

Blatz was happily engaged in discussing the nursery school movement in China with the Chinese ambassador when Shaw interrupted: 'In my opinion, far too much attention is being paid to the care of young children these days. They are hopelessly spoiled and ruined. I can remember in my young days in Kilkenny the young rolled around in the mud and the filth of the streets, ate what they could get, were cuffed a bit and, as far as I can see, were all the better for it.'

It was obvious that Shaw was teasing Blatz, and Blatz, who claimed to be enjoying it, shot back with, 'Mr Shaw, I have never heard such nonsense expressed, even in jest, in this so-called enlightened country.' A Canadian naval officer across the table became very upset as Blatz and Shaw tussled, and when dinner was over Shaw emerged (of course) triumphant and Blatz (for once) defeated.

After dinner Shaw sought Blatz out and asked him in detail about his work in Canada. Blatz was impressed by Shaw's grasp of modern psychology and psychiatry, though no mention seems to have been made of Shaw's earlier interest in eugenics.

The two talked for about an hour and a half; as Shaw took his leave of the group he said, 'Dr Blatz, have they many more psychologists like you in Canada?' 'No, sir, I am unique,' Blatz assured him. With a smile that Blatz said later he would like to be able to report as kindly, but that, as a matter of fact, was entirely enigmatic, Shaw declared: 'Well, perhaps we have something to be thankful for.'

As work at Garrison Lane progressed there was a general public curiosity about what was happening there. There were so many visitors the staff was forced to reserve Friday as visiting day, and one typical Friday Blatz counted 26 visitors, 42 students, the architect, the contractor, a representative of the water works, and an air raid warden. In one five-week period the number climbed to 375; thereafter all visits required permission from the Department of Education.

> You may wonder how the school carried on, with all this going on. So did I! But you can hardly realize as I do what a job the staff had done. To Dore goes all the credit for arranging, administering and organizing the dovetailing of courses. This she did, and kept all the students in good humour – besides lecturing. To Margaret goes the credit for running the school as smoothly as oiled silk. Every music circle was a public performance. Every washroom a spectacle and every meal a zoological episode. But – the routine carried on! And at the beginning of the month, every single child was sleeping in the sleeping room. Even the most recalcitrant – and there were some dandies. To the staff ... goes the credit for hard work, long hours, confusion of visitors and serene performance. No wonder the school has been a success.[8]

Students were in one door and out the other at Garrison Lane. The day after the advanced course graduated, a group of forty-two school principals started a special two-week orientation to nursery school practice. At the end of it they petitioned the Birmingham authorities to encourage Garrison Lane to carry on indefinitely as a Canadian venture. They also asked that the head teachers of not only the infant school (for children aged three to eleven) but also the junior school (for children aged eleven to fourteen) should be allowed to take the course.

A public health matrons' course followed for fifty nurses who would be in charge of residential nursery schools for children under five. The course was conducted at the children's hospital with relays of students observing and taking seminars at Garrison Lane. It was a strategic event, Blatz wrote to Hincks, because it was the first time a purely educational slant had been given to a subject that heretofore had been considered to be exclusively the concern of health.

Forty-two selected nursery school teachers who had already taken a child-care reserve course and had worked anywhere up to six months in an emergency nursery school were chosen for the wardens' course. After this training they would be assigned to a school in charge of the children from ages two to five during the usual nursery school day. This represented an attempt to improve the emergency nursery school care (which would ordinarily be wholly physical) and to give it a psychological and educational slant. Students were chosen from Birmingham and the counties surrounding it: Warwickshire, Leicester-shire, Staffordshire, Shropshire, Herefordshire, and Worcestershire.

Forty nursery teachers in the Birmingham system asked for an opportunity to study at Garrison Lane and were offered a one-week intensive course. This Blatz considered an interesting tribute, for all of them had already taken a training course at one of the private training schools in England, such as McMillan's or Gypsy Hill.

The course for His Majesty's inspectors involved taking forty-five inspectors to London and giving them a series of lectures by Anna Freud, Susan Isaacs, and Blatz. As Blatz wrote to Hincks: 'I attended all their lectures and answered their criticisms; they didn't attend mine and just said I was hopelessly in error.' After the course most of the inspectors went to Garrison Lane to see a school in action.

Blatz and his staff became busier and busier as the time approached for the first contingent of Blatz, Millichamp, Fletcher, and Harris to return to Canada, leaving the two Marys to work with the second group of Canadian nursery teachers (Margaret Hincks, Eleanor Hamilton, Alison Mack, Joyce Cornish-Bowden, and Nancy Griffin). Blatz addressed large audiences in Coventry, Wolverhampton, Exeter, and Birmingham itself. He advised the headmistress of Hereford College about initiating a nursery training course and demonstration nursery. Along with Millichamp, Fletcher, and Harris he gave a BBC broadcast about the Dionne quintuplets, and he prepared a thirteen week series of radio broadcasts on child care. He met with the exiled Polish minister of education to discuss plans for child care and nursery education in the post-war Poland that the minister envisaged. They were entertained at a whirl of luncheons and receptions in their honour by the lord mayor of Birmingham, the vice-chancellor of the university, and Lady Allen of Hurtwood. There were parties for the British nursery school association. The Canadian staff also entertained the parents of Birmingham children who had been evacuated to Toronto in order to be able to provide them with fresh news of their families.

Before they left they tried an experiment in teacher training. Three of the Canadian teachers (Griffin, McFarland, and Cornish-Bowden) would act as supervisors and teachers in the field. Each would be given ten emergency nursery schools, which they would visit for a week at a time. There they would observe, record, and attempt to resolve problems.

Blatz told Hincks that already the exercise had established its practicability and worth. 'The data that is [sic] being collected is amazingly valuable and the plan is being adopted in other regions – the same old story – only lack of highly trained personnel prevents wider spread.'⁹

The training of nursery personnel was indeed to continue at Garrison Lane throughout the next two years. When Blatz returned to Canada with Fletcher, Millichamp, and Harris, Mary Wright and Mary McFarland stayed with the new group of CCS workers. Mary Wright was set to lecturing – quite by accident, as she describes it:

> I expected to come home when the rest did. He [Blatz] never said anything. Then all of a sudden, he said, 'You're going to stay here; you're not going home.' I didn't have any money left with me. So he had me teach a couple of times and he said, ' You love teaching and you're going to do all the teaching.' I knew Dore and Margie were having fits and thought he was making a terrible decision and they were quite right. He was making a terrible decision. I said, 'But I don't know enough about what you think. Margie Fletcher taught me on the way over about the practice.' 'Oh,' he said, 'you're a natural on the practice,' and of course, I'd taken all the courses he offered that first year after everyone went overseas and I'd started on my PH D because I couldn't get a job. That's why I started on a PH D. Bill said, 'You know more about it than anyone else around here. You'll take all

of Dore's lectures and all of mine and you won't have to do anything in the school. You'll come up to Oxford with Anne and me and I'll talk to you all weekend about anything you want to know.' So that's what happened.[10]

There have been no follow-up studies of the Garrison Lane School, although for many years after the war the local doctor, Dr Beaumont, continued to keep in touch with the Canadian nursery workers. Some of the parents wrote, too, for a while, for this had been an unusual experience for them. The parents had been accustomed to a school system where parents kept away; but Garrison Lane was different. Blatz and his teachers had wanted to develop a close relationship between home and school, so that parents, unlike the public, had been encouraged to visit. Initially they had been suspicious, but gradually they had stayed to observe and learn. Informal chats led to parent education groups, which were organized as much for support as for information. There were no lectures as such; instead Blatz and his staff hoped the parents would learn by example when they saw the way the teachers planned and cared for the children's needs. The practice of bathing the children at school, for instance, did not have to go on for very long because the parents began to take enough pride in their children's appearance to make the considerable efforts involved in battling their inadequate plumbing facilities to cope at home. They began to welcome Blatz and the teachers into their houses. When Mary McFarland was married they produced a touching surprise. The parents had pooled their rations and managed to make her a real wedding cake.[11]

Several years later some of the CCS teachers went back to retrace old footsteps but found them largely erased. It was sad, for instance, to hear of an exceptionally bright and gifted child who had been apprenticed at fourteen and was living as an adult in much the same circumstances as his parents had before him. At the time of the Garrison Lane nursery it had been a revelation to see the swift effects an improved environment could have on a young child. All of them were tested at the beginning of their time in the nursery and again a year later. The gains were remarkable and virtually universal. Whether or not one believes in the validity of tests, there was certainly an observable difference in the children's way of showing interest and initiative in their activities. They had received almost nothing in the way of stimulation before. At Garrison Lane they had books and toys and music and conversation. They were well nourished. Instead of a diet emphasizing bread and dripping, fish and chips, jam and treacle, they were fed meat, milk, fruit, juice, and cooked and raw vegetables. ('Bring that back,' one of them said on being introduced to salad. 'It hasn't been cooked yet.')[12]

Blatz made two more trips to England during the war, visiting Garrison Lane and its satellites, calling in on London elementary schools where CCS teachers were working, and also speaking to groups of army officers on such topics as morale and the future of education.

The plan for *Understanding the Young Child* was outlined on a westbound transport with the help of Millichamp, Fletcher, and Harris when they were returning to Canada. The book carried Blatz's theories to a more sophisticated level. Along with elaborations on Blatz's earlier themes of discipline, motivation, persistence, social development, responsibility, work, and play, there were special words on nursery schools and parent education, significant new chapters on imagination and a philosophy of education, and a further outline of the security theory.

He saw security as a dynamic state marked by an ever-receding goal. When a specific goal is reached the solution beckons towards a future of further effort. 'Absolute independent security can be attained only by an individual who knows everything and can do everything ... thus, independent security can never be attained by man in any lifetime.'[13]

There were three ways in Blatz's plan (at that time) to cope with insecurity. The first would be to make an effort towards independent security through learning, the second to withdraw from the tendency to attack and return to the safety of an agency that had already proved to be satisfactory. The third would be to adopt a deputy agent and to rationalize, compensate, substitute, or sublimate instead of coping directly. If needed for temporary assistance, these devices might not be harmful; but if used persistently, Blatz warned, they would soon become mentally unhealthy reactions. It was the mark of healthy mental maturity to be able to accept the consequences of a decision; not to shift them away with an excuse or a stalling device.

Blatz was clear in his goal: from the point of view of mental health the first kind (independent security) is the type of activity we must attempt to instill in children.[14] There was still no room in his theory for the benefits of mature dependence. That would come later.

The Garrison Lane experience seemed to be an affirmation of the adaptability of the St George's School program to provide security in widely differing circumstances. Whether the program was for the children of Rosedale stockbrokers or Birmingham factory workers, the same patterns of play and routines gave structure and serenity to the nursery day. Blatz stressed in his speeches that nursery education was proving itself to be the most effective means of providing for a young child's physical and mental health as well as for social adjustment.

Back in Canada, Blatz was eloquent about the need for the Canadian government to intervene in the lives of children. 'England far ahead in child care – Blatz' read a headline in the *Toronto Daily Star*. In an address to the Royal Canadian Institute at Convocation Hall, Blatz declared Canada to be 'far behind Great Britain in recognizing the need of early education and care for children under school age, not only from the standpoint of a war emergency but also in giving every child an equal footing from babyhood, in education, feeding, recreation and medical care. England has already accepted this as part of her culture and as a social device for breaking down class privileges.'[15]

Speaking in Hamilton he laid out a four-point plan that he said must be instituted if 'democracy was not to remain hypocrisy.' It would be expensive, but would only cost about 10 per cent of what was being spent on the war. Canada should provide free medical services to all children, should give one balanced meal to children every day and a free holiday in camp to every child every year, and should educate them, by such means as day nurseries, on how to live in harmony with each other.[16]

Eighteen years after it had drawn its first shocked criticism, the idea that young children could beneficially spend part of their time away from home was becoming more generally accepted. No longer was it only in cases of strict necessity that they attended nursery school. Nursery education itself was beginning to be seen as useful. In particular, Blatz's Institute of Child Study was becoming recognized as the Canadian model for nursery education. Its three-quarter day with lunch and naptime could readily be applied to the longer hours of daycare. Already some of the graduates of its two-year MA in psychology were supervising crèches and nurseries in other parts of Canada. In the crèches these highly trained people were able to meld the principles of child study and nursery guidance with the particular demands of caring for the needs of children outside the home. Nevertheless, Blatz did not whole-heartedly endorse the idea of long hours in day-care. 'No child should be forced to stay in a day nursery for 11 consecutive hours,' he told the Big Sisters Association.[17]

Toronto had a long history of group care for the children of working mothers.[18] Its first crèche was opened in 1892 to give shelter to the pre-school children of mothers who were struggling to raise their families alone. There was often no alternative but to leave older children to care for the younger ones. This meant that school children sometimes had to miss their classes or would drag their younger brothers and sisters along with them to wait outside. Sometimes, if the teacher was merciful, younger siblings were allowed to sit or play quietly at the back of the schoolroom.

The first crèches concentrated simply upon giving physical care to their charges; but even so, it was a huge improvement in these young children's lives for them to be safe and warm and fed during the day. In 1930 the first child study graduate was employed by a crèche to add a mental health and nursery education component to custodial care. Gradually it became accepted practice in Toronto to attempt to model day-care on an extended nursery school program. It did not always work that way, but it did demonstrate an ideal of high-quality care for children.

Then wartime created a sudden need for more people in the workforce. Mothers were actually encouraged to take employment as their patriotic duty. This, in turn, created a new demand for more day-care facilities for both pre-school and older children. It was obvious that the small number of people already trained in child care could not be stretched to cover all the new centres that would be needed. The Ontario government entered into an agreement with the federal government to provide day-care for children whose mothers were employed in essential industries. It was easy enough to find buildings and equipment for the new nurseries, but staffing them was a different matter, and the rush was on to provide training. Blatz, Millichamp, Fletcher, and Harris were still in England when the agreement was made, but remaining staff at the institute immediately embarked on an emergency short course of four months along with a series of crash courses for volunteers. Five graduates of the institute's MA program set up a model school and training centre in an old house at 95 Bellevue Avenue, Toronto, giving demonstrations in day nursery administration to those who would be setting up day-care facilities. As soon as Blatz's group returned, Dorothy Millichamp was asked to take over the administration, organization, and expansion of day nurseries in Ontario.

The Dominion-Provincial Wartime Day Nursery Agreement of July 1942 made possible the establishment of three kinds of projects for the care of children of working mothers. There were to be nursery schools for pre-school children and organized programs for school-age children, providing care before and after school, with hot meals at noon; there would also be supervised foster-home day-care for individual children with special needs. Federal and provincial governments would share the costs equally.

A provincial committee with representation from the departments of Health, Welfare, Education, Public Works, and other selected services was established in Ontario to direct the projects in the province. In turn each municipality was asked to set up a local committee to survey the needs of its locality and submit proposals for child-care facilities to the provincial committee.

Plans provided for each nursery to look after from twenty to fifty children between the ages of two to five or six. The children would be able to spend practically the whole day in care if necessary, for the nurseries were open from 7:30 or 8:00 in the morning until 5:00 or 6:00 in the afternoon. Hot meals were provided both at noon and in the later afternoon, and these were supplemented with nutritious snacks. The original aim was to staff each day-care centre with two trained nursery school teachers and a corps of volunteers. This would mean that at all times there would be at least one professional staff member on duty along with three or more trained volunteers. (It soon became evident, however, that the professional staff would need to be increased to three, and sometimes four, in each nursery in order to carry the basic program in a consistent fashion.)

The program for school-age children was administered not through local committees but through the Board of Education of each community in order to ensure continuity with the organization of the schools. Each facility would be open from 7:00 a.m. to 6:00 or 6:30 p.m., sometimes in its own special classroom but more often moving from assembly hall to gymnasium to empty classroom and so on. Meal service was often arranged in nearby church or community buildings, and volunteers who could give instruction to the children in crafts and other special interests were encouraged. The centres were usually staffed by teachers pushing themselves to devote off-duty time to this aspect of the war effort. These staffing arrangements were not ideal, and a year or so into the program a few centres in larger cities were able to find regular staff members who were supplemented by trained volunteers.

Volunteers – always a crucial part of the day-care system for both school-age and pre-school children – were expected to prepare themselves for the job by attending a series of lectures and workshops. They consisted of housewives (many of whom were already involved in parent education classes), working women who gave time before or after work and in their lunch hours, and university and senior high school students.

At this stage nursery education was almost entirely in the hands of women. It was extremely rare for a male to be involved, even as a volunteer. Blatz was, as usual, an exception.

Elsie Stapleford, director of wartime day nurseries for Toronto and an institute graduate, estimated in a 1943 report that there were more than five hundred regular nursery school volunteers in Toronto. Although the volunteers' contributions were important, the number of day-care centres could not be increased to meet the demand without trained people to staff them. In the initial training course at the Bellevue Provincial Training Centre, there were thirty-four adults attending classes and working in rotation with the fifty pre-school children in its day-care centre. At the Institute of Child Study, in the autumn of 1942, four students enrolled for their second year of the regular two-year course for nursery school supervisors. Their graduate study would also be recognized by an MA degree in psychology. Another twenty-eight students registered to begin the first year of the same program, but because of the emergency, some of them (particularly those who already had a strong background of experience with children) were urged to take positions in day-care after completing only the first term. The others in this group were urged to finish the applied part of their studies and be ready for work in June.

It was a stop-gap measure. The students in the shortened courses received training, but not the kind of academic qualification expected in a university. Something was needed to bridge the gap between the expertise of graduates of the two-year MA program and the 'emergency outlook' of the influx of four-month-course practitioners.[19] In an effort to provide an answer, the one-year Diploma in Child Study was developed in 1944 and opened to university graduates. The course was constructed to give mature students a thorough understanding of the principles of child development and to demonstrate techniques for using this knowledge in practical situations. The first diploma students took courses in genetic psychology, methods of observation and research, parent education, and principles and procedures of nursery school practice. They studied physical development and patterns of family life, investigated the literature of child study, and observed children's agencies in the community. Their supervised practice was in the institute's nursery school and wartime day nurseries. They were taught by the staff of the institute (including, of course, Dr Blatz) and faculty from other departments, such as psychology, social work, and nursing. Each student spent two full days a week in the nursery school, with classes in the later afternoon after the nursery's three-quarter day. This program was supplemented with six weeks of apprentice work in the summer. (The same general format for the diploma course continued for another twenty years, until after Blatz's death.)

All prospective students were expected to have at least a university arts or home economics degree. The first year's group included a social worker, a dietitian, and an MA from Glasgow. All had previous practical experience with children in camps, playgrounds, or other community organizations. The first ten students graduated in June 1944 ready and eager to take on the challenge of organizing and staffing the day nurseries. Although the war was by no means over, however, an end was in sight, and the growth of day-care had reached its peak. As Mary Northway put it, 'Key appointments were already filled by excellent women from the emergency courses: [so] where were these people with high academic qualifications to be placed? ... The confusion between level of academic training and placement hovers over preschool education until this day.'[20]

Blatz was adamant that nurseries must be administered and staffed by qualified people who had a solid knowledge of child development and children's needs. Working with young children could not be left to kindly amateurs, for the result could only be confusion and upset, which would be dangerous to all children but particularly to those in a full-day program. When asked if he was in favour of day-care, his reply would focus on the situation and the staff and the insistence that a bad nursery school (or day-care centre) was worse for children than a bad home.[21]

The war's end meant, of course, a general readjustment to a new life by people everywhere and, most particularly, by servicemen returning to find themselves strangers in their own families. Blatz was ready for the challenge of helping to advise on the transition from soldier to civilian. He prepared an outline for the Canadian National Committee for Mental Hygiene to be used by army counsellors. He suggested group discussions to acquaint the returning servicemen with problems that they might not otherwise recognize and to help them to understand that other people were experiencing similar difficulties. Along with this, he believed, should go individual counselling of the men by an officer in the role of friend, confidant, and advisor. The more serious problems should be referred to clinicians. 'His client must leave him [the army counsellor] feeling that he has been sympathetically heard, that his problem is not insoluble, that the solution rests within himself and that he can return at any time to report progress and receive further encouragement.'[22] Blatz suggested that counsellors look at the client as soldier, citizen, spouse, and parent. He would have to adjust to new demands and different roles in most areas of his life. In his philosophy, for instance, he would have to change from a wartime attitude of hating the enemy and wanting to kill to a civilian attitude of being guided by religious dogma or working out his own system of values. In marriage, the returning soldier might find that he and his wife had developed divergent aims. If their relationship was a close one, they might be able to discuss their thinking, but sometimes changes might be wholly misunderstood and interpreted as dissatisfaction with the marriage. As a parent, the returned soldier might be impatient with formal instruction and leave the child in a vacuum with no idea of his father's views. Or he might, because of his army experience, attempt to dictate his values to the child, and resent any questioning on the part of the child. Blatz's outline for the army counsellors also covered the changing expectations of soldier, civilian, husband, and father in the areas of status, money management, responsibility, work, hobbies and leisure interests, relaxation, companionship, and personal adjustment.

The end of the war meant adjustments for civilian workers, too. As soon as the need for war workers stopped, federal support for daycare also stopped, and mothers were expected to pick up their children and go home. Some were perfectly happy to return to the traditional woman's world of kitchen and coffee club. But there were others who found that working outside the home had opened new doors and alleviated some of their major problems. Just as important, they saw positive benefits in the kind of day-care offered in the wartime programs. They wanted to continue at work, but to do so they needed satisfactory care for their children. A public outcry and a protest meeting in Massey Hall led the Ontario government to agree to continue the day-care program for pre-school children. Out-of-school care for older children was dropped entirely, however, except for a few centres in downtown Toronto.

Blatz was asked to submit recommendations to the provincial government for an act to govern the licensing of day nurseries. Working under pressure of time, he and his committee from the institute had no trouble defining requirements for space and equipment, but left the program regulations as a simple statement: 'Each procedure of the time table shall conform to the standards currently accepted by The Institute of Child Study of the University of Toronto.'[23]

The administration of the act came under the Department of Welfare, although Blatz had always assumed that a nursery system would be linked to education. Early in 1943, in a position paper outlining the costs of equipping and staffing a day-care unit, he had written: 'There is no question today as to the necessity of arranging for the administration of *all* preschool education under the proper educational authorities – local for immediate and direct responsibility, provincial for supervision, inspection and research, and federal for subsidy and control.

'The springing up of casual "nursery schools" in private homes, the need for a careful health programme, the qualification of teachers, can only be done under the type of machinery already functioning expertly in the educational field.'[24] That was not to be the case, but there was one compensating factor in placing the administration of day-care under welfare rather than education. The new unit was staffed by child study people – and Institute of Child Study people at that – headed by Elsie Stapleford, who replaced Dorothy Millichamp when Millichamp returned to the university from her wartime role in the day nurseries.

Of the schools themselves, Blatz had a lot to say towards the end of the war. Schools, the school-age child, and education *per se* became a major topic about which he spoke and wrote in the later years. He continued to be renowned for his understanding of the young child, but perhaps this shift in focus was an opportunity to look at unconquered territory and to try to bring the same kind of carefully elaborated system to school that he had brought to pre-school. He had applied the program of the St George's nursery first to the Dionne nursery, then to Garrison Lane, and ultimately to a whole structure of wartime day nurseries. Perhaps the time had come for the programs and principles of elementary school education, already in use at Windy Ridge, to stand a broader test.

For a while Blatz intended to work with his fellow psychologist William Line on a book about mental hygiene in the classroom; but, despite urgings from his publisher, promises to meet a deadline, and more nudges from William Morrow and Company, the book seems not to have progressed much beyond the preface and chapter outline.

'If I could believe what you said, I'd be a very, very happy man,' wrote Thayer Hobson (his editor) to Blatz; 'but I'm perfectly sure that before you get this one written, Nehru will have engaged you to go to India and establish a chain of nursery schools in India. It's going to be very interesting, though, my dear sir, to find out whether or not the Great Blatz who preaches about discipline and control applies the principles to his own life and writing career.'[25] Indeed the book was to have a whole chapter on discipline, along with chapters on intelligence, motivating factors, the home and school environments, the concept of adolescence, and a plan for mental hygiene services in the schools.

In *Understanding the Young Child* Blatz had outlined a complex plan for what was to be a revolutionary post-war educational system. It involved state intervention in assuring the child's health, optimum physical development, and recreational needs; it also involved a radical restructuring of the schools themselves. Some of his ideas are now taken for granted, although others have been so outdistanced by more recent knowledge that they are mere curiosities. Today, Canadians generally consider it a basic right to have access to pre-natal and post-natal care, to have preventive meas-.res taken against tuberculosis and other infectious diseases, or to have remedial and surgical care for sickness and accidents. However, when Blatz advocated such health coverage, without economic barriers, he was writing a good two decades before the Medical Care Insurance Act of 1960. Few would disagree with his call for playgrounds, community centres, and parks, or with his suggestion that leisure interests should be developed in childhood to carry into later life; but his assumption that middle age must be equated with entirely sedentary pursuits seems unnecessarily pessimistic by today's standards. The suggestion that the state should take complete responsibility for children's nutrition by providing their main meals at school might make for greater efficiency, but few parents today are ready to concede that 'the feeding of children requires a professional skill beyond the powers of the average parent.'[26]

As for the schools themselves, Blatz recommended that nursery schooling was usually appropriate for children age two and up; this was the best time for children to start learning social skills, and the best way was through a nursery school program. Nurseries need not be compulsory but should be universally available. For the later years, he outlined a system of testing and streaming that would begin at age five and culminate in a relatively permanent division by the age of seven. By then, Blatz wrote, the children's accomplishments, interests, and capacities should be accurately known, and they could be placed into academic and non-academic groups. The first essential for efficient administration of such a school system was the incorporation of a testing program to help in 'assigning the child to his educational niche.'[27] Writing in the *Bulletin of the Institute of Child Study* while *Understanding the Young Child* was still in press, Blatz had further thoughts on the educational scheme, this time extending it from *in utero* to university. Parent education was envisaged as the first step. 'The importance of direction during the prenatal and postnatal periods – by nurses, doctors, psychologists and social workers – cannot be over-estimated.'[28] Children would start nursery school at age two and go to kindergarten and the equivalent of the first two grades all in an infant school. These years would combine social and emotional development with an introduction to the three Rs in the last year or two. Just as important to Blatz, it would also give health officials an opportunity to organize preventive medical care and to promote a sturdy physique in the children. Repeated mental and aptitude tests in these early years would allow the children to be divided and proceed to one of four different types of schools. One group would learn the art and crafts of social living, being apprenticed at the age of twelve and at sixteen placed in full-time employment, though supervised by social agencies. The second group, the largest, would enter vocational schools, learn basic academic skills, and, at age twelve, be further divided, with one group learning skilled trades and the others attending a school of business administration leading to white-collar jobs in office or factory. The third group of seven-year-olds would begin a richer fare of academic subjects and at age twelve go on to a pre-college institution. The fourth group, comprising the deaf, the blind, and those with other disabilities, would have instruction adjusted to their particular requirements. At sixteen the business administration students could go to work, but would be expected to attend evening classes until the age of twenty. Their alternate route would be to go to a semi-professional college where they might be joined by those of their contemporaries from the academic stream who chose to go neither to university nor to a professional school. The highest educational school, for post-graduate work, would accept students from the semi-professional or professional schools or universities, and from these the best-trained students would be selected as teachers.

Such a rigid structure would now be judged not only unworkable but also offensive to our ideals of social mobility. To us, with today's greater awareness of the fallibility of tests and the dangers of classifying people, the plan sounds shocking. In fairness, though, Blatz's suggestions for re-schooling society were based on the humane consideration that children should be allowed to learn without external pressures. Even in his earliest work he gave more importance to interests, persistence, and motivation than to intellectual capacity, although he always thought there was an inherent ability basic to everyone's individual make-up. Environment would play a large role in how the children developed this ability, and they would do best if they were allowed to be enthusiastic learners. Unfortunately, however, adults tend to place their expectations either too high or too low and to stretch or squeeze their children in the process. Blatz promoted the idea of school as a place where confidence could be built, where individual differences would be considered, and where children would learn to conform to reasonable requirements, to co-operate with others to solve problems, and to explore new ideas with a healthy scepticism. 'Any rebuff is bound to affect the child adversely; arbitrary measures of discipline, sarcasm, humiliation, and unfair competition all serve to destroy his faith and confidence.'[29] In this, as elsewhere, he was Blatz the psychologist and Blatz the progressive educator.

# 10 Mature Security

In the fifteen years between the end of the war and his retirement in 1960, Blatz's pace became gradually slower. He still undertook major projects, but a good deal of the burden of carrying them shifted to his colleagues.

There was a major change in his personal life when he and Margery were divorced. Quite early in their marriage they had decided that when Gery grew up they would go their separate ways. It was a rational arrangement, completely without quarrelling or upsets, or else they could not have continued to live together for as many years as they did, he told June Callwood in an interview for *Maclean's* magazine.[1] They were both devoted parents and each other's good friends, willingly taking the consequences of an earlier, younger decision in order to give their daughter a relatively stable childhood until she was established in her own life. After the divorce, Margery married an old friend from Mental Hygiene, Harry Spaulding, and Blatz was free to marry Anne Harris. Their marriage was a tranquil, companionable one. They continued to work on the farm at Caledon and spent their evenings cooking, reading aloud, or with daughter Gery deRoux's two children, Jeffrey and Jimmy.

When the grandchildren were little, Blatz built them a real nursery school playground at Caledon, fully fenced and equipped. He and Anne would sit there in the evenings with their drinks watching the boys at play. Later he added what he called 'grandson bait,' such as a trampoline and a tennis court. The boys spent every available weekend and holiday with the Blatzes.

There were weekend parties at Caledon for city friends, too; one such was the annual reunion of his university bridge club, which went to Caledon ostensibly to fish, though in fact the members concentrated more on eating and drinking and playing horseshoes. Every year there was a large Blatz family picnic, a continuation of the peripatetic picnics that began before the First World War in Kitchener and Buffalo and Niagara Falls. There were also institute picnics for staff, students, and their families. Blatz kept tableware for more than a hundred people in special cupboards just for the picnics, and he cooked for the crowds himself, barking orders to a band of helpers.

His favourite reading was seventeenth-century English history, and he was particularly fascinated by the life of the unfortunate King Charles I. He never read novels, but sometimes he would relax with a detective story or something by Osbert Sitwell. He was a fast reader, and his knowledge of Greek and Latin along with an ability to speak German (fluently) and French (with a German accent) broadened his scope. When Gery was a child, Margery and he had continued his mother's custom of sitting with their daughter while she did her homework. With Gery grown, he and Anne became the mentors for neighbourhood children studying for their grade thirteen examinations. If children were having difficulties, Blatz would guide their studies by helping them to set schedules for review. He would require them to get a notebook for each subject and to return at regular intervals for further discussions and to set new goals.

Mary Northway has conjectured that perhaps Blatz was so content in his new marriage that some of the dynamism went and he no longer had the drive to accomplish as much as he had before.[2] Certainly some of the common health frailties of fifty and beyond were beginning to catch up with him. A severe case of pneumonia in 1955 left him weak, looking old, and newly vulnerable to other respiratory illnesses. Although he took a six-month leave of absence after the illness and went to Europe with Anne, he never properly regained his strength.

Blatz remained in the public eye as the central figure at the Institute of Child Study, but increasingly the research, the writing, and the day-to-day work were quietly assumed by such co-workers as Dorothy Millichamp and Mary Northway. Was this an exploitation of intelligent women? Dorothy Millichamp feels it was quite the contrary. At a time when women were expected to be seen rather than heard she found the atmosphere of the institute liberating. Although the universities of the day did little actively to encourage the advancement of women, it was nevertheless possible, particularly at the institute, for a woman to be accepted on her own merits and to have her ideas and efforts taken seriously. This might count as only a crumb or two by today's thinking, but it was significant in the context of the time.[3]

In the post-war years, Blatz himself had become something of a wise elder statesman and less of a controversial figure. His ideas were rarely a surprise. Most of his advice was widely accepted as the common-sense way of doing things. The general thinking about child raising had travelled to the point where Blatz's theories had become mainstream methods. If fairly knowledgeable parents stopped to reflect on a problem for a minute or two, it was quite likely that they would find a solution that was perfectly in line with Blatz.

When Benjamin Spock published his *Commonsense Book of Baby and Child Care* in 1945, Blatz had helped to make the world ready for it. Along with Spock's precise instructions on handling the tumbles and traumas of childhood there was a clear new message: parents could rely on their own judgment to solve behaviour problems. They were comforting words, and generally it was easier to utter them in 1945 than it would have been in 1925. Child study pioneers such as Blatz had shifted thinking into a new alignment that did indeed make common-sense care acceptable. It was not necessary for Spock to tackle basic questions about sparing the rod, about encouraging children to make responsible decisions, about listening to children, and about allowing oneself to enjoy them. The groundwork had already been laid for a more liberated kind of child-care.

The post-war years were still years of involvement for Blatz, of course, although not to the same degree as earlier. The institute grew in size and complexity, he continued to teach at the university, and his speeches were still well-attended, although they rarely made headlines any longer. His writings were popular, too – popular as opposed to academic. The publications were almost entirely in the institute's own in-house journal, the *Bulletin of the Institute of Child Study*, or in mass-circulation magazines such as *Chatelaine* or *Maclean's*. He spoke on the radio and was an amusing gladiator on early editions of CBC television's 'Fighting Words.' He continued at the Juvenile Court and helped to develop Thistletown Hospital School for emotionally troubled children. This was a natural outgrowth of his clinical counselling, which absorbed a good deal of his time in the later years.

Blatz's classes at the University of Toronto were usually over-subscribed, for he remained a stimulating, witty lecturer; furthermore, he was a non-believer in exams and always gave his students the questions in advance, so that no one need fail. His former students tend to rank him as one of their best teachers, partly because of the way he used words and also for his grasp of the subject and his memory. There was never a prepared lecture, but there was always a plan. 'He was a really skilled arguer. If our thinking was not clear he would back us into the corner. Even when I knew what was happening, I'd watch him pick out the holes in my thinking in a way I'd never seen anyone else do. And yet you'd never feel you had been had. You never felt resentful. He was not authoritarian or overpowering or in any way critical. You just looked at the subject again and tried to figure out a way he wouldn't get you the next time. He was the kind of teacher who just set you on a path and then made you go as far as you could, and further, which is what a teacher ought to be.'[4] Others describe the way he loved to get a student up against the wall. 'He would try to make you back down but if you wouldn't back down then he was delighted.' That was his teaching style. 'He wanted to know why you thought as you did and if you had thought it out.'[5] Mary (Salter) Ainsworth remembers him as very definite in his beliefs and very explicit in the way he expounded them. 'He would come in to give a lecture and it was never this business of "Well, we'll go on to that next day." He would come to the end of what he had to say and then he would pop out, and off he would go to something else.'[6]

The *Bulletin of the Institute of Child Study* appeared quarterly and usually contained an article by Blatz. His contributions ranged from variations on the theme of security to pithy essays on Santa Claus (Blatz was in favour), the joy of eating (Blatz was a keen gourmet), and George Bernard Shaw (Blatz told of his weekend with him at Clivedon). The *Chatelaine* articles embraced such topics as: homework (self-imposed homework such as a hobby is the ultimate goal of all education); a child's allowance (getting it, getting rid of it, keeping it); summer camp (not a luxury but a necessity); Santa Claus again (to adults: if you know of a better myth go to it); relaxation (sleep is instinctive, relaxation is a learned pattern); discipline (clear, concise requirements with consistent consequences directed towards teaching, not punishing); dawdling (a sign of bad training and a child's refuge against inconsistent routine); eating problems (the high chair was not a sensible invention, it is too tempting to the average adult to criticize,

nag, ignore, rebuff, flatter, or stimulate a child at meals); responsibility (you don't toss responsibilities and freedom at her; you give her as
much as she can carry and stand close by to help her if she should
stumble a little); emancipation (the amalgam that holds people together
must be respect based on freedom); competition (co-operation in
learning, emulation of skills, and admiration of the attainment of others
could be as easily learned as the present-day 'dog-eat-dog' behaviour);
special talents (general capacity is inborn but special qualities are
entirely learned, depending upon interest, effort, and opportunity);
lying (the psychological lie is unavoidable and can be minimized by
the absence of prejudice; the lie of fantasy is important and should be
fostered; the lie of loyalty is indispensable and the child must be
carefully tutored in its use, while lies of self-protection are completely
dispensable and can be avoided through a consistent plan of discipline
and a satisfying opportunity for development); bedtime (we spend the
first decades of our lives trying to stay out of bed and the rest of our
lives trying to get back in); and nagging (parents are prone to be reluctant in giving up their children as they grow up. Nagging is a form of
compensation for this apparent loss.)[7]

Blatz had a tenacious interest in the Toronto Juvenile Court Clinic,
an interest that spanned his whole professional life. Several times the
clinic nearly foundered for lack of staff, but he continued to make his
best effort to keep it afloat during the war years and during the long
illness of its director, George Anderson. He persuaded one of his pupils,
psychiatrist Donald Atcheson, to take a position there, and during the
ten or eleven years Atcheson remained, the court grew. Eventually
there was the possibility of a new court on Jarvis Street. 'Bill was in
and out two or three times a week offering his piece as he did so well,
often with what appeared to be sarcasm but usually with what was
great intelligence. It was his way of impressing people with the need.'

Eventually discussions about moving the court seemed to come to
an impasse, because those who were financing it were not prepared to
see the court move forward to focus on treatment and research. It
seemed to Atcheson that some intelligent protest should be made, and
he spent hours with Blatz discussing the most effective way of stating
his position. His course of action became clear, and he resigned.

'I think Bill had some regrets about that. He thought he'd led me
on and then I took the bit and ran. He always used to say "live dangerously" and God, I can remember saying, "Bill, I can't live any more
dangerously than this," ' Atcheson recalls.

Blatz continued his work at the clinic for as long as his own health allowed. Nine years after Blatz's death, Atcheson evaluated his contribution. By then the court clinic had become an effectively functioning operation, separated from the court, involved with families and the community, doing assessments, and working closely with police and probation officers, all almost exactly as Blatz had urged. For all this he gave Blatz the lion's share of the credit. 'Every now and again we rediscover the wheel and talk of community psychiatry, but I think it was discovered long ago and I think that Blatz made a great contribution in his time to what appears to be a new thing.'[8]

In these years Blatz's counselling occupied increasing amounts of his energy and involved private patients from all walks of life as well as work with disturbed children at Thistletown Hospital School. Thistletown was designed to be a place where children with major problems could live while receiving both therapy and schooling. Blatz was in charge of the elementary school itself for the first few years and, although it came under the aegis of the institute, it was very much his own project. His principle was that the children should be introduced to the school as a place where their state of being well could be fostered. If at any time they were upset, they would be taken out of the schoolroom by the child-care workers and later brought back to try again. In this way their behaviour in the classroom was always kept acceptable, and gradually most children learned to stay in school for longer and longer parts of the day. Blatz made the point consistently that the teachers and therapists each had quite different roles to play. It was important for therapists to know what had brought the child into treatment and what extreme conditions of his life (or his perception of his life) were apt to lead him into psychotic behaviour; but Blatz wanted the Thistletown teachers to play a separate role based on prevention of further problems. He wanted the teachers to set up expectations in their classrooms of what a classroom was like and to use this as the measure of improvement. The aim was to bring the children to the point where they could accommodate a regular school day. There were graduated stages of treatment: one for children in a state of extreme disturbance, another for those who were getting on a little better, and a third leading to eventual integration into regular schools in the community. This provided a series of reasonably manageable goals. Often there would be a transition time when some of the children would need the structure of Thistletown school in the day although they could return to their homes at night. Others would need just the opposite. They could cope with a regular school but needed the therapeutic setting as a substitute for home until they could learn to adjust to the outside world.

Although the fifteen years from the end of the war to Blatz's retirement marked a steady decline in his personal strength, he put his efforts into the institute (rather than into major publications) during this time, and it flourished in its schools, its training programs, and its research.

Blatz had long wanted to incorporate an elementary school into his educational model, thus making the Institute of Child Study a school for children from age two up to about age twelve. Windy Ridge went only as far as grade two, but he decided it could be the base for a further extension of grades if it were joined to the institute. In 1951 he worked with his long-time friend, architect Eric Haldenby, whose firm, Mathers and Haldenby, usually designed the university's buildings. The two of them drew up plans for a new child study building. It would combine Windy Ridge with the institute and give plenty of space for an expansion of research projects, parent education, and student training. They intended the building to be on St George Street, very near the projected new arts building.

Blatz's negotiations with the university authorities and Board of Governors were lengthy ones, but they seemed to proceed smoothly. His spirits were particularly buoyed when the institute celebrated its twenty-fifth anniversary to the accompaniment of high praise from the university community. The president of the university, Sidney E. Smith, declared that the institute had become a model of what an institute should be and what it could do. It had helped to make the ideal of the university as a community of scholars into a reality. 'At twenty-five years of age the Institute has attained maturity, and it is now recognized as a full-fledged member of the academic family. Zealous for its own progress, it is jealous for the welfare of the University. *Maneat, crescat, floreat!*'[9]

But the new institute was not to grow and flower exactly where Blatz had hoped. Despite the heady celebrations of the previous year, the university turned down his plans. (Today the Sidney Smith building sits on the proposed site.) Blatz was upset enough at the decision that he talked seriously to his staff about taking the institute away from the University of Toronto and setting it up at McMaster.[10]

A few months later, however, the university held out an olive branch. A substantial house on Walmer Road had been left to the university and, if Blatz agreed, this could become the new home of an enlarged Institute of Child Study. The house had belonged to the Honourable Leighton G. McCarthy, a former ambassador to the United States. It was set on a large property, and the house itself was vast, with a series of individual suites for each member of the large McCarthy family. The rooms were spacious and sunny, and both basement and attic were bright enough to be useful. Certainly it was much more extensive than the old St George Street premises, although it would still take a bit of squeezing to accommodate everyone from both the institute and Windy Ridge. Modifications were needed at once to adapt the building for use by young children. These included extra steps, handrails, fire-doors, and other safety features. A downstairs study was turned into a traditional Blatz-style nursery washroom with miniature plumbing fixtures, while upstairs some of the plumbing fixtures were removed from excess bathrooms and dressing-rooms in order to convert them into offices for the research and parent education people. (The parent education staff had been further strengthened by the addition of Nan Foster, a young war widow who was raising her two children as a single parent and who was responsible for much of the application of Blatz's ideas to special situations.) The small entrance garden retained much of its formality, but most of the grounds were planted with slides, swings, jungle gyms, and sand-boxes, interwound with concrete pathways for trikes and wagons.

The new institute opened in September 1953 with the children and staff from two nursery schools combined into one, two school principals (Margaret Fletcher was now joined by Rachel Minkler from Windy Ridge), and several extra grades (kindergarten to grade three). With one hundred school children, a staff of forty-five, and a varying number of university students, parents, and visitors, there was no room to spare.

Nineteen fifty-three, the year the institute moved house, was generally a year of expansion and revision in programs as well, both at the institute and at Mental Hygiene headquarters. Clarence Hincks retired as director, and J.D. Griffin, a former student of Blatz, took his place. Mental Hygiene now became the Canadian Mental Health Association (CMHA), changing its orientation to become more of a community-based organization with responsibility resting in local groups and the Toronto headquarters helping to co-ordinate efforts.

Student training in child study at the institute had grown in the post-war years. As well as offering the graduate Diploma in Child

Study, the institute was also being used by the CMHA to educate groups of mature teachers to be mental health consultants. At the end of their training these liaison officers returned to their school districts across Canada to promote principles of mental health in the classrooms. The first three groups of these teachers did not receive any university credit for their training, but in 1953 the diploma course at the institute was revised to assimilate the school mental health program. The diploma then had three options: mental health in education, designed for experienced teachers who had been recommended by their local boards of education; mental health in the home, preparing students for parent education; and childhood mental health for those planning to work with young children.

It was also the year that research at the institute received a boost when Blatz was awarded the first of five annual grants from the federal government for developmental studies in mental health. The grants were assigned to Blatz personally; in fact, however, although the institute remained part of the university, these grants constituted virtually the entire budget of child study for the next five years and made the institute relatively free of university constraints.

One of the purposes in uniting Windy Ridge and the institute nursery school under one roof was to enable developmental studies to continue until children reached adolescence. It was evident to Blatz that the Walmer Road house would need an addition almost immediately to extend the Windy Ridge curriculum to include grades four to six, to relieve the pressure of crowding caused by the new research projects that were under way, and to make room for a demonstration and model nursery school to support the teaching and research programs.

Blatz raised the necessary funds for the addition almost single-handed, by, as he described it, begging money from his friends. Windy Ridge already had a roster of wealthy supporters who were willing once again to contribute generously to a project that would be of direct benefit to the education of their children or grandchildren. The new wing opened in 1956. It included, on the ground floor, a self-contained nursery school with three playrooms and one-way-glass observation windows lining the corridors. On the second floor were three new classrooms, and partly below ground level was a dual-purpose dining-room and meeting-room. The children who entered the new institute thus were able to continue into the elementary school years, and the institute acquired a stable population that could be followed through the longitudinal research projects. It was a small school, staffed by highly skilled teachers, who put a great deal of emphasis on knowing each child very well. This concern with the well-being of children as individuals gave a safe opportunity to experiment with the curriculum. The teachers could judge the appropriateness of any innovation almost at once. After being put to the test with a small group many of the methods were adopted by the general school system. Today it is no surprise to hear of French in the nursery school, science in the kindergarten, story-book writing in the early grades, or trips outside the classroom to consider such topics as water and waste, or producing and consuming. But these were bold experiments in learning at a time when most teachers taught prescribed lessons from a blackboard and children wrote or crayonned in identical workbooks.

The institute's mental health studies of the mid-fifties integrated this practical work in the schools with the more theoretical aspects of research. Theory and practice had always supported each other, and the nursery school staff had been involved in research from the earliest days on St George Street; now this responsibility was extended further to the teachers in its new elementary grades.

The research under Federal Health Grant 605-5-147 was focused on formulating a definition of mental health. On the assumption that the pathology of mental life was already being explored elsewhere, Blatz and his colleagues undertook to learn more about the positive side of the picture. They would try to ascertain how a person manifests mental health while functioning in the world; and, in particular, they would look at children who were essentially well, in order to observe how they coped with life's inevitable vicissitudes. The security theory would be the central point of view for the research, and the majority of the studies would be longitudinal. The children in the institute's schools would be followed for at least the first decade of their lives, while teachers, parents, parent educators, child study students, and researchers would all contribute to the study from their own perspectives. It was, in essence, an opportunity to refine the security theory, apply its precepts to daily life in the school and at home, and begin to put the theory to the test of measurement.

Since Blatz had first outlined his theory in *Understanding the Young Child*, it had been the subject of a running debate between Blatz and his staff. In his early scheme Blatz had contended that dependence was something of a poor relation of independence, and of relatively little value in itself. Inasmuch as he recognized it, he tended to rank it on a level with deputy agents: simply a temporary device for fending off consequences. His colleagues insisted that independence could only grow with dependence firmly established and growing alongside it. The position of dependent trust would give the foundation for an infant to explore the world. When the going became too tough, the young child could return to the safety of dependence, recover, and set forth again with the assurance that there would be a sound haven available if needed again. But Blatz was reluctant to yield his position that only the independent explorations were significant. He did not want security to be associated with bovine contentment; instead his definition of maturity focused on the ability to cope with constant changes and to be able to combine living dangerously with accepting the consequences of one's decisions.

By the end of the five-year mental health study Blatz had modified his security theory to give more respectability, though not yet total acceptance to dependence. The change in his thinking came about partly because of the heated discussions in his weekly seminars for senior staff. The debates started there would continue throughout each ensuing week, with his colleagues reorganizing their arguments for the next battle. The other significant influence came from the analysis of nursery school records. In routine situations it was quite evident that the children who accepted directions and followed procedures were also the ones taking responsibility and showing ample evidence of adventurous spirit in their play.[11] Furthermore, simple observations reinforced this idea. The children who struggled with a shoelace or overcoat and angrily brushed off an offer of help may have appeared at first glance to be independent; but their skill in dressing lagged behind those who could accept assistance. Betty Flint and Dorothy Millichamp, who were working with a group of institutionalized babies in an effort to help them adjust to adoptive homes, were finding similar evidence. The mental health of the babies was not to be found in how much independence they showed but rather in the kind of trusting relationship they built up with the people taking care of them. Eventually Blatz was convinced that dependence and trust should have stronger emphasis in the security system. (It was not until *Human Security*, however, that he presented the newly elaborated theory in full written form).

The increased status for dependence that arose out of these discussions broadened the scope of the security theory to allow it to grow in two directions. No longer did it discuss just the side of security that was involved with decisions and skills and accepting consequences; it now put equal emphasis on learning about trust in oneself and in other people. Willingness to accept the consequences of behaviour was still considered the basis of independent security, but there was also beginning to be room in the scheme for sharing of responsibility. It was now considered mentally healthy for a young child to return to the security of trusting dependable adults when the consequences became too much to assume. This revision and refinement of the theory had two direct effects on the research under way in the federal health study; it made space within the institute's philosophy for a variety of research interests, and it gave a focus to the great mass of data collected in the longitudinal research.

With the expansion of the theory, it could now comfortably accommodate broader areas of investigation than before. Blatz had always chosen his staff from those who were basically in accord with the institute's outlook, but beyond that had left them free to develop their own research interests. In the new institute, and under the new grants, researchers simply continued their projects much as they had previously, although they were now expected to consider the implications of mental health in every study and to relate their individual research to the overall project. The idea of interdependence as a significant part of security now encouraged the investigation of social adjustment, which was a particular interest of Mary Northway's while the new emphasis on the development of trust supported Betty Flint and Mary Kilgour in their theoretical and practical work with infants. These varied studies had all been long-term projects of the individual researchers, but the revised theory integrated their work with the overall plan.

Although some of the research was designed to give immediate results, most of it involved the long-term collection of data. One of the major problems with longitudinal research is that it produces a huge mass of information that is often difficult to use in any effective way. With the redefinition of the security theory, there were now some clear starting points in the search for mental health, and researchers could approach what might have been an avalanche of data with an improved sense of direction and purpose.

The institute's project was to be a co-ordinated study of mental health with all data collected on the children made available to all the other researchers. The teachers played a variety of roles in addition to their regular classroom responsibilities. They protected the children from over-exposure to tests and observations; they provided information on the children through questionnaires, records, and reports; and they were engaged in a continual analysis of their own knowledge and techniques. The diploma students selected research projects that could contribute to the whole effort yet be small enough to be completed in their single year of graduate study. Parents kept records at home, and some worked on research studies of their own. The parent educators attempted to translate the research findings into a form that would be understood by the public. Even the children were aware of the research. All the tests were designed to be enjoyable and free of stress, but were never passed off as only a game. The children were told that the researchers were trying to discover more about how they learned in order to help other children in other schools.[12]

The years of the mental health studies were five golden years during which those at the institute had a united sense of purpose and enough money to spread thinly but thoroughly. There were two setbacks, however, that had an influence on the institute's future. Late in 1955 Blatz became ill with pneumonia and never was able to work at full strength again. Also, during the Christmas holidays that year a pipe froze in the basement of the Walmer Road building. The resulting flood was one of the worst disasters that can befall longitudinal research. Much of the old material from St George Street was drenched, and early photographs were ruined. There was an effort to dry out as much as possible, but it was too late for most of it. The material from the five-year study survived because it was kept upstairs ready for active use. The awareness of the fragility of such documents, which need long-term preservation, may have been one of the factors in influencing the university's later decision to discontinue longitudinal research at the institute.

There was no new written statement of the modified theory arising out of the mental health studies (that did not come until *Human Security*, ten years later), but the emphasis on the interaction of theory, practice, and research led immediately to several publications, which, although they did not involve Blatz directly, were significant in the institute's history. Mary Northway and Lindsay Weld published the results of their sociometric testing. Margaret Fletcher wrote about the adult and the nursery school child, Dorothy McKenzie and Jocelyn Raymond about children's parties. Betty Flint discussed the security of infants, M.F. Grapko devised a test to evaluate the security of school children, and Mary and Len Ainsworth measured security and insecurity in adult adjustment.[13]

Later, Carroll Davis published her investigations of parent-child relationships in *Room to Grow*,[14] and Flint wrote an account of a group of babies who were helped to adjust to foster and adoptive families after living in an institution. This rescue was guided by Flint and Millichamp, who, in turn, were applying the precepts of the security theory. The story is told in Flint's *The Child and the Institution: A Study of Deprivation and Recovery*.[15]

The move to Walmer Road in 1953 had separated the institute geographically from the rest of the campus, and its outside funding, commencing the same year, had allowed it considerable freedom to chart its own course, outside the university's budget. Furthermore, the old order was changing, and by the time Ned Bott retired from the psychology department, with Roger Myers becoming the new head, it had become increasingly obvious that child study and psychology were travelling in very different directions. Myers emphasized a tighter, more controlled approach to research, with the emphasis on experimental design and statistical evaluation. The institute's method was more diffuse, with a focus on long-term studies of children and applications to the community and to mental health.

When the five years of federal health and welfare grants were drawing to a close in 1959 there was some apprehension about the institute's future. Blatz asked that it be brought back within the university's financial fold, and eventually the university agreed to resume responsibility for the child study budget. 'Dr Blatz rejoiced greatly,' Mary Northway wrote, 'believing that the Institute was established forever as a University faculty. He had accomplished what he set out to do.'[16] And so he had, although the bonds that anchored the institute safely in academe were also to fetter its freedom.

Blatz retired in 1960 as director of the institute, although he remained as its consultant and as a part-time professor in the psychology department. His health was failing seriously, and he was diagnosed as having emphysema. He managed to meet his commitments to the Juvenile Court, to Thistletown, and to the people he counselled, but it was a struggle. 'It was to me a very painful experience to see him coming in [to Thistletown] with his difficulty in breathing and still coming,' Dr Don Atcheson recalls. 'Anne used to drive him out and come and get him, and he was certainly not well.'[17]

He continued to visit the institute very frequently in the first year of his retirement, for he was involved in developing a new longitudinal study, which got underway in 1962. His counselling clinic was in the old Leighton McCarthy garage on the institute's grounds, and his grandsons, Jeffrey and Jimmy, were pupils in the institute's elementary school. He also spent a good deal of time in the psychology department, more than he had in years, for now he had time on his hands. He made new friends among the bright young psychologists who were involved in laboratory studies of animal behaviour, and for a while he became quite interested in hearing about their experiments with rats.[18] It was nearly forty years since he had last worked with white rats at Chicago.

The new longitudinal research project being developed at the institute, however, was an entirely different kind of project from the ones he heard about at coffee time in the psychology department. The new research was a complex charting of the development of several groups of children in an attempt to answer a broad set of questions arising from Blatz's security theory: Is there a core of security in each person? If there is, within what limits does it fluctuate? At what point of development is it established? Do dependence and independence supplement each other, or are they complementary? What is the optimal relationship between dependence and independence, and does this vary at different levels of maturity?[19]

The new longitudinal study was to be a twelve-year project involving the groups of twenty children who would enter nursery school for each of five consecutive years, and was to follow them through their first six grades of elementary school. Altogether it would study one hundred children in all aspects of their development, using standard measurements and tests, along with those constructed at the institute. Twelve members of the research staff and most of the teachers would work on their particular interests within the study, but all the resultant data would be shared. The intention was for a variety of studies to be published separately using the same material on the same children but looking at it from different perspectives.

One of the problems of such a complex study would be in the tedious calculations necessary to analyse data, and those designing the study decided to see if use could be made of a new tool, the university computer. When a number of the first institute tests were finished, the computer was given the task of coping with some of the data. Almost at once it sent forth card after miraculous card showing means, standard deviations, and co-ordinations of the measurements. It seemed that the difficulties of longitudinal research had been overcome.[20] It was not the sort of study that the psychology department would have undertaken, but with the solution to such a major statistical problem, perhaps the time was ripe for longitudinal research to come into its own. A few years earlier Blatz had been reassured about the future of the institute when the university resumed the underwriting of its budget; he was now able to feel confidence in the future of his type of research.

In the last year of his life Blatz was unable to continue most of his activities on any regular basis. He visited the institute, but more as a grandparent or an honoured guest at tea than as the retired director. He kept on with his interest in Thistletown, the Juvenile Court Clinic, and his counselling of private patients, as his strength allowed, but in the last months he channelled his limited energies into the one major remaining task in his life, a complete statement of his security theory.

The theory had been the guiding structure for Blatz and his colleagues since long before their work with the Dionne quintuplets, and it had been outlined many times in his writings and in those of his co-workers. But he had not completed a book since he had included the chapter on security in *Understanding the Young Child* some twenty years before. The security theory needed its own clear forum in a book of its own.

He worked out a method with Mary Northway for the logistics of getting it down on paper. His daughter, Gery, recalls that he would get up very early at Caledon and go downstairs to work while his energy was highest. He would write in the kitchen, which was directly under her bedroom, and she would hear the chair creak and his coughing. Northway would arrive later, and he would dictate his morning's work into a portable Dictaphone. Northway would take the bulky records back to Toronto to be transcribed and return the pages to him the next day for polishing and rewriting, every word written by hand in his tiny writing.

So, bit by bit, the first draft of *Human Security* was pieced together into a book, and by late 1964 it was nearly finished. Northway arranged for Blatz to meet with Francess Halpenny of the University of Toronto Press on 4 November to discuss its publication, but on 1 November 1964 Blatz died at his home in Toronto. He was sixty-nine years of age. As the *Globe and Mail* described it, his had been 'a lifetime of professional dissent.'[21] The *Canadian Medical Association Journal* said, 'He was never dull ... He could be devastating in debate but was never malicious. He exercised his sharpness of wit to deflate pomposity, but he was the essence of kindliness and graciousness in his personal relationships.'[22]

At the time of his death the two major concerns of Blatz's last years appeared to be well under control: the future of the institute seemed assured with university funding, and the new longitudinal research was under way. As well, the book outlining his philosophy of development and adjustment was nearly completed.

In fact, although the book was published posthumously, the structure of the institute as Blatz knew it began to fall apart.

# 11 Consequences

After Blatz's death, Mary Northway was left to tidy up the details of the book. She added a preface and a postscript and changed the order of some paragraphs to improve continuity, but otherwise she tried to have it appear as it would if Blatz had been given the opportunity to say the last word. Blatz had often said he wanted William Line and Bruce Quarrington of the psychology department to read the manuscript before it went to press, but Line died shortly before Blatz, so Quarrington and Northway worked out the revisions together.

Quarrington suggested both a foreword, to put Blatz's views in a current perspective of child psychology and personality theory, and an additional chapter, to relate the theory to contemporary research findings and develop some of the implications of these views for future studies.[1] The idea of an introduction was ultimately rejected on the basis that Blatz 'had never needed an apologia and had always been capable of defending himself. To interpret him in his own book would be no compliment.'[2] The postscript, however, did give a list of studies arising from the security theory and attempted to give an answer to some of the recurrent questions arising from the theory. It also made the very important point that the security theory would continue to evolve as people worked with it and that the book did not pretend to present it in final form.

In this last book Blatz dwelt on two new points that had scarcely been mentioned in his earlier writings. True to his roots in functional psychology he placed consciousness as the foundation of his security theory. This commitment to the importance of consciousness clearly put an end to speculation that linked him with functionalism's popular offspring, behaviourism. He avoided giving a definition of consciousness, on the grounds that if a person is conscious, that is simply that. He saw emotions as the most highly conscious aspect of our lives, and dismissed the Freudian idea of subconscious influences as merely a scapegoat to allow an excuse for any type of behaviour. Blatz's form of consciousness always had thought content and was in part involved in providing background and organizing material ready for selection. Because a person is conscious he begins to ask questions about himself and his world. He asks such questions as: which? when? where? who? how? and why? The questions appear more or less in that developmental sequence. The last question is asked only by humans, and is the origin of all religions and philosophies. A person consciously selects the answer to any of these questions from his particular experience. Blatz considered this phenomenon of conscious selection to be the most important aspect of the security theory, because selection means making decisions, and because, for Blatz, security was defined as the state of mind in which one is willing to accept the consequences of one's decisions.

*Human Security* also marked two decades of development in thinking about mutual trust as an important part of mental health. In *Understanding the Young Child* Blatz had made short work of dependent security, declining to endow it with any worthwhile purpose other than to forestall insecurity for a while until independence could be established. In the years between the two books, Blatz's position had been under attack by some of his colleagues, particularly Dorothy Millichamp, Betty Flint, and Carroll Davis, and especially during the federal mental health studies of the mid-fifties. They had argued that dependent security is not only important in the development of independence but vital in itself at all stages of development; it is from basic trust in oneself that trust in others is able to grow, and this underlying good feeling is what allows a person to accept consequences.

At first Blatz had resisted the recognition of any benefits of dependent security (apart from its role as an infantile place of refuge), holding the line that independence was the only mature form of security. His colleagues had been tenacious, and he had been won over little by little, capitulating first on the salutary role of immature dependent security as a way of learning to trust. In the debates of a few years earlier he had not been able to accept the idea of dependence in its mature form, but by the time he wrote *Human Security* he had been convinced enough to be willing to include a whole chapter on the subject. His colleagues have said that this is probably one of the very few arguments in which Blatz ever conceded defeat.

This inclusion of mature dependent security gave a new balance to the entire theory, and in *Human Security* Blatz was able to explain the dynamics of development far more broadly than ever before. For the first time he acknowledged that interpersonal relationships are as important as the thoughtful decision-making that is characteristic of independent security. Willingness to accept the consequences of one's behaviour was still the basis of independent security, but in the revised scheme there was also room for sharing the load on a give-and-take basis, and, in fact, this could be a sign of maturity. For young children it would be perfectly healthy to return to the security of depending on the help and support of trustworthy adults if the consequences were too much for them to assume.

In Blatz's new form of the security scheme, both dependence and independence supplemented and interacted with each other and reflected the stages of growth. At first infants are entirely dependent on an agent (usually a parent) and feel secure because the agent is responsible for all decisions. This is immature dependent security. No matter how comfortable this world may be, however, there is still a basic need unmet – the need for activity and change – and this drives children to explore the world that lies outside the nest of absolute dependence. Gradually, as they emerge into exploration, they emerge also into a state of insecurity and anxiety. When they have had enough of the new situation they can extricate themselves by returning to their state of immature dependent security. It is 'a regressive mechanism which is wholly salutary in infancy and depends for its efficacy upon the adequacy of an "immature agent" (usually the parent).'[3] It is a one-way relationship but an important cornerstone of later security. In later childhood, too, this return to a state of immature security can be an entirely healthy process, providing a safe haven when the explorations become too vigorous or dangerous. Simply because the base is secure it allows new and inevitable crises to be met, and, in this way, leads to effective emancipation.[4]

A second way of coping with the anxiety of insecurity is to put forth effort to learn, to acquire knowledge, and to accept consequences, hence becoming independently secure. A third route is to acquire a mature agent and establish a reciprocal relationship. This is mature dependent security and involves a mature agent from outside the family, each person in the relationship contributing to the security of the other. Paradoxically, it is only when a person is firmly launched on the road to independence that it is possible to develop maturely dependent relationships. Such a mutually supportive alliance, with neither person controlling the other, would be the ideal basis for marriage or for a solid friendship. Another factor in mature dependence, Blatz wrote, is the acceptance of a code of ethics and an appreciation that it is part of being a mature human to be able to accept one's own inadequacies.

The fourth device for avoiding insecurity is to employ a deputy agent in order to avoid the real consequences, at least temporarily. Postponement, reinterpretations (such as reasoning or arguing), redirection of the blame, and denial can all be used as short-term, but relatively healthy, ways of solving problems. (For instance, postponement can appear as caution, and denial, in its healthy form, as a sense of proportion.) These mechanisms become increasingly dangerous, however, if they are used so often that they become permanent or pathological. In their ultimate form any of these deputy agents would imply the complete lack of insight that is characteristic of serious mental illness. (The less extreme maladaptions such as indecision, obsessions, or the minimizing of responsibility were frequent problems for the patients Blatz met in his clinical counselling.)

Blatz presented a diagram of the security model, picturing it as a four-pointed star with insecurity as its pivotal point, and the four kinds of security (mature dependent, independent, immature, and the use of deputy agents) as its radial arms. Blatz contended that any kind of security becomes boring after a while, driving people to seek the thrill of insecurity. In turn, insecurity soon becomes too much to bear, so it is a choice of returning to the same type of security as before or looking for another kind. When that particular type of security becomes boring, the process starts all over again, sometimes as a matter of choice, and sometimes as a result of circumstances. In Blatz's theory this is the whole basis of learning. For example, when people accept the challenge of boredom and move out into a state of insecurity, one of their choices is to expend effort and to learn. If they do so, they move into a state of independent security, until another challenge comes along and the balance shifts them back to insecurity again.[5] The diagram is in almost constant motion, as insecurity is resolved temporarily then reappears.

The process proceeds from primitive to more mature patterns, as well. As the child grows he develops patterns of security, first within the family, and later outside it. At about four or five, his interests begin to solidify. In the third stage, at about eight or nine, as well as continuing to be concerned with intimacies and avocation, he begins, more or less, to accept the routine requirements of his world (vocation), and finally, in addition, to acquire a philosophy and sense of purpose. At any time, and in any of these areas, the balance between security and insecurity may be at different points.

*Human Security: Some Reflections* was published in 1966 and received mixed reviews. 'Blatz' book is exasperating ... He was obviously flamboyant and an *ipse addixit* with a fine disregard for details when he felt that an exaggeration was closer to the spirit of the truth than the immediate facts at hand' commented one reviewer.[6] While another stated: 'The reader of this book will come away enriched in his understanding of the complexities of the human relationship.'[7] Ivor McCollum in *American Psychologist* listed *Human Security* as one of his students' favourite 'psychological thrillers,'[8] while a CBC reviewer said he was inspired by the book to suggest that, as a centennial project, Canada should create a hall of fame for champions of children, with Blatz as its first candidate.[9]

At Blatz's funeral, MacGregor Grant, the minister of Rosedale United Church, had delivered a ringing eulogy declaring that Blatz had left behind him a monument more abiding than any of brass or stone – the Institute of Child Study. The institute, however, was not to survive for long in the form in which Blatz had known it.

Blatz had been succeeded upon his retirement by Karl Bernhardt, a solid and competent worker, respected by his colleagues, but without the fire or fireworks of Blatz. Bernhardt had planned to use the seven years before his own retirement to consolidate the institute's programs and to find a young Canadian to prepare to take over as director. Almost immediately, however, Bernhardt's health began to fail, and he was forced to retire the January before Blatz died. The institute was left without a director, and none was appointed. Without a leader, it was vulnerable to attack. The differing approaches to research taken by the psychology department and the institute led to the withdrawal of support for the longitudinal study.

In a statement in the *University Bulletin* of December 1968, University of Toronto President Claude Bissell said: 'We have been unable to make a satisfactory provision for the continuation of the Institute of Child Study. The Institute's approach, and its way of organizing research, are said to be no longer useful, since long-term developmental research with a highly selected child population has been replaced by other approaches that have been found more fruitful.'

This statement confirmed two of Blatz's long-time colleagues, Dorothy Millichamp and Mary Northway, in their decision to retire early in order to salvage some of the possibilities for development that would be lost by a radical change in the institute's direction. They then founded the Brora Centre, to give people from a variety of professions an opportunity to carry on with their previous research and to develop new projects on aspects of human growth, with the focus on child development, education, and mental health. The centre opened in 1969, planning to continue for five years. It lasted for eight. Many of its activities arose out of projects started in the Blatz era.

Ten years later, still angry about the university's decision against child study's research program, Northway wrote: 'My view is that the blockage of the innovative plan of a new approach to longitudinal study which we had introduced in 1962 and adapted to the computer age was a tragedy for the progress of human research. It is understandable that the research plan of a small faculty that had no access to the "secret" committee investigating the Institute, was lost. That the participants were never consulted nor allowed to express their views was a travesty of the democratic process.'[10]

With the change in emphasis, the institute's focus was largely directed to its schools and its student training, and although individual faculty members continue today to do research, the vast and far-reaching projects of Blatz's day have virtually disappeared. Today child study is part of the University of Toronto's Faculty of Education, which gives programs in early childhood education, along with childhood assessment and counselling, in its two-year post-graduate course for diploma students. The laboratory school is used for student practice and as a place to try out ideas in programming, scheduling, and preparing new curricula. There is still a major effort to keep continuous records on each child's developmental and educational growth, because this allows student teachers to check their own judgments of the children they teach.[11] Neither is Blatz entirely forgotten at the institute. In 1985 it organized a seminar on Blatz's security theory, and one of its faculty, Richard Volpe, is investigating the Regal Road Public School files and following up those children he was able to trace nearly half a century later.

Mary Wright of the University of Western Ontario considers that the longitudinal studies will be a much-valued find for historians, with interest likely to extend outside Canada. 'The Institute's longitudinal study is classical in the sense that it was not only the first in Canada, but among the first of its kind on this continent and elsewhere. This work was well-known in the United States and the goals of the study were consistent with those of other comparable research programmes, at, for example, the University of California at Berkeley.'[12]

Mary Ainsworth of Johns Hopkins University, talking to Roger Myers, for the Oral History of Psychology in Canada project was not as convinced of the use of the longitudinal files, saying that very little could be done with 'somebody else's old data, especially data collected at an earlier time with earlier methods, earlier hypotheses and problems. The only reason I am hesitating in the slightest is the fact the Berkeley study has, after these many, many years, been mined, and I am interested that people with new problems are going to Berkeley study data and using it for their own purposes.'[13] Wright's view is that it is simply a matter of technical problems in the handling of multiple variables coupled with a lack of financial resources that have delayed the data from being properly worked. The budgetary problems have not been solved, but the computer and the development of increasingly sophisticated statistical techniques have now gone a long way to solve the other half of the problem, and such technology has allowed Berkeley to begin to yield a rich return.[14]

The Laura Spelman Rockefeller Memorial funds, of course, emphasized longitudinal research. Lawrence Frank likened longitudinal research to films from a movie camera giving a more vivid and complex account of a person than could the results of experimental design, results that he compared to snapshots. Frank also made the practical suggestion that longitudinal records of children and youth, identified in adulthood, would make invaluable subjects for the study of aging, for they would focus on a unique group for whom records would be available of their earliest years and their subsequent development.[15] The first Blatz babies of the mid-1920s are at retirement age today and might, if they were willing, shed light on the establishment of lifelong patterns of coping with the world.

When the longitudinal research was initiated in the 1920s it was taken for granted that the children's records would be kept confidential. Blatz and his staff assumed personal responsibility for seeing that access to the subjects' records would be monitored and the children's identities protected.

With Blatz's death, followed soon after by termination of the institute's longitudinal studies, the question arose of whether to destroy the data or preserve them for the use of historians and scientists in the future. The eventual plan was to preserve the records for safe-keeping in the Rare Books and Special Collections Department of the University of Toronto Library. The present-day ethical procedures required for research with human subjects have been incorporated into the plan. Special permission must be sought to use the documents for

historical or any other kind of research – for individual clinical purposes, for a biography of one or more of the subjects, or if the subjects
themselves make a request to see their own records. The data are filed
under individual research numbers, which assure privacy when researchers are using the material. There is a master list matching the
identities of subjects with their research numbers, but access to the
code is retained by the chief librarian and released only for certain
specified purposes.

This transfer of material from the institute to the library further
marked the end of an era. The major question remains of why it took
so long after Blatz's retirement for the university to decide on the
future of the Institute of Child Study. The question was debated again
and again by those who worked with Blatz. Many put the blame straight
on Blatz himself for failing to share his territory with someone who
might eventually have locked antlers with him and assumed leadership.
Roger Myers said that, although Blatz was a rebel in the child field, in
his own life he was conservative and opposed to change. He did not
provide for his own successor, and as he grew older he seemed to feel
threatened by the kind of bright and brash young person that he had
once been himself.[16]

Mary Wright called it a tragedy that Blatz had not nurtured the
career of someone who would grow to challenge him. Millichamp took
the different view that he had indeed fostered the start of other strong
people, but had used the institute to launch them on to much larger
enterprises. For example, both Griffin and Atcheson had been his
protégés, he supported them in what they did, and they remained
close friends. But the institute was always short of funds; although
Blatz was clever at carving loaves and slicing fishes, there was never
enough to put together salaries that were even approaching adequate
for these two highly qualified psychiatrists. So they moved away
eventually to take other major work in the community: Griffin as director of the Canadian Mental Health Association and Atcheson as
director of the Thistletown Hospital School and professor at the Clarke
Institute of Psychiatry.[17] It was on this very question of salaries that
Blatz and the institute have been accused of exploiting women by
paying them very little for taking major responsibility. He used to say
he could more easily find a competent woman than a competent man.
He said this at a time when women's salaries were much lower than
men's and no one stopped to question it; there was no thought of equal
pay for equal work. Women's career choices were limited, and although
conducting research at the institute might not bring much more money

than working in the secretarial pool, the women at the institute were at least using their minds to their full potential. Over and over again, the women Blatz worked with – Millichamp, Northway, Fletcher – said they felt liberated.

Karl Bernhardt was widely respected, but he, like the rest of Blatz's close colleagues, was not much younger than Blatz. Michael Grapko was considerably younger, but his youth meant inexperience in the increasingly complex university administration of the 1960s, and he waited in the role of assistant director as a conscientious caretaker until a decision could be made one way or the other about the institute. The choices facing the university seemed to be to close the whole operation, to bring in a brilliant director (probably with accompanying staff and possibly from the United States), or to make it a division of the Faculty of Education at the university.

Roger Myers saw it as his responsibility as head of the psychology department to find at least two first-rate researchers in child psychology for the staff of the department, on the assumption that two or more people in an area will stimulate productivity. Certainly he thought the institute would need the prestige of a major name to keep it going, and perhaps someone from the psychology department could take over. Myers tried to get young blood into the department, but his attempts consistently failed. As Myers remarked, Blatz had never been one to tolerate fools gladly, but he especially could not tolerate bright young fools. In his retirement, Blatz had seemed quite amenable to Myers's plan of departmental rejuvenation and had set up a system to get to know the new members of the department. On a certain day of each week he would take one of the new staff to lunch at the York Club and ask him questions. Some passed muster; some did not. But Blatz was always interested in their affairs, and it was characteristic of him that he dropped little personal notes to them about this and that – if they published a book, got married, or had a baby. He made a lot of friends this way, but they did not really get to know Blatz and none of them was ready to make the transition to the institute.[18]

There was consideration given for a while to an interdisciplinary committee to run the institute with representation from the paediatrics, psychology, nutrition, dentistry, and other departments, but this idea fell through. The university also struck a search committee under Ernest Sirluck to find a new director after Bernhardt's retirement, but its deliberations were again inconclusive.

Roger Myers's son, who was one of the St George's School children and is now dean of Henson College, Dalhousie University, in a recorded discussion of the matter with Wright, Northway, and Millichamp, asked rhetorically, 'Who could have done Bill's act again? Nobody.'[19]

As Carl Williams (a pupil of Blatz who was later the president of the University of Western Ontario) said: 'It reminds me of that dictum of Emerson, "A great institution is but the length and shadow of a great man." And I think the Institute was very much of a kind of a one man band in that sense. The Institute in the public mind was very much identified with Bill and I think when Bill withdrew there was very much a question in the University – or at least its administration's mind, was there enough without him for it to carry on under its own steam or would it be better just to wrap it up and just say it's a one man band?'

Roger Myers felt that the institute was going downhill before Blatz vacated the chair. It was coming under criticism and people were wondering if it was sufficiently productive. The institute's house journal (the *Bulletin*) Myers considered to be a mistake; scholars publishing for themselves did not have to survive the 'awful red pencil of the open literature.' Neither would Blatz ever admit an intellectual debt to anyone. But could he have played his cards differently? 'Certainly. We all could – looking back. When the controversy died his influence dwindled.'[20]

Elsie Stapleford, director of the Day Nurseries Branch of the Ontario Department of Welfare, considered Blatz a victim of his own genius because his mind ran so fast that he had neither time nor patience to return and back up his ideas with time-consuming research. He would check out his ideas with further experience, but would not wait for meticulous cross-checking, which meant that he got out of step with research. Millichamp added that he was so often right that he got the feeling he did not need to prove anything.[21] Mary Ainsworth expressed regret that Blatz did not seem to have the impact on American psychology that his security theory should have had, that it had neither the recognition nor the influence that it deserved. She attributed it to two factors: first, that Blatz usually failed to quote sources; and second, that in his search to be original he not only refused to allow himself to be labelled but also would never integrate his material into any kind of perspective in the literature.

Yet there was a time when Blatz and the institute stood in the forefront of their field. Milton J. Senn in his *Insights on the Child Development Movement* states unequivocally that for the first quarter century of child study, 'the field could be defined almost entirely in terms of a few places and the persons located there – Iowa, Minnesota, Berkeley, Antioch, Yale, Toronto, Detroit, Columbia. The discipline was created outside of psychology and remained there until the 1950s ... while learning theory and research became the predominant motif of psychology proper ... the child institutes were pursuing a somewhat different tradition, a maturational orientation, accumulating longitudinal and cross-sectional normative data on the growth of child behaviours.'[22]

Williams spoke of the discussion Blatz's theories evoked among graduate students and of the way they would try to compare them to other personality theories. 'Nobody else [at the University of Toronto at the time] was evolving theories of this order, of this scale which invited discussion. Everybody else was eclectic, criticizing what others had produced but not producing any [theories] themselves.' Williams could see no direct persistent influences of Blatz's theory of education upon the field of psychology: 'I have the feeling it's the fate of all good theories to be superceded by better ones. I don't know that theories are upset by facts but they are replaced by others that explain more, are more comprehensive or go into things in greater depth. This is not to say the new theory is right and the old one wrong. This is clearly a series of building blocks. I think of Bill's notions now as being built into the foundations of contemporary psychology. Without that, this would be the less.'[23]

Atcheson put it with great eloquence in an interview with the author: 'Blatz was one of the greats who did not leave a well identified monument. His contribution was more subtle. He gave of himself freely but he is difficult to use as a teaching model because whatever skills I have with patients I have learned from him and have tried to teach my students: to be sensitive, concerned, humanitarian. He was a great man. You knew you learned a great deal from him but it was difficult to clarify what it was. One could only hope to pass something on from him. Blatz was a unique and unsung hero. He was a member of La Scala when alive but his voice does not echo today. Instead we get the ripple effect of Blatz in psychiatry, education, child life.'

# Notes

The following abbreviations are used in the notes.

TFRBL   Thomas Fisher Rare Book Library, University of Toronto
UTA     University of Toronto Archives

## 1 The Educator Educated

1 W.E. Blatz, *Human Security: Some Reflections* (Toronto: University of Toronto Press 1966) 3
2 V. Carson, interview with M.L. Northway (Mar. 1973) and V. Carson and Margery deRoux, *W.E. Blatz: His Family and His Farm* (Toronto: Brora Centre 1975). (This booklet was compiled from the reminiscences of Carson and deRoux as given during interviews with M.L. Northway. Early biographical material is based on information from the booklet, supplemented with tapes and transcripts of the interviews themselves and with an interview by the author with Lee Blatz Nihill.)
3 Norman MacDonald, *Canada: Immigration and Colonization, 1841–1903* (Toronto: Macmillan 1966) 214–15
4 M. Katz, *The People of Hamilton, Canada West: Family and Class in a Mid-Nineteenth-Century City* (Cambridge, Mass.: Harvard University Press 1975) 5–6; also see M. Katz, 'The Social Structure in Hamilton, Ontario,' in Michiel Horn and Ronald Sabourin, eds, *Studies in Canadian Social History* (Toronto: McClelland and Stewart 1974) 164–85
5 See Joy Parr, *Labouring Children: British Immigrant Apprentices to Canada, 1869–1924* (Montreal: McGill-Queen's University Press 1980);

Phyllis Harrison, ed., *The Home Children: Their Personal Stories* (Winnipeg: Watson and Dwyer 1979); Kenneth Bagnell, *The Little Immigrants: The Orphans Who Came to Canada* (Toronto: Macmillan 1980); and Ivy Pinchbeck and Margaret Hewitt, *Children in English Society*, vol. 2, *From the Eighteenth Century to the Children's Act, 1948* (London: Routledge and Kegan Paul 1973).

6 Katz, *People of Hamilton* 23, 25, 337

7 Most of the early biographical information about Wilhelm (William) Blatz has been supplied by Eva's daughter, Victoria (Mueller) Carson, and Elizabeth 'Lee' Nihill, the youngest daughter in the Blatz family.

8 Carson and deRoux, *W.E. Blatz* 21

9 June Callwood, 'The Dr William Blatzes,' *Maclean's* 3 Jan. 1959

10 Carson and deRoux, *W.E. Blatz* 7

11 Ibid. 11

12 Callwood, 'The Dr William Blatzes'

13 TFRBL, W.E. Blatz Coll., Box 1, Regulations for Special Entry in Canada into the Royal Naval Air Service (9322) – Item 7, enclosed with application, 19 Dec. 1916

14 TFRBL, W.E. Blatz Coll., Box 1, Vice-Admiral C. Kingsmill, letter To whom it may concern (17 Mar. 1917)

15 M.I. Fletcher, interview with J.K. Raymond (May 1979)

16 Ibid.

17 Blatz, *Human Security* 4

18 E.A. Bott, 'Founding of the Institute of Child Study,' in Karl S. Bernhardt, Margaret I. Fletcher, Frances L. Johnson, Dorothy A. Millichamp, and Mary L. Northway, eds, *Twenty-five Years of Child Study* (Toronto: University of Toronto Press 1951) 16

19 E.A. Hartman, W.E. Blatz, and L.G. Kilborn, *Studies in the Regeneration of Denervated Mammalian Muscle* (Ottawa: Research Committee Medical Service Department of Militia and Defence 1919)

20 W.E. Blatz, 'The Freshman's Credo,' and 'The Student's Litany,' *Epistaxis* 24 Feb. 1921

21 Carson and deRoux, *W.E. Blatz* 10

22 TFRBL, W.E. Blatz Coll., Box 1, Blatz, letter to V. Carson (25 Apr. 1919)

23 TFRBL, W.E. Blatz Coll., Box 1, Blatz, letter to V. Carson (12 Jan. 1921)

24 Blatz, *Human Security* 4

25 Thomas W. Goodspeed, *The Story of the University of Chicago, 1890–1925* (Chicago: University of Chicago Press 1925), and Richard J. Storr, *Harper's University, The Beginnings* (Chicago: University of Chicago Press 1966)

26 Robert S. Woodworth and Mary R. Sheehan, *Contemporary Schools of Psychology* (New York: Ronald Press, 3rd ed. 1964) 15
27 Ibid. 31
28 A.A. Roback, *A History of American Psychology* (New York: Collier Books 1964) 240
29 'James Rowland Angell,' in Carl Murchison, ed., *A History of Psychology in Autobiography*, vol. 3 (Worcester, Mass.: Clark University Press 1936) 23
30 Harvey Carr, *Psychology: A Study of Mental Activity* (New York: Longmans, Green and Co. 1925)
31 Hamilton Cravens, *The Triumph of Evolution: The Heredity-Environment Controversy, 1900–1941* (Baltimore: Johns Hopkins University Press 1988) 253, 258
32 The history of psychology at the University of Chicago has been compiled from: Cravens, *Triumph of Evolution*; Murchison, ed., *Psychology in Autobiography*; Roback, *History of American Psychology*; Woodworth and Sheehan, *Contemporary Schools of Psychology*; Edna Heidbreder, *Seven Psychologies* (New York: Appleton, Century Crofts 1933); Raymond E. Fancher, *Pioneers of Psychology* (New York: W.W. Norton 1979); Leonard Zusne, *Names in the History of Psychology: A Biographical Sourcebook* (New York: John Wiley 1975).
33 W.E. Blatz and W.T. Heron, 'The Effect of Endocrine Feeding upon the Learning Performance of White Rats,' *Journal of Experimental Psychology* 8: 4 (Aug. 1924)
34 W.E. Blatz, 'A Physiological Study of the Emotion of Fear,' (Dissertation abstract, Department of Psychology, University of Chicago 1934)
35 TFRBL, W.E. Blatz Coll., Box 1, Blatz correspondence (Nov. 1924)

2 Childhood Ready for Change

1 'James Mark Baldwin,' in Carl Murchison, ed., *A History of Psychology in Autobiography*, vol. 1 (Worcester, Mass.: Clark University Press 1930) 3
2 C. Roger Myers, 'Psychology at Toronto,' in Mary J. Wright and C.R. Myers, eds, *History of Academic Psychology in Canada* (Toronto: C.J. Hogrefe Inc. 1982) 76
3 The material on the history of the psychology department at the University of Toronto is based on the following sources: Edward Alexander Bott, taped interview with C. Roger Myers, 17 Jan. 1962 (Canadian Psychological Association Archives); Clarence Hincks,

*Autobiography* (unpublished); Wright and Myers, eds, *Academic Psychology in Canada*.

4 Neil Sutherland, *Children in English-Canadian Society: Framing the Twentieth-Century Consensus* (Toronto: University of Toronto Press 1976) 72

5 Helen MacMurchy, *The Almosts: A Study of the Feeble-Minded* (Boston: Houghton Mifflin 1920) 177, 1

6 Sutherland, *Children in English-Canadian Society* 71–8

7 Sources for the history of the mental hygiene movement are: Sutherland, *Children in English-Canadian Society*; Norman Dain, *Clifford W. Beers: Advocate for the Insane* (Pittsburgh: University of Pittsburgh Press 1980); Hincks, *Autobiography*; Wilbur Cross, *Twenty-five Years After: Sidelights on the Mental Hygiene Movement and Its Founder* (New York: Doubleday, Doran 1934); Nina Ridenour, *Mental Health in the United States: A Fifty Year History* (Cambridge, Mass.: Harvard University Press 1961).

8 G. Stanley Hall, *Life and Confessions of a Psychologist* (New York: D. Appleton and Company 1923) 392

9 William Scott, 'What Child Study Has Done for the Teaching World,' Dominion Educational Association *Proceedings* (1901), in Douglas Lawr and Robert Gidney, eds, *Educating Canadians: A Documentary History of Public Education*, 2nd ed. (Toronto: Van Nostrand Reinhold 1973) 185

10 Hamilton Cravens, *The Triumph of Evolution: The Heredity-Environment Controversy, 1900–1941* (Baltimore: Johns Hopkins University Press 1988) 80

11 P. Collier and D. Horowitz, *The Rockefellers: An American Dynasty* (New York: Signet–New American Library 1976) 59

12 The story of the child study movement, and the Laura Spelman Rockefeller Memorial fund's part in fostering it, is based on the following accounts: John E. Anderson, 'Child Development: An Historical Perspective,' *Child Development* 27 (Mar.–Dec. 1956); Lawrence K. Frank, 'The Beginnings of Child Development and Family Life Education in the Twentieth Century,' *Merrill-Palmer Quarterly of Behaviour and Development* 8: 4 (Oct. 1962); Elizabeth Lomax, 'The Laura Spelman Rockefeller Memorial: Some Contributions to Early Research in Child Development,' *Journal of the History of the Behavioural Sciences* 12: 3 (July 1977); P. Keith Osborne, *Early Childhood Education in Historical Perspective* (Athens, Ga: Education Associates 1975); Steven L. Schlossman, 'Philanthropy and the Gospel of Child Develop-

ment,' *Proceedings of the Rockefeller Archive Center* 8 June 1979; Milton J. Senn, *Insights on the Child Development Movement in the United States*, Monographs of the Society for Research in Child Development 49: 3–4 (Aug. 1975) (Chicago: University of Chicago Press 1975).

13 Schlossman, 'Philanthropy and the Gospel of Child Development'
14 Hincks, *Autobiography* 57
15 Ibid. 58–62
16 W.E. Blatz, *Hostages to Peace: Parents and the Children of Democracy* (New York: William Morrow 1940) 123
17 Ibid. 123
18 Helen MacMurchy, *The Canadian Mother's Book*, Little Blue Books Mother's Series No. 1 (Ottawa: Dominion of Canada Department of Health 1923) 67
19 Helen MacMurchy, *How to Take Care of the Children*, Little Blue Books Mother's Series No. 5 (Ottawa: Dominion of Canada Department of Health 1923) 40
20 Helen MacMurchy, *How to Take Care of the Mother*, Little Blue Books Mother's Series No. 4 (Ottawa: Dominion of Canada Department of Health 1923) 5
21 Roy Lubove, *The Professional Altruist: The Emergence of Social Work as a Career, 1880–1930* (Cambridge, Mass.: Harvard University Press 1965) 106
22 Ibid. 89
23 Ridenour, *Mental Health in the United States* 83
24 Andrew Jones and Leonard Rutman, *In the Children's Aid: J.J. Kelso and Child Welfare in Ontario* (Toronto: University of Toronto Press 1981) 125–32
25 Patricia T. Rooke and R.L. Schnell, *Discarding the Asylum: From Child Rescue to the Welfare State in English Canada (1800–1950)* (Lanham, Md.: University Press of America 1983) 347–50. See also Patricia T. Rooke and R.L. Schnell, *No Bleeding Heart: Charlotte Whitton, A Feminist on the Right* (Vancouver: University of British Columbia Press 1987).
26 Lubove, *Professional Altruist* 162
27 Ibid. 121
28 Jones and Rutman, *In the Children's Aid* 36
29 In *Discarding the Asylum*, Rooke and Schnell have detailed the changing patterns of intervention from institution to foster home to family reorganization.
30 MacMurchy, *The Almosts* 173, 175–6
31 Daniel J. Kevles, *In the Name of Eugenics: Genetics and the Use of*

*Human Heredity* (New York: Alfred A. Knopf 1985) 184
32 Cravens, *Triumph of Evolution* 78
33 Ibid. 179–80
34 Ibid. 247–50, and Christopher Lasch, *Haven in A Heartless World: The Family Besieged* (New York: Basic Books 1977) 32–4
35 Cravens, *Triumph of Evolution* 230
36 'Angell,' in Murchison, ed., *Psychology in Autobiography*, vol. 3, 28
37 'Jean Piaget,' in Edwin G. Boring, Herbert S. Langfeld, Heinz Werner, Robert M. Yerkes, eds, *History of Psychology in Autobiography*, vol. 4 (Worcester, Mass.: Clark University Press 1952) 245–6
38 Lori Rotenberg, 'The Wayward Worker: Toronto's Prostitute at the Turn of the Century,' in Janice Acton, Penny Goldsmith, and Bonnie Shepard, *Women at Work: Ontario, 1850–1930* (Toronto: Canadian Women's Educational Press 1974) 45
39 TFRBL, W.E. Blatz Coll., Restricted File, Juvenile Court Clinic Reports, 1925–6, and Social Studies Conferences, Edited Reports
40 Ibid.
41 Ibid.
42 Ibid.
43 Lasch, *Haven in a Heartless World* 16, 17
44 TFRBL, W.E. Blatz Coll., Box 16, *Toronto Daily Star* 17 May 1934
45 Norman MacDonald, *Canada: Immigration and Colonization, 1841–1903* (Toronto: Macmillan 1966) 50
46 Kenneth Bagnell, *The Little Immigrants: The Orphans Who Came to Canada* (Toronto: Macmillan 1980) 204–5
47 Sutherland, *Children in English-Canadian Society* 35
48 Joy Parr, *Labouring Children: British Immigrant Apprentices to Canada, 1869–1924* (Montreal: McGill-Queen's University Press 1980) 82
49 Rotenberg, 'Wayward Workers' 45
50 Sutherland, *Children in English-Canadian Society* 240
51 J. Bowlby, *Maternal Care and Mental Health* (Geneva: World Health Organization 1951)

3 The Blatz Babies

1 TFRBL, W.E. Blatz Coll., Tape, Margaret Hincks, interview with M.L. Northway (3 Dec. 1973)
2 Milton J. Senn, *Insights on the Child Development Movement in the United States* Monographs of the Society for Research in Child Development 40: 3–4 (Aug. 1975) (Chicago: University of Chicago Press 1975)

3 E.A. Bott, interview with Roger Myers (17 Jan. 1962); transcript, in Canadian Psychological Association Archives, Ottawa

4 Frederick Tracy and Joseph Stimpfl, *The Psychology of Childhood* 7th ed. (Boston: D.C. Heath 1909)

5 D.A. Millichamp and M.I. Fletcher, 'Goals and Growth of Nursery Education,' in Karl S. Bernhardt, Margaret I. Fletcher, Frances L. Johnson, Dorothy A. Millichamp, and Mary L. Northway, eds, *Twenty-five Years of Child Study* (Toronto: University of Toronto Press 1951) 58

6 Elizabeth Cleveland, *Training the Toddler* (Philadelphia: J.P. Lippincott 1925)

7 Neil Sutherland, *Children in English-Canadian Society: Framing the Twentieth-Century Consensus* (Toronto: University of Toronto Press 1976) 174

8 TFRBL, W.E. Blatz Coll., Box 15, *Toronto Daily Star* 29 Mar. 1927

9 R.G.N. Laidlaw, 'A Note on the Origins of Blatz' Security Theory,' *Merrill-Palmer Quarterly of Behaviour and Development* 6:1 (Fall 1959) 17

10 TFRBL, W.E. Blatz Coll., Box 15, Dora Smith Conover, 'The Nursery School in Canada,' *New Outlook* 20 Apr. 20 1927

11 TFRBL, W.E. Blatz Coll., Box 15, Frances L. Johnson, 'Where a Child Can Be a Child,' *Chatelaine* Mar. 1928

12 TFRBL, W.E. Blatz Coll., Box 15, Mabel Crews Ringland, 'The New Child Study Movement: The Message of the Nursery School to Modern Parents,' *Toronto Star Weekly* 23 June 1928

13 TFRBL, W.E. Blatz Coll., Box 15, 'Spanking Is Barred at Nursery School,' *Toronto Daily Star* 29 Mar. 1927

14 TFRBL, W.E. Blatz Coll., Box 15, 'Mothers Would Spank Less if at Home More,' *Toronto Daily Star* 30 Mar. 1927

15 TFRBL, W.E. Blatz Coll., Box 15, Ringland, 'The New Child Study Movement'

16 TFRBL, W.E. Blatz Coll., Box 15, W.E. Blatz, Press release to Toronto newspapers, 18 Nov. 1925, published in part as 'Catch Wild Infant at the Age of Two,' Toronto *Telegram* 27 Nov. 1925

17 TFRBL, W.E. Blatz Coll., Box 15, Johnson, 'Where a Child Can Be a Child'

18 TFRBL, W.E. Blatz Coll., Box 17, Minutes of staff meeting (20 Oct. 1926)

19 Ibid. (5 Jan. 1926)

20 Ibid. (3 Nov. 1926)

21 Ibid. (5 Jan. 1926 and 26 Jan. 1927)

22 Ibid. (3 Nov. 1926)

23 Ibid. (20 Sept. 1926)

24 TFRBL, W.E. Blatz Coll., Tape, Reba Cohen, interview with M.L. Northway (6 Feb. 1973)

25 TFRBL, W.E. Blatz Coll., Box 17, Minutes of staff meetings (5 Jan. 1926 and 3 Nov. 1926)

26 Ibid. (3 Nov. 1926)

27 Ibid. (19 Jan. 1927)

28 Ibid. (12 Jan. 1926)

29 Ibid. (20 Oct. 1926)

30 Ibid. (26 Jan. 1927)

31 Ibid. (3 Nov. 1926)

32 Ibid. (19 Jan. 1927)

33 Ibid. (19 Jan. 1927)

34 Ibid., Box 18 (27 Feb. 1929)

35 Ibid., Box 17 (5 Jan. 1926)

36 William Blatz and Helen Bott, *Parents and the Pre-School Child* (London and Toronto: J.M. Dent and Sons 1928) 6, 41, 42

37 Ibid. 214–17

38 TFRBL, W.E. Blatz Coll., Box 49, General Directions for Use of the Three Day Continuous Record Form

39 TFRBL, W.E. Blatz Coll., Restricted File, Direction for Keeping Records of Vocalization

40 TFRBL, W.E. Blatz Coll., Restricted File, Institute of Child Study Monthly Developmental Record

41 TFRBL, W.E. Blatz Coll., Box 49, Introductory Guide to the W.E. Blatz Research Documents, W.E. Blatz Longitudinal Study, 1926

42 TFRBL, W.E. Blatz Coll., Box 8, W.E. Blatz, 'The St George's School for Child Study,' *University of Toronto Monthly* (June 1926)

43 Ibid.

44 TFRBL, W.E. Blatz Coll., Box 15, Blatz, 'Catch Wild Infant at the Age of Two'

45 TFRBL, W.E. Blatz Coll., Box 15, Conover, 'The Nursery School in Canada'

46 TFRBL, W.E. Blatz Coll., Box 15, Johnson, 'Where a Child Can Be a Child'

47 TFRBL, W.E. Blatz Coll., Box 15, Ringland, 'The New Child Study Movement'

48 Among the authors who decry the influence of the 'experts' on raising children are Veronica Strong-Boag, 'Intruders in the Nursery: Childcare Professionals Reshape the Years One to Five, 1920–1940,' in Joy Parr, ed., *Childhood and Family in Canadian History* (Toronto: McClelland

and Stewart 1982), and Daniel Beekman, *The Mechanical Baby: A Popular History of the Theory and Practice of Child Raising* (New York: Meridian Books 1977).

49 Lawrence Frank, 'The Beginnings of Child Development and Family Life Education in the Twentieth Century,' *Merrill-Palmer Quarterly of Behaviour and Development* 8: 4 (Oct. 1962) 221–2, and Steven L. Schlossman, 'Philanthropy and the Gospel of Child Development,' *Proceedings of the Rockefeller Archive Center* 8 June 1979, 30

50 TFRBL, W.E. Blatz Coll., Box 25, Nellie Chant, 'Early Parent Education,' undated typescript

51 TFRBL, W.E. Blatz Coll., Box 17, Minutes of staff meeting (19 Jan. 1926)

52 TFRBL, W.E. Blatz Coll., Box 21, Nellie Chant, letter to Mary Northway (7 Feb. 1973)

53 TFRBL, W.E. Blatz Coll., Box 17, Minutes of staff meeting (19 Jan. 1926)

54 Frances L. Johnson with H. Bott, N.I. Chant, A.M.R. Foster, M.W. Brown, K.S. Bernhardt, and D.M. Douglas, 'Activities and Aims of Parent Education,' in Bernhardt et al., eds, *Twenty-five Years of Child Study*

4 Fame without Fortune

1 TFRBL, W.E. Blatz Coll., Tape, J.D. Griffin, interview with M.L. Northway (3 Dec. 1973)

2 TFRBL, W.E. Blatz Coll., Tape, C.D. Williams, interview with M.L. Northway (30 Mar. 1974)

3 TFRBL, W.E. Blatz Coll., Tape, M.I. Fletcher, interview with M.L. Northway (3 Oct. 1973)

4 M.I. Fletcher, interview with J.K. Raymond (June 1979)

5 TFRBL, W.E. Blatz Coll., Tape, M.I. Fletcher, interview with M.L. Northway (3 Oct. 1973); and interview with J.K. Raymond (June 1979)

6 D.A. Millichamp with M.L. Northway, *Conversations at Caledon: Some Reminiscences of the Blatz Era* (Toronto: Brora Centre 1977) 6

7 Ibid. 7

8 William Blatz, Dorothy Millichamp, and Margaret Fletcher, *Nursery Education: Theory and Practice* (New York: William Morrow 1935) 31–3, 168

9 Dorothy A. Millichamp, Notes for an Address to a Security Theory Seminar: A Meeting to Discuss and Apply the Ideas of W.E. Blatz (University of Toronto 15, 16 Nov. 1985)

10 Margaret L. Husband, 'The Food Preferences of Nursery School

Children' (MA diss., University of Toronto 1933)
11 Blatz, et al., *Nursery Education* 56
12 Ibid. 15–16
13 Ibid. 20
14 Millichamp, Notes for an Address to Security Theory Seminar
15 Blatz et al., *Nursery Education* 259
16 Alida Starr, 'Emotional Episodes in Nursery School Children,' (MA diss., University of Toronto 1930)
17 TFRBL, W.E. Blatz Coll., Box 18, Minutes of staff meeting 20 Mar. 1929
18 TFRBL, W.E. Blatz Coll., Box 49, Introductory Guide to the W.E. Blatz Research Documents. W.E. Blatz Longitudinal Study, 1926, folder five: 'The Nursery School Records'; folder six: 'The Testing Program' and 'Mental and Personality Test Reports'
19 TFRBL, W.E. Blatz Coll., Box 25, St George's School for Child Study and Canadian National Committee for Mental Hygiene, *Organization of Parent Education Groups*, pamphlet (Toronto: University of Toronto Press 1930) 4
20 Ibid. 6
21 Ibid. 8
22 TFRBL, W.E. Blatz Coll., Box 25, Organization of Parent Education in a Mental Hygiene Program, undated mimeographed course description (1931?)
23 E.A. Bott, Introduction to W.E. Blatz and E.A. Bott, 'Studies in Mental Hygiene of Children: I. Behaviour of Public School Children – A Description of Method,' *Pedagogical Seminary and Journal of Genetic Psychology* 34:4 (Dec. 1927) 552–82
24 Ibid. 5
25 Ibid. 9
26 W.E. Blatz, 'Delinquency,' *Parent Education Bulletin* 30 (Winter 1944–5)
27 Blatz and Bott, 'Studies in Mental Hygiene of Children,' 30
28 TFRBL, W.E. Blatz Coll., Tape, Elsie Stapleford, interview with M.L. Northway (25 Mar. 1974)
29 TFRBL, W.E. Blatz Coll., Tape, J.D. Griffin, interview with M.L. Northway (3 Dec. 1974)
30 Blatz and Bott, 'Studies in Mental Hygiene'
31 Ibid. 30
32 'Robert S. Patterson,' in Robert S. Patterson, John W. Chalmers, and John W. Friesen, eds, *Profiles of Canadian Educators* (Canada: D.C. Heath 1974) 299
33 TFRBL, W.E. Blatz Coll., Tape, Eleanor Hamilton, interview with M.L.

Northway (22 Oct. 1972)

34 The history of Windy Ridge is compiled from: M. L. Northway's interviews with Carroll Davis (13 Feb. 1973) and Eleanor Hamilton (22 Oct.
1972); Margaret Findley, interview with Carroll Davis (Dec. 1972);
Eleanor Hamilton's scrapbooks filed in the TFRBL; and the Windy Ridge
notes in TFRBL, Blatz Coll., Box 34.

35 Millichamp and Northway, *Conversations at Caledon* 7

36 M.I. Fletcher, interview with J.K. Raymond (May 1979)

37 TFRBL, W.E. Blatz Coll., Tape, Reba Cohen, interview with M.L.
Northway (6 Feb. 1973)

38 TFRBL, W.E. Blatz Coll., Tape, M.I. Fletcher, interview with M.L.
Northway (3 Oct. 1973)

39 TFRBL, W.E. Blatz Coll., Tape, Bruce Quarrington, quoted by Carl
Williams, interview with M.L. Northway (30 Mar. 1974)

40 TFRBL, W.E. Blatz Coll., Box 15, J. David Ketchum, 'The Saga of Bill
Blatz,' typescript 9 Apr. 1930

41 TFRBL, W.E. Blatz Coll., Box 15, 'Russia Threatens Complacent Selfish-
ness of Industrial Order,' *Varsity* 49 (25 Feb. 1931)

42 TFRBL, W.E. Blatz Coll., Tape, Gery deRoux, interview with M.L.
Northway (8 Aug. 1973)

43 W.E. Blatz and H.M. Bott, *Parents and the Pre-School Child* (London
and Toronto: J.M. Dent and Sons 1928) v

44 Ibid. viii

45 TFRBL, W.E. Blatz Coll., Box 1, William Morrow, letter to William Blatz
(25 Oct. 1929)

46 Ibid., Blatz, letter to Morrow (2 Nov. 1928)

47 Ibid., Morrow, letter to Blatz (5 Nov. 1928)

48 Ibid., Morrow, letter to Blatz (10 Nov. 1928)

49 Ibid., John B. Watson, letter to William Morrow (1 Mar. 1929)

50 William Blatz and Helen Bott, *The Management of Young Children*
(Toronto: McClelland and Stewart 1930) v

51 Ibid. vi

52 TFRBL, W.E. Blatz Coll., Box 1, William Morrow, letter to Blatz (3 Dec.
1930)

53 Steven Schlossman, 'Philanthropy and the Gospel of Child Development,' *Proceedings of the Rockefeller Archive Center* 8 June 1979, 26–9

54 Frederick Tisdall, *The Home Care of the Infant and Child* (New York:
William Morrow 1931)

55 William J. Perlman, ed., *The Movies on Trial: The Views and Opinions of
Outstanding Personalities about Screen Entertainment Past and Present*

(New York: Macmillan 1936)

56 Colin Sabiston, review in the *Narrator* 3:7 (Sept. 1936)
57 Material for this brief story of the McGill University Nursery School and Child Laboratory was gathered from Roger Myers, interview with J.K. Raymond (May 1979); Carroll Davis, interview with M.L. Northway (13 Feb. 1973); M.L. Northway, 'Child Study in Canada: A Casual History,' in Lois M. Brockman, John H. Whiteley, and John P. Zubek, eds, *Child Development: Selected Readings* (Toronto: McClelland and Stewart 1973).
58 W.E. Blatz, in *National Parent Teacher* (Nov. 1958)
59 TFRBL, W.E. Blatz Coll., Box 21, Nellie Chant, letter to M.L. Northway (22 Feb. 1973)
60 Blatz et al., *Nursery Education*
61 Marjorie Poppleton and William Blatz, *We Go to Nursery School* (New York: Morrow 1935)

5 In the Dionne Nursery

1 UTA, Norma Ford Walker Coll., B79-0045/003, 004, Dionne scrapbooks
2 William E. Blatz, *The Five Sisters: A Study of Child Psychology* (Toronto: McClelland and Stewart 1938) 4
3 Ibid. 6, 7, 8
4 M.I. Fletcher, D.A. Millichamp, and Roger Myers, interviews with J.K. Raymond (May 1979)
5 TFRBL, W.E. Blatz Coll., Box 37, Edna Guest to W.E. Blatz (16 Sept. 1937)
6 TFRBL, W.E. Blatz Coll., Box 38, *New York Times Magazine* 10 Oct. 1937, Section 8
7 Blatz, *The Five Sisters* 203–5
8 D.A. Millichamp, interview with J.K. Raymond (Dec. 1980)
9 Blatz, *The Five Sisters* 137
10 Ibid. 88
11 D.A. Millichamp, interview with J.K. Raymond (May 1979)
12 Ibid.
13 M.I. Fletcher, interview with J.K. Raymond (May 1979)
14 D.A. Millichamp, interview with J.K. Raymond (May 1979)
15 Ibid.
16 TFRBL, W.E. Blatz Coll., Box 36, Dorothy Millichamp, 'Nursery School Plans – Observation Set-up' (20 Sept. 1936)
17 D.A. Millichamp, interview with J.K. Raymond (May 1979)
18 TFRBL, W.E. Blatz Coll., Box 36, Dorothy Millichamp, Memorandum to Dionne Staff (Sept. 1936)

19 UTA, Norma Ford Walker Coll., B79-0045/003, *Evening Telegram*, 2 Sept. 1936
20 Anne Harris Blatz, interview with J.K. Raymond (Nov. 1979)
21 W.E. Blatz, N. Chant, M.W. Charles, M.I. Fletcher, N.H.C. Ford, A.L. Harris, J.W. MacArthur, M. Mason, and D.A. Millichamp, *Collected Studies on the Dionne Quintuplets*. Child Development Series, Nos 11–16 (Toronto: University of Toronto Press 1937) 3
22 TFRBL, W.E. Blatz Coll., Box 35, D.A. Millichamp to J. Noel and C. Tremblay (8 Jan. 1937)
23 Blatz, *The Five Sisters* 94
24 TFRBL, W.E. Blatz Coll., Box 36, Memorandum (May 1936)
25 Ibid., Memorandum (Sept. 1936)
26 Ibid., Memorandum (Nov. 1936)
27 Ibid., Memorandum (23 Jan. 1936)
28 Ibid., Suggested Routine Reorganization (Feb. 1937) 4
29 TFRBL, W.E. Blatz Coll., Restricted File
30 Blatz, *The Five Sisters* 81
31 TFRBL, W.E. Blatz Coll., Box 36, Memoranda (Nov. 1936, Jan. 1937)
32 Ibid., Memorandum (6 Nov. 1936)
33 Ibid., Suggested Routine Reorganization (Feb. 1937)
34 TFRBL, W.E. Blatz Coll., Restricted File, Developmental Report (30 Mar. 1936)
35 TFRBL, W.E. Blatz Coll., Box 36, Memorandum (3 Jan. 1937)
36 Ibid.
37 TFRBL, W.E. Blatz Coll., Box 36, Millichamp Report from Dafoe Hospital (23 Jan. 1937)
38 Blatz, *The Five Sisters*, 37
39 Ibid. 68
40 Ibid. 80
41 TFRBL, W.E. Blatz Coll., Box 36, Suggested Changes (6 Nov. 1936)
42 Ibid., Suggested Routine Reorganization (30 Jan. 1937)
43 Ibid., Suggested Routine Reorganization (Feb.1937)
44 Blatz, *The Five Sisters* 35
45 TFRBL, W.E. Blatz Coll., Box 36, Report by Margaret Fletcher, Dafoe Hospital (13 May 1937)
46 Blatz, *The Five Sisters* 132

6 Studying the Five Sisters

1 UTA, Norma Ford Walker Coll., B79-0045/003, 004, Dionne scrapbooks

2 William E. Blatz, *The Five Sisters: A Study of Child Psychology* (Toronto: McClelland and Stewart 1938) 23

3 TFRBL, W.E. Blatz Coll., Box 38, *Globe and Mail* 18 Sept. 1937

4 TFRBL, W. E. Blatz Coll., Box 37, Minutes of Research Committee

5 J.W. MacArthur and N.H.C. Ford, 'A Biological Study of the Dionne Quintuplets – An Identical Set,' in W.E. Blatz, N. Chant, M.W. Charles, M.I. Fletcher, N.H.C. Ford, A.L. Harris, J.W. MacArthur, M. Mason, and D.A. Millichamp, *Collected Studies on the Dionne Quintuplets*. Child Development Series, Nos 11–16 (Toronto: University of Toronto Press 1937) 35–6

6 Blatz, *The Five Sisters* 5

7 Ibid. 25

8 TFRBL, W.E. Blatz Coll., Box 37, Untitled, undated note on research

9 William E. Blatz, 'Mental Growth of the Dionne Quintuplets,' in Blatz, et al., *Collected Studies on the Dionne Quintuplets* 3

10 Ibid. 5

11 Ibid. 6

12 Blatz, *The Five Sisters* 24–44

13 Ibid. 30

14 Blatz, 'Mental Growth of the Dionne Quintuplets,' 7

15 Blatz, *The Five Sisters* 38

16 Ibid. 40

17 Ibid. 41

18 Blatz, 'Mental Growth of the Dionne Quintuplets,' 9

19 Ibid. 11

20 Blatz, *The Five Sisters* 192–3

21 UTA, Norma Ford Walker Coll., B79-0045/003(01), Press clipping, name of newspaper omitted, dateline: Detroit (24 Feb. 1939)

22 TFRBL, W.E. Blatz Coll., Box 37, Minutes of First Meeting of the Research Committee on the Dionne Quintuplets (18 Jan. 1936)

23 Ibid. 4

24 Ibid. 4

25 Ibid., Program of Conference on Dionne Quintuplets

26 Ibid., Mary Dabney Davis to W.E. Blatz (4 Nov. 1937)

27 Ibid., Resolution by delegates to Conference on Dionne Quintuplets (Oct. 1937)

28 Ibid., Allan Roy Dafoe and William Dafoe, 'The Physical Welfare of the Dionne Quintuplets'

29 TFRBL, W.E. Blatz Coll., Box 38, Mary Dougherty, 'What about the Other Five Dionnes?' *Pictorial Review* (May 1935)

30 Blatz, 'Mental Growth of the Dionne Quintuplets,' 3

31 TFRBL, W.E. Blatz Coll., Box 36, 'Miscellaneous Notes Re Dafoe Hospital, Callander'
32 James Brough, with Annette, Cecile, Marie, and Yvonne Dionne, *We Were Five: The Dionne Quintuplets' Story from Birth through Girlhood to Womanhood* (New York: Simon and Schuster 1965) 55
33 TFRBL, W.E. Blatz Coll., Box 36, Note by J. Noel (17 Feb. 1937)
34 TFRBL, W.E. Blatz Coll., Box 38, Dougherty, 'What about the Other Five Dionnes?'
35 Blatz, *The Five Sisters* 6
36 TFRBL, W.E. Blatz Coll., Box 35, Blatz, letter to Mrs W.J. Hanna of Sarnia (15 June 1935): 'Your suggestion of a Catholic psychologist I think was very timely and when we meet in the fall I will certainly include Father Furfey.'
37 TFRBL, W.E. Blatz Coll., Box 36, Staff notes (1936)
38 TFRBL, W.E. Blatz Coll., Box 36, Memorandum (Sept. 1936)
39 TFRBL, W.E. Blatz Coll., Box 35, Claire Tremblay to D.A. Millichamp, and D.A. Millichamp to various Montreal booksellers
40 TFRBL, W.E. Blatz Coll., Box 36, Memorandum (Sept. 1936)
41 Blatz, *The Five Sisters* 86
42 TFRBL, W.E. Blatz Coll., Box 37, Leon Barreau, letter to W.E. Blatz (7 Mar. 1938)
43 Brough, *We Were Five* 88–9
44 TFRBL, W.E. Blatz Coll., Box 38, *Globe and Mail* 7 Apr. 1938
45 Ibid., *Toronto Daily Star* 14 Apr. 1938
46 TFRBL, W.E. Blatz Coll., Box 35, W.E. Blatz, letter to Allan Roy Dafoe (11 Oct. 1937)
47 Brough, *We Were Five* 89
48 Ibid. 55, 58, 70, 119–20, 191
49 D.A. Millichamp, interview with J.K. Raymond (Dec. 1980)
50 M.I. Fletcher, interview with J.K. Raymond (May 1979)
51 D.A. Millichamp, interview with J.K. Raymond (Dec. 1980)

7 The Practical Counsellor

1 TFRBL, W.E. Blatz Coll., Tape, Roger Myers, interview with M.L. Northway (30 Apr. 1973)
2 TFRBL, W.E. Blatz Coll., Box 49, Introductory Guide to the W.E. Blatz Research Documents, W.E. Blatz Longitudinal Study, 1926, Follow up Records, folder seven; and J. Partridge, W.E. Blatz Longitudinal Study, 1926: Method of Collecting Longitudinal Information (1951)
3 M.L. Northway, 'Child Study in Canada: A Casual History,' in Lois M.

Brockman, John Whiteley, and John Zubek, eds, *Child Development: Selected Readings* (Toronto: McClelland and Stewart 1973)

4 This is a recurrent theme in the recent literature of child study, but for an early mention of the idea see Elizabeth Lomax, Jerome Kagan, and Barbara Rosenkranz, *Science and Patterns of Child Care* (San Francisco: W.H. Freeman 1978).

5 William E. Blatz, *Hostages to Peace: Parents and the Children of Democracy* (New York: William Morrow 1940) 183

6 Ibid. 185

7 Ibid. 186

8 Ibid. 192

9 D.A. Millichamp with M.L. Northway, *Conversations at Caledon: Some Reminiscences of the Blatz Era* (Toronto: Brora Centre 1977) 33

10 TFRBL, W.E. Blatz Coll., Tape, D. Atcheson and J.D. Griffin, interviews with M.L. Northway (3 Dec. 1973)

11 TFRBL, W.E. Blatz Coll., Box 49, D.A. Millichamp, Introductory Guide to the W.E. Blatz Research Documents, folder 12, Clinical correspondence 1950–9

12 Millichamp and Northway, *Conversations at Caledon*

13 June Callwood, 'The Dr William Blatzes,' *Maclean's* 3 Jan. 1959

14 TFRBL, W.E. Blatz Coll., Tape, Carl Williams, interview with M.L. Northway and D.A. Millichamp (30 Mar. 1974)

15 M.L. Northway, Postscript to William E. Blatz, *Human Security: Some Reflections* (Toronto: University of Toronto Press 1966) 127

16 Blatz, *Human Security* 16

17 R.G.N. Laidlaw, interview with J.K. Raymond (May 1979)

18 Donald Ford and Hugh B. Urban, *Systems of Psychotherapy: A Comparative Study* (New York: John Wiley and Sons 1963). See also R. Herink, ed., *The Psychotherapy Handbook* (New York: New American Library 1980); J.O. Prochaska, *Systems of Psychotherapy: A Transtheoretical Analysis* (Chicago: Dorsey Press 1984); William S. Sahakian, ed., *Psychotherapy and Counselling: Studies in Technique* (Chicago: Rand McNally 1969).

19 Jan Ehrenwald, *The History of Psychotherapy: From Healing Magic to Encounter* (New York: J. Aronson 1976) 391

20 TFRBL, W.E. Blatz Coll., Tape, Roger Myers, interview with M.L. Northway (30 Apr. 1973)

21 Millichamp and Northway, *Conversations at Caledon* 31

22 J.D. Griffin, interview with M.L. Northway (3 Dec. 1973)

23 Roger Myers, interview with M.L. Northway (30 Apr. 1973)

24 Millichamp and Northway, *Conversations at Caledon* 31
25 J.D. Griffin, interview with M.L. Northway (3 Dec. 1973)
26 TFRBL, W.E. Blatz Coll., Restricted File, Clinical correspondence
27 Ibid.
28 Ibid.
29 Ibid.
30 D. Atcheson, interview with J.K. Raymond (Mar. 1981)
31 J.D. Griffin, interview with J.K. Raymond (Mar. 1981)
32 D. Atcheson, interview with J.K. Raymond (Mar. 1981)
33 M.L. Northway, interview with J.K. Raymond (May 1979)
34 D.A. Millichamp, interview with J.K. Raymond (May 1979)
35 TFRBL, W.E. Blatz Coll., Restricted File, Clinical correspondence
36 Mary L. Northway, *Tribute to William Emet Blatz: M.A., M.B., PH. D.,
   1958–1964, from the Institute of Child Study, University of Toronto,
   Canada. January 1965* 3; see also abstract of Blatz's address to CPA
   conference, 13 June 1958, in *Canadian Journal of Psychology* 12:3
   (Sept. 1958).
37 Blatz, *Human Security* 110
38 Ibid. 109
39 TFRBL, W.E. Blatz Coll., Restricted File, Clinical correspondence
40 M.L. Wright, interview with J.K. Raymond (Nov. 1979)
41 Millichamp and Northway, *Conversations at Caledon* 32
42 Howard Kirschenbaum, *On Becoming Carl Rogers* (New York: Delacorte
   Press 1979) 258
43 Blatz, *Human Security* 12
44 Ibid. 114
45 TFRBL, W.E. Blatz Coll., Restricted File, Clinical correspondence
46 Ibid.
47 W.E. Blatz, 'Curing and Preventing,' *Bulletin of the Institute of Child
   Study* (73) 19: 2 (June 1957) 6
48 Blatz, *Hostages to Peace* 51
49 Ibid. 200, 201
50 Ibid. 200
51 Ibid. 201
52 Ben Wicks, *No Time to Wave Goodbye* (Toronto: Stoddart Publishing 1988)
53 Blatz, *Hostages to Peace* 201, 202

8 The Nursery Overseas

1 Tom Harrison, *Living through the Blitz* (Harmondsworth, Middlesex:

Penguin Books 1978) 19–35

2 TFRBL, W.E. Blatz, Coll., Box 9, Blatz's undated notes on lectures to Canadian Army Officers (Jan. and Mar. 1942)
3 Ibid., Blatz, pamphlet on morale (typescript)
4 Walter Gordon, interview with J.K. Raymond (4 Oct. 1979)
5 TFRBL, W.E. Blatz Coll., Box 31, *Telegram, Toronto Daily Star, Globe and Mail* 13 Mar. to 4 Apr. 1942
6 Ibid., *Globe and Mail* 2 Apr. 1942
7 Ibid., Scrapbook, clipping from *The Times* (London) Jan. 1942
8 Ibid., *Globe and Mail* 14 July 1942
9 D.A. Millichamp, interview with J.K. Raymond (May 1979)
10 TFRBL, W.E. Blatz Coll., Tape, M.I. Fletcher, interview with M.L. Northway (3 Oct. 1973)
11 TFRBL, W.E. Blatz Coll., Box 31, W.E. Blatz report to Clarence Hincks, July 26, 1942. This and the ensuing excerpts are all from Blatz's report to Hincks.

9 Day-care Begins at Home

1 TFRBL, W.E. Blatz Coll., Box 31, W.E. Blatz, letter to C.M. Hincks (30 Aug. 1942)
2 Ibid.
3 Ibid.
4 Ibid.
5 Ibid.
6 Ibid.
7 W.E. Blatz, 'A Vignette of George Bernard Shaw,' *Bulletin of the Institute of Child Study* 47 (Fall 1950), tells the story of Blatz's weekend at Clivedon.
8 TFRBL, W.E. Blatz Coll., Box 31, Blatz, letter to Hincks (2 Oct. 1942)
9 Ibid.
10 TFRBL, W.E. Blatz Coll., Tape, Mary Wright, interview with M.L. Northway (25 Mar. 1974)
11 Margaret Fletcher, interview with J.K. Raymond (May 1979)
12 Dorothy Millichamp, interview with J.K. Raymond (Dec. 1980)
13 W.E. Blatz, *Understanding the Young Child* (Toronto: Clarke Irwin 1944; New York: William Morrow 1944) 168
14 Ibid. 169
15 TFRBL, W.E. Blatz Coll., Box 31, *Toronto Daily Star* 30 Nov. 1942
16 Ibid., Hamilton *Spectator* 1 Feb. 1943

17 Ibid., *Toronto Daily Star* 3 Feb. 1943
18 Material on the growth of day-care is based on the following sources: *Bulletin of the Institute of Child Study* (Autumn 1942); E.M. Stapleford, *History of the Day Nurseries Branch* (Toronto: Ontario Ministry of Community and Social Services 1976); M.L. Northway, 'Child Study in Canada: A Casual History,' in Lois M. Brockman, John Whiteley, and John Zubek, eds, *Child Development: Selected Readings* (Toronto: McClelland and Stewart 1973); D.A. Millichamp with M.L. Northway, *Conversations at Caledon: Some Reminiscences of the Blatz Era* (Toronto: Brora Centre 1977).
19 Northway, 'Child Study in Canada' 30
20 Ibid.
21 Mary L. Northway, in Millichamp and Northway, *Conversations at Caledon* 15
22 TFRBL, W.E. Blatz Coll., Box 9, 'The Adjustment of the Returning Soldier into Civilian Life: Outline for Army Counsellors' Course,' for CNCMH
23 Day Nursery Act, Ontario, 1946, 7 C111
24 TFRBL, W.E. Blatz Coll., Box 9, 'The Nursery School in the Canadian Educational Scheme,' Manuscript (30 Jan. 1943)
25 TFRBL, W.E. Blatz Coll., Box 9, Thayer Hobson to W.E. Blatz (28 Oct. 1949)
26 Blatz, *Understanding the Young Child* 232
27 Ibid. 234
28 W.E. Blatz, 'A Scheme for Post-War Education,' *Parent Education Bulletin of the Institute of Child Study* (Dec. 1943, Feb. 1944, Apr. 1944); reprinted as 'Thoughts on Education Written Fifteen Years Ago,' *Bulletin of the Institute of Child Study* (77) 20:2 (June 1958)
29 Ibid.

10 Mature Security

1 June Callwood, 'The Dr William Blatzes,' *Maclean's* 3 Jan. 1959
2 M.L. Northway, interview with J.K. Raymond (Mar. 1979)
3 D.A. Millichamp, interview with J.K. Raymond (Mar. 1979)
4 TFRBL, W.E. Blatz Coll., Tape, Joanne Briggs, interview with M.L. Northway (3 Dec. 1973)
5 TFRBL, W.E. Blatz Coll., Tape, Mary Wright and Elsie Stapleford, group discussion with M.L. Northway (25 Mar. 1974)
6 Mary (Salter) Ainsworth, interview with Roger Myers at the annual

meeting of the American Psychological Association (2 Sept. 1969);
transcript, Canadian Psychological Association Archives, Ottawa

7 W.E. Blatz, 'Training Your Child' series, *Chatelaine* (Mar., June,
Aug., Oct., Nov., Dec. 1944; Feb., Mar., Apr., May 1945; Jan., Feb., Mar.,
Apr., May, July, Nov., Dec. 1946; Feb., Mar., Apr., May 1947); also
'Cut an Apron String,' 'Marriage in Canada Today' series, *Chatelaine*
(June 1956)

8 TFRBL, W.E. Blatz Coll., Tape, D. Atcheson, interview with M.L.
Northway (3 Dec. 1973)

9 Sidney E. Smith, 'The Contribution of Child Study to the University,' in
Karl S. Bernhardt, Margaret I. Fletcher, Frances L. Johnson, Dorothy
A. Millichamp, and Mary L. Northway, eds, *Twenty-five Years of Child
Study* (Toronto: University of Toronto Press 1951)

10 D.A. Millichamp with M.L. Northway, *Conversations at Caledon: Some
Reminiscences of the Blatz Era* (Toronto: Brora Centre 1977) 19

11 Ibid. 26

12 M.L. Northway, ed., *Well Children: A Progress Report* (Toronto: Institute
of Child Study 1956), and M.D. Ainsworth, 'The Significance of the Five
Year Research Programme of the Institute of Child Study,' *Bulletin of
the Institute of Child Study* (84) 22:1 (Mar. 1960)

13 M.L. Northway and L. Weld, *Sociometric Testing* (Toronto: University of
Toronto Press 1957); M.I. Fletcher, *The Adult and the Nursery School
Child* (Toronto: University of Toronto Press 1958); D. MacKenzie and
J.K.M. Raymond, *Parties for Preschoolers* (Toronto: University of
Toronto Press 1958); B.M. Flint, *The Security of Infants* (Toronto:
University of Toronto Press 1959); M.F. Grapko, *The Story of Jimmy*
(Toronto: Institute of Child Study, University of Toronto 1957); M.D.
Ainsworth and L.H. Ainsworth, *Measuring Security in Personal Adjust-
ment* (Toronto: University of Toronto Press 1958)

14 Carroll Davis, *Room to Grow: A Study of Parent-Child Relationships*
(Toronto: University of Toronto Press 1966)

15 B.M. Flint, *The Child and the Institution: A Story of Deprivation and
Recovery* (Toronto: University of Toronto Press 1966)

16 Millichamp and Northway, *Conversations at Caledon* 24

17 TFRBL, W.E. Blatz Coll., Tape, D. Atcheson, interview with M.L.
Northway (3 Dec. 1973)

18 R.G.N. Laidlaw, interview with J.K. Raymond (May 1979)

19 M.L. Northway and the Research Staff, 'The Research Programme and
the Longitudinal Study,' *Bulletin of the Institute of Child Study* (100)
26:1 (May 1964)

20 Millichamp and Northway, *Conversations at Caledon* 26
21 TFRBL, W.E. Blatz Coll., Box 16, *Globe and Mail* 2 Nov. 1964
22 *Canadian Medical Association Journal* 91 (26 Dec. 1964) 1375

11 Consequences

1 TFRBL, W.E. Blatz Coll., Box 13, Bruce Quarrington, associate professor of psychology, letter to Francess Halpenny, editor, University of Toronto Press (26 Jan. 1965)
2 M.L. Northway, Preface to William E. Blatz, *Human Security: Some Reflections* (Toronto: University of Toronto Press 1966) xii
3 Blatz, *Human Security* 112
4 Ibid. 52
5 Ibid. 34–44, 63
6 TFRBL, W.E. Blatz Coll., Box 13, Reprint from (complete title indecipherable) *Quarterly* (Jan. 1967)
7 Ibid., *Psychology in the Schools* (July 1971)
8 Ibid., I.N. McCollum, in *American Psychologist* 226 (1971) 921–7
9 Ibid., 'Champion of Children: Dr W.E. Blatz,' book review by David Critchley, broadcast on 'Trans-Canada Matinee,' 14 June 1966
10 TFRBL, W.E. Blatz Coll., Box 41, M.L. Northway, J. Hodgson, and D.A. Millichamp, *Why the Brora Centre?* (Toronto: Privately printed May 1980)
11 TFRBL, W.E. Blatz Coll., Box 28, M.F. Grapko, 'The Place of the Institute of Child Study in Canadian Education,' paper presented at annual conference of the Canadian Society for the Study of Education 1973
12 TFRBL, W.E. Blatz Coll., Box 40, Mary Wright, letter to D.A. Millichamp (24 June 1971)
13 Mary (Salter) Ainsworth, interview with Roger Myers at the annual meeting of the American Psychological Association (2 Sept. 1969); transcript, Canadian Psychological Association Archives, Ottawa
14 TFRBL, W.E. Blatz Coll., Box 40, Wright to Millichamp (24 June 1971)
15 L. Frank, 'The Beginnings of Child Development and Family Life Education in the Twentieth Century,' *Merrill-Palmer Quarterly of Behaviour and Development* 8:4 (Oct. 1962) 220
16 Roger Myers, interview with J.K. Raymond (May 1979)
17 TFRBL, W.E. Blatz Coll., Tape, Mary Wright, D.A. Millichamp, M.L. Northway, Douglas Myers, and M.F. Grapko, interviews and group discussion on the Blatz era (25 Mar. 1974)
18 Roger Myers, interview with J.K. Raymond (May 1979)

19 TFRBL, W.E. Blatz Coll., Tape, Douglas Myers, in group discussion (25 Mar. 1974)
20 TFRBL, W.E. Blatz Coll., Tape, Roger Myers, interview with M.L. Northway (30 Apr. 1973)
21 TFRBL, W.E. Blatz Coll., Tape, Elsie Stapleford, group discussion with M.L. Northway (25 Mar. 1974)
22 Milton J. Senn, *Insights on the Child Development Movement in the United States*, Monographs of the Society for Research in Child Development 40:3–4 (Aug. 1975) (Chicago: University of Chicago Press 1975)
23 TFRBL, W.E. Blatz Coll., Tape, D.C. Williams, interview with M.L. Northway and D.A. Millichamp (30 Mar. 1974)

# Index

www.ingramcontent.com/pod-product-compliance
Lightning Source LLC
Chambersburg PA
CBHW070615030426
42337CB00020B/3804